We Need to Talk about Pornography

A Resource to Educate Young People about the Potential Impact of Pornography and Sexualised Images on Relationships, Body Image and Self-Esteem

VANESSA ROGERS

Jessica Kingsley *Publishers*
London and Philadelphia

First published in 2017
by Jessica Kingsley Publishers
73 Collier Street
London N1 9BE, UK
and
400 Market Street, Suite 400
Philadelphia, PA 19106, USA

www.jkp.com

Library of Congress Cataloging in Publication Data
A CIP catalog record for this book is available from the Library of Congress

British Library Cataloguing in Publication Data
A CIP catalogue record for this book is available from the British Library

ISBN 978 1 84905 620 5
eISBN 978 1 78450 091 7

Printed and bound in Great Britain

Contents

About the Author

Vanessa Rogers is a qualified youth worker and teacher with an MA in Community Education who managed local authority services for children and young people for over 15 years before becoming an independent trainer/consultant. She is a recognised expert in youth work and personal, social and heath education (PSHE) and is regularly commissioned by statutory and voluntary sector organisations across the UK and Ireland to provide high-quality training for those working with young people aged 11–19 (up to 25 with additional needs).

The fact that she still regularly works with young people ensures that Vanessa's work is always engaging, informative and timely. Her consultancy roles include project development, interim service management and external evaluations and quality assurance, ensuring that her operational and strategic knowledge is up to date too.

Vanessa has over 20 social education resource books published by the National Youth Agency (NYA) (UK) and Jessica Kingsley Publishers (worldwide). Her writing credentials include being a regular features writer for *Children & Young People Now* and being commissioned to devise teaching and learning packs for a wide range of organisations, including teachers' packs for the BBC3 series, 'The Baby Borrowers' and 'Underage and Pregnant'.

Vanessa has written a number of popular resource books for those working with young people, including the following published by Jessica Kingsley Publishers:

- *Let's Talk Relationships: Activities for Exploring Love, Sex, Friendship and Family with Young People*

- *Working with Young Women: Activities for Exploring Personal, Social and Emotional Issues Second Edition*

- *Working with Young Men: Activities for Exploring Personal, Social and Emotional Issues Second Edition*

- *A Little Book of Alcohol: Activities to Explore Alcohol Issues with Young People*

- *A Little Book of Drugs: Activities to Explore Drug Issues with Young People*

- *A Little Book of Tobacco: Activities to Explore Smoking Issues with Young People*

Her website gives detailed information about further titles, training and consultancy visits.[1]

---

1   www.vanessarogers.co.uk

Overview

The learning resources in this book are designed to inform and educate young people aged 13–19 (up to 25 with additional learning needs) about pornography and its potentially negative impact on real-life relationships, mental health and emotional wellbeing. This timely addition to the PSHE curriculum also meets aspects of spiritual, moral, social and cultural (SMSC) education as it focuses on values and attitudes, both personal and cultural, and the spiritual challenges and moral dilemmas that young people face throughout adolescence and beyond.

Included are lesson plans and group work activities to build the self-confidence and personal skills to make healthy choices and stay safe by:

- challenging the myths and stereotypes surrounding the porn industry

- exploring the negative impact watching online porn can have on body image and emotional wellbeing

- considering how personal and societal values and attitudes are informed from a wide range of competing influences, including family, peers, faith, culture, gender and the media

- discussing how pornography can impact on real-life relationships and shape sexual expectations

- considering the short- and longer-term risks of engaging in 'homemade' and 'revenge' porn

- identifying the risks of taking, sending or receiving naked 'selfies' or 'nudes' on social media

- raising awareness about sexual bullying and domestic abuse and ensuring that young people understand the meaning of sexual consent

- informing young people about the laws that govern the making and distribution of pornographic material

- providing information about where to go for further help and support.

Although the focus of this resource is often considered a taboo subject, the ethos throughout is supporting young people to build healthy relationships based on mutual respect, affection and trust. As such it is an inclusive resource suitable for all young people, regardless of their gender identity or sexual orientation.

PART 1

Introduction

It sometimes seems that sexual images are all around us, from storylines of love, lust and betrayal on mainstream TV to seductive cinema adverts and raunchy music videos featuring scantily clad women and glistening, muscled men. Added to this, with just a few clicks on a PC, tablet or phone, intimate pictures and porn videos can be streamed or downloaded with ease any time, anywhere, any place – even within the safety of school and privacy of home.

Most young people are likely to encounter sexual images and porn in one form or another, whether they actively seek them or not. One of the big questions is: does it matter? Many would argue that viewing adult content is harmless fun, or simply part of the well-paved path to adulthood. Others say that its effects are dangerous and we should do all we can, as educators, parents and society, to protect young people from harm. My starting point for the months of research that underpin this book is to explore these questions:

> Can a bombardment of provocative or sexual images, in some cases long before experiencing a real-life relationship, affect the self-image, romantic expectations and ultimately longer-term relationships of children and young people? After all, everyone knows porn is not real, don't they?

I think these questions should be explored as part of a robust whole-school and youth services approach to sex and relationships education (SRE). Educators, health and social care practitioners, parents and community leaders need to work together to challenge the growing influence of porn on young people, potentially affecting their values and attitudes to sex and relationships, and offer another perspective based on reality. Simply maintaining a wall of silence means that any negative effects and misinformation will go largely unchallenged. It may be an uncomfortable topic to discuss, but research suggests that watching porn can leave young people anxious about the sort of sexual activities they are expected to engage in, regardless of age, gender or experience, and confused about how real-life relationships work. This includes issues surrounding sexual consent, relationship bullying and newer concerns associated with social media including 'sexting', nude 'selfies' and revenge porn. Combined, these add to the existing well-documented stress of adolescence, threatening to impact negatively on the physical, spiritual, moral, cultural and emotional wellbeing of young people already struggling to make sense of the world around them.

As an alternative, this book aims to increase young people's understanding of how pornography can potentially distort views of what is normal – both in terms of body image, size and shape and relationships – and explore the myths behind the adult entertainment industry to see where truth lies, meaning that young people get to make informed decisions, which has got to be a good thing.

So it seems the right time for educators to step forward to help young people understand some of the potential dangers inherent in viewing unfiltered material and discuss ways that porn can distort reality, including accepting Photoshopped pictures and routinely edited videos as the 'perfect' body.

In short, why should we leave it to the pornographers to do all the teaching?

Identifying the Need

Why do we need to talk about porn now?

Pornography is nothing new; it has been around for centuries with the historical evidence to prove it, meaning that generation after generation has grown up looking at sexual images, secretly or otherwise. In fact, lots of adults in the UK continue to watch and enjoy adult entertainment perfectly legally. To support this view, a journalist for the *Independent* newspaper researching for an article: 'The truth about pornography', undertook a 'Twitter and Facebook trawl of about 45,000 people [that] turned up a vanishingly small number of men – six – who never watched porn'.[1]

So if porn is a well-established phenomena, legally enjoyed by thousands and written about openly in national newspapers, why do we need to talk to young people about it now? What has changed? Well, quite simply, the big change is accessibility. Back in 2009 the Terrence Higgins Trust/UNICEF survey, 'Young people's views on sex and UK sexual health services', found that three-quarters of young people said they would use the internet to get information on sex and sexual health.[2] Fast forward 15 years and with improved technology young people can, and do, regularly access pornography without any filters via the internet, smart phones and video streaming.

Pre-internet generations had to actively seek out porn and put some effort into finding it. 'Top shelf magazines', so called because of their shelf placement in a shop, were sold strictly to those over the age of 18 and so were less casually available. Visiting a sex shop in the 1960s and 70s probably involved going to a well-known area, such as Soho in London, and trying to sneak a look past the doormen, or staring at a poster outside, which was likely to have any nipple shots covered by a paper star (in line with decency laws of the age), until a potential customer had proof of being over 18.

Even the advent and rise of the video in the 1980s and 90s was reliant on a) being able to get hold of a film, b) having the money to pay for it and c) finding somewhere to watch it undisturbed. So, porn was harder to get hold of, though definitely not impossible.

Fast forward to today where young people are increasingly exposed to sexual images from a young age through the media, music and TV/films, everyday viewing of sexy underwear in the windows of established high street sex and lingerie shops, plus easy access to the internet via phones, computers, laptops and tablets. Although some porn costs money or needs a credit card to sign up for full access, there are still plenty of free websites available to anyone who says they are over 18, plus a wealth of material in the form of still photographs and computer games. Much of this can be streamed or

---

1   www.independent.co.uk/news/uk/politics/the-truth-about-pornography-its-time-for-a-rude-awakening -8735043.html

2   https://www.cornwallhealthyschools.org/documents/Sexual%20health%20rights%20and%20staying%20safe.pdf

downloaded straight to a device of choice, often on a contract paid for by unsuspecting parents, thus removing many of the blocks to previous generations' viewing.

With numerous young people saying that indecent images have just 'popped up', without them doing or typing anything into the search bar, and anecdotal evidence suggesting that children sometimes find pornography by accident while looking for legitimate information about sex and relationships,[3] I decided to do a bit of research of my own. I can now honestly say that the only way that I found access to porn was by looking for it. Type in 'porn' or 'sex' into a search engine and immediately there are thousands of results just waiting to be clicked on. Suspicious teachers, youth workers and parents can easily check the web history of any device to see which pages are being returned to most, and if a young person has deliberately cleared the history, then it does beg the question why.

However, just because it is out there and freely available doesn't mean that all young people are viewing pornographic material or reading erotic literature. A bit like sex and drugs misuse, it is important for young people to understand that not 'everyone' is doing it, and not everybody wants to do it. But with a 2014 BBC3 documentary 'Porn: What's the Harm?'[4] identifying children as young as eight being regular viewers of online porn, it is clearly too important an issue to be ignored.

---

3   The Education Committee inquiry into Personal, Social, Health and Economic education (PSHE) and Sex and Relationships Education (SRE) in schools, http://data.parliament.uk/writtenevidence/committeeevidence.svc/evidencedocument/education-committee/pshe-and-sre-in-schools/written/10259.html

4   'Porn: What's the Harm?' BBC3 (broadcast 16 April 2014), www.bbc.co.uk/programmes/b040n2ph

Purpose of this Resource

The lesson plans in this book provide youth workers and teachers with a set of interactive materials with which to deal sensitively with issues around pornography and the impact that it potentially has on real-life relationships, body image and attitudes to sex. They contribute to the spiritual, moral, social and cultural education of pupils, as defined by Ofsted,[1] which all schools in England must demonstrate development in.

Intended for use with Key Stage (KS) 3 and KS 4 pupils, the activities, projects, quizzes and discussions are equally relevant in post-16 classes and informal education settings such as youth clubs. Each exercise has an age-appropriate recommendation, for example Years 8–13+, but this is dependent on maturity, existing knowledge and ability so is intended only as a guide.

The exercises for lesson plans are written with reference to the Sex Education Forum's core values for good quality SRE:

- mutual respect

- loving and happy relationships

- rights to information, safety and health

- equality; particularly on the basis of gender and sexual orientation

- responsibility for oneself and others.[2]

Context for learning

The National Association of Headteachers (NAHT) says more young people are educating themselves about sex online, which it anticipates will only increase as technology gets faster and easier to use.[3] This suggests that although young people definitely want to learn, the sex education they currently receive from school, parents and youth services is not enough, or does not include the things they really want to know.

Pornography as an issue is a legitimate subject area for workers to discuss with young people because of the effect it can have on young people's sex and relationships education, their understanding of sex and sexual health and the impact on their self-esteem and body image.[4]

---

1   'Promoting fundamental British values as part of SMCS in schools – Departmental advice for maintained schools' – Department for Education (2014) p.5, www.gov.uk/government/uploads/system/uploads/attachment_data/file/380595/SMSC_Guidance_Maintained_Schools.pdf

2   www.sexeducationforum.org.uk/resources/practice/faith,-values-sre.aspx

3   www.bbc.co.uk/newsbeat/20009247

4   'Young people and pornography: A briefing for workers' (Brook, Centre for HIV and Sexual Health, FPA, The National Youth Agency 2009)

A recent NAHT poll revealed parental consent for this addition to the content of SRE with 83 per cent of parents saying they want SRE lessons to address issues about pornography[5] so that their children are clued up rather than reliant on hearsay, gossip and playground myths. Sex Education Forum policy adviser Sion Humphreys says:

> We would support children being taught in an age-appropriate way about the impact of pornography as part of a statutory personal, social and health education (PSHE) programme.[6]

In addition to these collective concerns about the easy accessibility to porn and the potentially damaging effects it can have, mental health charity Young Minds engaged 5600 young people through focus groups, surveys and online consultations, revealing that easy access to explicit images adds to the stress and pressure of growing up, with over half of 11–14-year-olds saying that they had viewed online pornography, and four out of ten believing it has affected their relationships.[7]

National Curriculum links

This resource is primarily for educating young people at Key Stages 3 and 4 (11–19) through PSHE[8] both in formal and informal education environments about the potential impact and influence of pornography on individuals and wider society. The Government's PSHE education review in 2013 concluded that PSHE would remain non-statutory on the National Curriculum, despite campaigns by educators (including the Sex Education Forum,[9] Brook,[10] the FPA,[11] and The National Youth Agency), the Association of Headteachers and parents who feel that it is an important part of preparing young people for the adult world. PSHE topics include drug and alcohol awareness, budgeting and finance, voting and democracy (through Citizenship), emotional health and wellbeing and sex and relationships education (SRE).

Though not statutory, the Department for Education (DfE) advice for local authority maintained schools (and recommended good practice for grant maintained or free schools) is that 'all schools should make provision for PSHE, drawing on good practice. Schools are also free to include other subjects or topics of their choice in planning and designing their own programme of education'.[12] This includes the addition of education about the potential impact of pornography on young people to SRE lessons.

Although SRE is a topic within PSHE it is also a statutory part of the curriculum in maintained secondary schools from the age of 11. However, not all topics are statutory and parents have the right to withdraw their children from those non-statutory lessons, which are often those that contain education about the emotional aspect of relationships rather than just the facts of reproduction.

---

5   National Association of Headteachers (2013). Research carried out in April 2013 by Research Now and commissioned by the National Association of Headteachers (NAHT) and press released by NAHT in May 2013 www.naht.org.uk/welcome/news-and-media/key-topics/parents-and-pupils/parents-want-schools-to-manage-dangers-of-pornography-says-survey

6   Pornography impact lessons 'should be taught' in school – NAHT, www.bbc.co.uk/newsbeat/20009247

7   Young Minds Vs. Sexed Up (2013) www.youngmindsvs.org.uk/assets/0000/0136/YM_Vs_A4_SEXED_UP_info_sheet_INTERACTIVE.pdf

8   PSE in Wales

9   www.sexeducationforum.org.uk

10   www.brook.org.uk

11   www.fpa.org.uk

12   www.gov.uk/government/publications/personal-social-health-and-economic-education-pshe

SRE can be delivered within a range of core curriculum subjects as well as through dedicated lessons. These include science, to learn about the biology of sex, religious education/ethics, to consider personal values and attitudes, and vocational subjects such as health and social care. Cross-curricular links can be made with other subjects, including drama, English, history and politics to enrich learning and add value so that young people see how SRE contributes to other areas of their life. This choice is dependent on the school, but must be delivered with regard to the Secretary of State's guidance.[13] Academies do not have to provide SRE but if they choose to they must also have regard to the Secretary of State's guidance.

The main principles of SRE in schools are:

- Effective sex and relationships education is essential if young people are to make responsible and well-informed decisions about their lives.

- The objective of sex and relationships education is to help and support young people through their physical, emotional and moral development.

- To help pupils develop the skills and understanding they need to live confident, healthy, independent lives.

- To learn the significance of marriage and stable relationships as key building blocks of community and society.

- To be given accurate information and helped to develop skills to understand difference and respect themselves and others.

- Sex and relationships education should contribute to promoting the spiritual, moral, cultural, mental and physical development of pupils at school to prepare them for adulthood.

- Effective sex and relationships education does not encourage early sexual experimentation.

SRE should also enable young people to develop assertiveness skills, to understand the potential consequences of decisions made, to build a sense of personal responsibility and develop the ability to discern fact from fiction.

In the absence of a national DfE programme of study (PoS), the PSHE Association (the leading national support body for PSHE teachers), has developed a curriculum that includes a PoS for Key Stage 3 and 4 SRE that contributes to a whole-school approach across the UK:

- *England:* PSHE (Personal, Social and Health Education)

- *Northern Ireland:* Learning for Life and Work (Personal Development and Religious Education)

- *Scotland:* Health and Wellbeing (Relationships, Sexual Health and Parenthood)

- *Wales:* Personal and Social Education (Health and Emotional Wellbeing).

This PoS is also useful for school-based youth workers who are increasingly tasked with supporting formal education by delivering high quality SRE to meet a wide range

---

13   Available to download from www.gov.uk/government/publications/sex-and-relationship-education

of learning styles and abilities, alternative education programmes for pupils requiring additional support and within pupil referral units.

This book is aligned to the PSHE Association's three overlapping core themes for PSHE Association Programme of Study in a number of ways:

1. **Health and wellbeing** e.g. by developing young people's ability to make informed choices and take personal responsibility for their own decisions about sexual health, consent and relationships; by encouraging emotional wellbeing and exploring trust, respect and sexual identity; by challenging negative ideas about body image and promoting healthy self-esteem.

2. **Relationships** e.g. by identifying what a positive relationship is and the difference between this and those that may be damaging or abusive; understanding that the media portrayal of relationships may not reflect real life; promoting healthy relationships based on trust and respect for all young people, regardless of gender identity or sexual orientation; learning risk-management skills.

3. **Living in the wider world** e.g. by learning verbal and non-verbal communication skills, looking at the impact that greater access to pornography and erotic images can have in terms of altering social norms and learning how to get their opinions heard through youth democracy.

Whist there are no formal attainment targets in SRE it is important to make baseline assessments of young people's knowledge, experience and understanding in order to ensure that education is age-appropriate and relevant. Tools for reflection and review to assess and reinforce learning are suggested at the end of each lesson plan within this resource.

The full PSHE Association guidance for schools, including a 2016 update, can be downloaded and read in full online and it is suggested that all teachers read this carefully as part of their planning process.[14]

Contribution to spiritual, moral, social and cultural education

All state-funded schools must offer a balanced curriculum that promotes the spiritual, moral, social and cultural (SMSC) development of pupils and society. This aims to prepare them for the opportunities, responsibilities and experiences of later life. The lesson plans in this teaching resource contribute to SMSC education (as defined by Ofsted) by promoting:

1. **Spiritual development** e.g. through exploring and reflecting on beliefs and values about sex, relationships and pornography; understanding personal feelings and building empathy for those of others; considering how and why people may have different views on pornography and how these may impact on their behaviour.

2. **Moral development** e.g. recognising right and wrong and respecting the laws that govern sexual consent, appropriate and inappropriate online content and pornography; understanding consequences; investigating moral and ethical issues relating to sex, gender and porn; considering sexual stereotypes and learning to debate offering reasoned views.

---

14 Available at www.gov.uk/government/uploads/system/uploads/attachment_data/file/283599/sex_and_relationship _education_guidance.pdf

3. **Social development** e.g. through developing a range of social skills including communication, listening and assertiveness; recognising the right to have an opinion and appreciate diverse viewpoints; promoting respect of self and others; practicing resolving relationship conflict without resorting to bullying or aggressive behaviour; experiencing democracy though participation in a basic voting system and building respect for the law.

4. **Cultural development** e.g. by better understanding the impact of cultural influences on personal values; discussing how social norms are shaped by popular culture and the media; understanding more about different types of relationships and developing respect and tolerance for others and celebrating diversity.

To find out more about how exploring the potential impact of pornography on children and young people fits within SMSC read the Ofsted guidelines.[15]

Youth work curriculum and accredited outcomes

This is a resource that enables young people aged 13–19 (up to 25 with additional needs) to learn about the potential impact and influence of pornography, both on the individual and wider society, by exploring values and attitudes, as well as giving factual information and sparking debate. It is appropriate for use by school-based youth workers that contribute to formal education or those who work in community education settings, including outreach and detached.

The key focus of youth work is to 'enable young people to develop holistically, working with them to facilitate their personal and educational development, to enable them to develop their voice, influence and place in society and to reach their full potential'.[16]

This book aims to facilitate a dialogue between youth workers and young people about the impact pornography can have on real-life sex and relationships, encouraging them to explore the potential consequences of different actions before making decisions.

Youth work helps young people learn about themselves, others and society, through informal educational activities which combine enjoyment, challenge and learning.[17]

'Informal education' certainly does not mean 'unplanned' and youth workers plan learning opportunities within a curriculum that meets the approval of Ofsted. This includes life skills, one of which is the ability to form and maintain healthy relationships and make informed decisions about when, where and with whom to have sex and to fully understand the concept of consent.

Personal and social development can be accredited through a range of different methods. These include:

- The Duke of Edinburgh's Award

- Award Scheme Development and Accreditation Network (ASDAN) short courses

---

15 Guidance for inspecting schools under the common inspection framework from September 2015, with a myth buster document on common misconceptions, available to download at www.gov.uk/government/publications/school-inspection-handbook-from-september-2015

16 National Occupational Standard 2008 cited in 'A narrative for youth work today': www.gov.uk/government/uploads/system/uploads/attachment_data/file/210380/a-narrative-for-youth-work-today.pdf

17 National Youth Agency 2015, www.nya.org.uk/wp-content/uploads/2014/06/The_NYA_Guide_to_Youth_Work_and_Youth_Services.pdf

- City & Guilds in employability and social skills (Unit 77546)
- Local awards
- AQA units
- UK Youth, Youth Achievement Awards.[18]

Examples of projects that could be accredited include peer education projects and awareness raising campaigns, for example about domestic abuse or the risks of engaging in nude self-made images or 'selfies'.

---

18   www.ukyouth.org/youth-achievement-awards.html

How Young People Learn about Sex and Relationships

In the UK, SRE teaches the facts about reproduction and sexual health, but not necessarily about the emotional elements of a relationship. This includes mutual respect and pleasure within consensual sex, building trust and falling in love, and on the negative side, learning the skills to cope with rejection, break-ups, peer pressure and understanding that sex in porn bears little or no resemblance to real-life relationships.

> Positive sexual experiences are related to health and well being throughout the life course, and it's time for this to be given wider recognition by health workers, educators, and society as a whole. We need to do more to create an environment in which it is easier for people to discuss sexual well being as an integral part of the conversation we have with people about our health.[1]

Parents can choose to withdraw their children from the non-compulsory parts of SRE[2] for a variety of reasons, including faith, culture or because they choose to educate their children themselves. While acknowledging that parents do have an important role to play in preparing their children for adult life, this can mean that young people are given different levels of information on which to base their choices.

It is generally recognised that talking about sex and relationships can be a daunting or embarrassing prospect for both young people and their parents, with many young people reporting that talk about sex is 'banned' in their house. Focus groups for this book said that periods, masturbation and pornography were also on the list of things never to be mentioned and that old-style double standards are often still applied to what is acceptable behaviour for sons and daughters to engage in.

So it is unsurprising that a recent YouGov survey confirmed that outside school more than a third of teens rely on getting advice about sex from their friends, the internet, magazines and via pornography.[3] This raises concerns about the mixed messages young people are receiving as porn relationships bear no resemblance to fairytale happy endings or the Disney cartoons children grow up watching. The lack of romance in most porn is a sharp contrast to the quest to find 'the one' central to the plot of literally thousands of Hollywood 'rom-com' movies, all of which are quietly internalised by millions of young viewers worldwide. Although some erotic novels, dubbed by the media 'mommy porn',[4] offer readers a marriage of romance and explicit sex, porn often depicts sex in ways

---

1   Professor Dame Anne Johnson. See more at www.ucl.ac.uk/news/news-articles/1113/26112013-Results-from-third-National-Survey-of-Sexual-Attitudes-and-Lifestyles#sthash.l0NQ5NoO.dpuf
2   www.gov.uk/national-curriculum/other-compulsory-subjects
3   YouGov (2011)
4   www.urbandictionary.com/define.php?term=Mommy+Porn

that are threatening, misogynistic, violent and without boundaries, leaving both young women and men feeling confused as they absorb conflicting information about sex and relationships from school, home, friends, faith, culture and the outside world.[5]

Further research is still needed to establish if there is a conclusive link between education and a reduction in the number of children and young people accessing pornography. However UK-based charity Safety Net claims evidence that pornography has a detrimental impact on children and young people, including premature sexualisation, negative body image and unhealthy notions about relationships.[6]

All of which adds weight to the Sex Education Forum's ongoing campaign 'SRE – It's My Right',[7] supported by organisations including UK Youth, the National Union of Students (NUS) and the UK Youth Parliament, to include the effects of pornography in SRE and urging political parties to commit to statutory SRE in their manifestos.

Supporting LGBT+ young people

All young people are entitled to high-quality, age-appropriate SRE both in school and within other services for young people. However, research by the University of Cambridge for Stonewall revealed that more than half of LGBT+ (lesbian, gay, bisexual and trans) young people say the focus of sex education remains firmly on heterosexual sex and traditional boy/girl relationships.[8]

Facilitators are reminded to think carefully about the language used within group activities and to be mindful that although some young people are open about their sexuality, others may be questioning, not ready to come out or simply don't want to talk about it. This book makes no assumptions about gender identity or sexual orientation and specifically uses the inclusive term 'partner' as well as offering examples of same sex couples for discussion scenarios. Using non-gender specific terms, for example using 'they' instead of 'him' or 'her' can also be useful.

The laws relating to lesbian and gay pornography are included alongside other legislation, and opportunities are created to challenge LGBT+ stereotypes and correct common mistakes, for example not knowing that the age of sexual consent in the UK is 16 for all.[9]

Challenging any homophobic comments, pointing out that this could be considered a hate crime or hate incident[10] and is therefore unlawful, should make it clear that this behaviour will not be tolerated. Referring back to ground rules to remind everyone that asking personal questions and sharing details of intimate experiences is off-limits should mean that no one feels uncomfortable while learning.

The following organisations may provide useful information:

- The website for the charity Avert has a great section on 'coming out', giving information, case studies and support.[11]

5   www.psychologytoday.com/blog/sex-lies-trauma/201107/effects-porn-adolescent-boys
6   www.safetynet.org.uk/thefacts.php#sthash.fMxj1GY9.dpuf
7   www.sexeducationforum.org.uk/policy-campaigns/sre-its-my-right.aspx
8   www.stonewall.org.uk/sites/default/files/The_School_Report__2012_.pdf
9   www.fpa.org.uk/factsheets/law-on-sex#age-consent
10   www.stonewall.org.uk/help-advice/hate-crime
11   www.avert.org

- Families and Friends of Lesbians and Gays provides support and information to young people and their families, before, during and after 'coming out'.[12]

- Stonewall is a UK organisation that campaigns for the rights of gay, lesbian, bi and trans people.[13]

SRE for young people with additional needs

Young people with disabilities have as much right to high-quality SRE as anyone else, including exploring the impact access to pornography can have on their self-image and expectations of sex.

> Sex and relationships education should focus on dignity and respect, providing information on safe sex and making it possible for young adults with SEN to safely experience what millions of other young people take for granted.[14]

The word 'disability' is a collective term for such a huge range of physical, sensory and mental disabilities, including 'invisible' disabilities like diabetes and deafness, that it is impossible to prescribe for all. Along this continuum, pupils will have different learning needs and abilities, as well as differing levels of experience and understanding of sex, relationships and pornography.

This resource is not specifically aimed at students with special educational needs (SEN) but many of the ideas can be easily adapted, for example by swapping words for pictures, using a larger type font or inviting students to draw, not write, their discussions. In some of the lesson plans, specific additional suggestions have been included, while others will need individual adaptation.

For more information about teaching SRE to children and young people with additional needs please see the DfE website for guidance.[15]

12 www.fflag.org.uk
13 www.stonewall.org.uk
14 Quote from online article http://senmagazine.co.uk/articles/896-sex-and-the-special-child-how-do-we-educate-young-people-with-sen-about-sex.html
15 https://www.gov.uk/government/uploads/system/uploads/attachment_data/file/283599/sex_and_relationship_education_guidance.pdf

Sex, Porn and the Law

Sex and the law

The age of sexual consent in the UK for men and women is currently 16 years old, which is reinforced throughout this book. In 2013 the National Survey of Sexual Attitudes and Lifestyles (NATSAL) confirmed that the median age for people in Britain to first have sex is 16, which means that although 'young people today have sex at an earlier age than previous generations did'[1] not everyone has sex underage. This suggests that for many young people their first encounter with sex of any kind will be through porn.

Another underlying message throughout this resource is that the decision to have a physical relationship, who to have it with and whether it includes penetrative sex or not, is a personal one. Abstinence should always be promoted as an option, along with the message that even if someone has had sex, they do not necessarily have to do it again if they aren't ready or don't want to. Coercion to engage in the taking and sharing of explicit pictures or films by using emotional pressure, aggressive tactics or deception is unacceptable in any form and could result in the law being broken.

Teachers should ensure they promote that a loving relationship does not have to be a sexual relationship and if one person says no, then that is what they mean and no attempt should ever be made to charm, bully or beg them to change their mind. No is always no, whatever the context and any form of sexual activity without the express consent of both partners is illegal. Activities to explore the meaning of consent, the impact that alcohol or misusing substances can have on decisions made and how to set and maintain relationship boundaries can be found in Chapter 4 of Part 5.

An overview of the UK laws governing pornography

In the UK there are laws governing pornography and the making and sharing of explicit images. These laws are there to protect children and young people, for whom pornography is deemed unsuitable. Basically you need to be over 18 to buy or view porn, for example going into an adult shop to buy films rated R18 (the 'R' means restricted) or membership of an online porn site. However, some porn is illegal to make, distribute or watch at any age in any format, regardless of who you are. This includes streaming or downloading images of extreme pornography, such as sex involving animals, children or extreme violence.

There are certain types of pornography that can only be described as extreme; I am talking particularly about pornography that is violent and that depicts simulated rape.

---

1   www.ucl.ac.uk/news/news-articles/1113/26112013-Survey-examines-changes-in-sexual-behaviour-and-attitudes-in-Britain#sthash.vlas0YbI.dpuf

These images normalise sexual violence against women and they're quite simply poisonous to the young people who see them.[2]

The Audiovisual Media Services Regulations 2014 introduced a series of restrictions on pornography produced and sold in the UK for online paid-for video on demand (VoD). This aims to bring British VoD up to the same standards that already apply to porn distributed on DVD, which must have an R18 marked clearly on it.[3] This defines the film as suitable only for viewers aged 18 or over.

It is illegal to take a sexually explicit picture or to film anyone naked (or engaging in a sex act) under the age of 18, with or without that person's consent. This includes consenting young couples in an under-18 relationship who film or take intimate photos of each other, which amounts in law to creating child pornography. It is also illegal for those under the age of 18 to take 'naked selfies' even if they don't intend to share them and only mean to store them on their own phone.

It is also illegal to 'incite' underage porn in any way, including in the guise of a loving relationship or where the subject is complicit. The law is further broken if this material is shared with friends, for example via text, or posted online, and the perpetrator could be charged with distributing child pornography, even if they are under 18 too. Once shared a photo can very quickly go 'viral' and it is almost impossible to be 100 per cent sure that every copy is traced and removed, even if the original is reported to the website or social media company and taken down.

Please note that no money needs to exchange hands for any of the above to be considered a serious crime by the police.

Revenge porn is explored in more detail later in the book. However, it should be pointed out that it is not just teenagers creating this form of homemade porn, a *Daily Telegraph* article written to explain the change in law reported that a McAfee study (in the US) 'found that 36% of people have sent or intend to send intimate content to their partners, and that one in ten ex-partners threatened to expose risqué photos online – a threat carried out 60% of the time'.[4] There have been high profile celebrity stories reported where pictures or sex tapes have been 'leaked'.

While it is arguable that engaging in sex tapes has enhanced not harmed the careers of some celebrities, many people come to regret their actions. This includes Kim Kardashian who, during an interview with Oprah Winfrey,[5] confessed that she regrets the way she became famous after a sex tape she made in 2003 with then-boyfriend, musician Ray J, was 'leaked' online. 'It was a negative way, so I felt like I really had to work ten times harder to get people to see the real me.' She also talked about the impact it had on her family, admitting the X-rated clip was 'humiliating'. Now she is a wife, mother and reality TV star, but her explicit home-shot sex film is still regularly downloaded by millions and watched globally without her consent or knowledge.

In real life, it is unlikely that an online sex tape will enhance anyone's CV and it could present an additional challenge for those hoping to work in a teaching, policing or caring capacity, as well as create constant fear about who has seen it.

---

2   Cabinet Office, Prime Minister's Office, 10 Downing Street and The Rt Hon David Cameron MP (13.07.2013) www.gov.uk/government/speeches/the-internet-and-pornography-prime-minister-calls-for-action

3   For more information on this story go to www.independent.co.uk/news/uk/a-long-list-of-sex-acts-just-got-banned-in-uk-porn-9897174.html

4   www.telegraph.co.uk/news/uknews/law-and-order/11531954/What-is-the-law-on-revenge-porn.html

5   *The Sun* www.thesun.co.uk/sol/homepage/showbiz/4381835/Kim-Kardashian-admits-to-Oprah-that-she-was-put-on-birth-control-aged-14.html

Where to find more detailed information

Please note: all UK legal information is correct at the time of publishing but the law is subject to change, so check to ensure that it is up to date and/or relevant to your area before using.

- The Crown Prosecution Service – www.cps.gov.uk/legal/d_to_g/extreme_ pornography

- UK Parliament website – http://researchbriefings.parliament.uk/Research Briefing/Summary/SN05078

- Child Exploitation and Online Protection Centre (CEOP) – http://ceop.police.uk

PART 2

Teaching

Guidelines for Teaching SRE that Includes Pornography

Reflecting on personal values and attitudes

Good quality SRE, offered in a balanced, knowledgeable way that doesn't seek to shame or blame, is one of the few structures in place to challenge what is becoming part of the everyday for thousands of teenagers in the UK so it is vital that those doing the teaching feel confident and assured.

As with all emotive topics, for example religion, ethics or politics, it is important for teachers and youth workers to spend time reflecting on where they stand in the pornography debate *before* stepping into the classroom. Some people are anti-porn based on a whole spectrum of reasons, including the politics of gender equality and arguments about the objectification of women. Others consider the choice to watch legal porn or not simply a matter of personal taste. The crucial point is that while everyone is entitled to an opinion, which is likely to reflect personal values shaped by faith, culture and life experience, this should not influence how or what they teach. Facilitators need to feel comfortable discussing porn-related issues with young people and develop strategies to ensure that personal feelings do not influence the way they do it.

Additional consideration should be given to anyone who feels particularly sensitive to teaching this element of SRE and opportunities provided for additional support from either a line manager or headteacher (whichever is most appropriate). There is a suggested outline for continuing professional development included in the next chapter of this section which provides opportunities to discuss any obstacles to good practice that should also help to build confidence.

Teaching with confidence

While the basic biological content of SRE may not produce many blushes among those familiar with teaching it, talking about sexting, revenge porn and naked selfies might make even the most seasoned teacher or youth worker feel a bit uncomfortable or embarrassed. The idea of this book is not to talk with KS3 and KS4 about the contents of the pornographic material in detail, i.e. who did what to whom, but to enable professionals to have an open dialogue with young people and educate them about the way it can potentially shape and influence opinions, feelings and actions towards sex and relationships. This falls within the remit of SMSC education, which focuses more on values, attitudes and discussions about the impact that wider acceptability of pornography may have on culture and society.

It is important to stress that there is absolutely no need for anyone to research by looking at pornography. Equally, *young people should not under any circumstances be shown pornographic images* to illustrate what is being discussed.

The use of distancing techniques

Discussing the issues surrounding pornography within an educative environment should be done using clear language that presents a non-judgemental attitude, while reflecting the whole-school or youth services SRE policy and guidelines.

If there are any questions a facilitator feels uncomfortable with, or doesn't know the answer to, the simplest solution is to buy time by offering to look into it and come back with an answer. If necessary, ask for support and guidance from sexual health professionals or check the PSHE Association guidelines before responding. While it is fine not to have all the answers, it is not OK to give out advice based on personal opinions or experiences.

Wherever possible avoid being entangled in discussions where young people demand to know your opinion or the answer to embarrassing personal questions. While the use of ground rules that specifically include not asking or answering personal questions should reduce the likelihood of this happening, if it does, the use of deflective techniques is recommended. These include asking and answering questions in the third person or using hypothetical scenarios to enhance and check out learning. For example, 'If Tom takes a topless picture of his girlfriend on his phone, would he be breaking the law if he passed it on to his best friend? What is likely to happen if he sends the pictures on to several friends? How might Sian, his girlfriend, feel if she finds out he has shared their special pictures? What could happen if he gets caught with the pictures on his phone?'

Using this technique means that nobody has to reveal personal information and sensitive topics can be discussed in detail safely within appropriate boundaries. This includes examining the potential consequences of different choices and agreeing ways to stay safe.

All of the scenario-based work in this book is set out in this way as experience has shown that young people usually find it easier to problem solve effectively for abstract people rather than to talk about their own dilemmas.

Continuing Professional Development

PSHE coordinators, youth work trainers and other professional development professionals may find it useful to offer some continuing professional development (CPD) workshops to prepare teachers and youth workers to feel confident using this resource.

Below is a suggested framework to deliver three hours CPD, either as one workshop or divided up by topic into 'bite-size' learning. This mirrors the main topics within this resource and the relevant pages where more information can be found are referenced in the grid.

The aim of the workshop is to familiarise practitioners with the style and content of the lessons in this resource and to develop the confidence to explore the potential impact that pornography can have on the emotional, physical and spiritual health with young people.

In addition all professionals should be familiar with the SRE curriculum, safeguarding and confidentiality policies and child protection procedures of their school or youth service.

CPD workshop outline

	Task	How	Purpose
1	Setting ground rules (see pages 42–43)	Developed and owned by the group to enable them to feel comfortable, safe and valued.	Creating an ethos of trust and open dialogue so that children and young people can learn effectively and safely. Explaining confidentiality and boundaries.
2	Exploring personal values and attitudes to pornography (see pages 26, 72, 96 and 133)	Considering the difference between personal and professional opinion. Exploring how personal values are established. Discussing diversity issues and how social, cultural and emotional difference can affect learning. Understanding how personal values can impact on attitudes and beliefs about pornography.	The importance of role modelling positive behaviour and not offering opinion as fact. Offering a balance of different views for young people to explore the issues, backed by research and evidence. Remaining impartial while discussing sensitive issues.

	Task	How	Purpose
3	Pornography and the law (see pages 22–24, 59, 69, 87 and 92)	To know the basics about the law that controls the making, viewing and distribution of pornography and adult material. To have a working knowledge of the Criminal Justice Act 1988, Public Order Act 1994, the Sexual Offences Act 2003 and the Criminal Justice and Immigration Act 2008 (section 63).	Being clear that: • the legal age for watching, buying or distributing porn is 18 • some pornography is illegal at any age • possession of indecent images of children (under-18s) is illegal. This includes computer imagery and simulated imagery. It also includes pictures taken with both parties consent.
4	Confidentiality and safeguarding (see pages 43, 244 and 252)	Considering parental concerns and identifying challenges. Clarifying school policy and safeguarding procedures in relation to disclosure or concerns about risky behaviour. Agreeing boundaries and acceptable behaviour.	Managing parents/carers expectations and responding to concerns. Ensuring that pupils understand the meaning of confidentiality and when things need to be passed on and to whom. Setting and maintaining clear boundaries.
5	Determining learning needs (see pages 11, 19–21, 40 and 97)	Identifying how much young people already know. Considering how different topics can be discussed in an age-appropriate way. Building confidence in supporting young people in good decision making, even if their existing knowledge is more than the facilitators.	Involving young people in decision making and consulting with them about this part of the PSHE curriculum, based on Ofsted evidence that demonstrates how learning and motivation are enhanced when pupils are consulted about their learning.
6	Managing sensitive issues and controversial responses (see pages 27, 32–34, 244, 247–249 and 251)	Discussing techniques including: • 'car parking' ideas • the use of distancing techniques • role-play • using drama or music • collective discussions • referring back to ground rules set and maintaining boundaries.	Developing strategies for managing sensitive or controversial issues both in the classroom and with parents.
7	Measuring learning (see pages 41, 203 and 253)	Using the quizzes and reflection activities in this resource. Accreditation, where appropriate e.g. peer education. Recognising the development of new skills, wider knowledge and positive reinforcement of choices made. Identifying additional and ongoing learning needs.	Reviewing attitudes, values and knowledge expressed at the start and comparing them with those at the end of the lessons. Enabling young people to recognise learning that has taken place using quantitative methods (e.g. accreditation) and qualitative (e.g. positive reinforcement). Peer mentoring and peer education. Evaluation. Targeted development of further learning.

Additional guidelines are available to download free of charge from the PSHE Association[1] and the Sex Education Forum,[2] as well as the Department for Education.[3] It is suggested that facilitators and PSHE coordinators read these documents as part of the preparation for delivering the lessons.

1   www.pshe-association.org.uk/curriculum-and-resources/resources/sex-and-relationship-education-sre-21st-century

2   www.sexeducationforum.org.uk/schools/the-best-teaching-methods-and-resources.aspx

3   www.gov.uk/government/uploads/system/uploads/attachment_data/file/283599/sex_and_relationship_education_guidance.pdf

Keeping Parents and Carers Informed

Sex and relationships education

Some parents and carers find it very difficult to talk to their children about sex and relationships and are perfectly content to leave this to professional educators. Others hold the opposite view, believing that it is solely their right and responsibility to educate their children about sex, as and how they see fit. As previously discussed, this right is upheld to a certain extent by the Department for Education, with only core elements of SRE being statutory, allowing those with parental responsibility to remove their children from the rest if they choose.

Research suggests that the most effective way for young people to learn about the birds and the bees (and all the bits in between) is not at either end of this scale, but within a learning partnership developed between home and school. This approach recognises that those with parental responsibility have a wealth of expertise and experience to draw on and are likely to know how their child will respond best. Working together and pooling the knowledge and skills of both parents and teachers creates a more equal partnership, enabling and encouraging young people to learn in school with reinforcement of the same clear, consistent messages at home.

Inviting parents (or those with parental responsibility) into school to inform them of the topics that will be covered and to share the contents and ethos of this book, producing information sheets and sending letters home that give a curriculum outline can all help to allay fears and clarify the purpose of this learning. An example letter is included in the back of this book (Appendix 1) that can be adapted by schools for use.

Some youth services will need parental consent to deliver sessions that could be of concern to parents. While consent in schools for pupil to take part (or not) in PSHE is routinely sought, within informal education this is not always required. A template for a parent/carer consent form is provided in the appendices (Appendix 2) which can be easily altered to specify what will be covered.

Online and mobile safety

Parents are encouraged to set boundaries to internet use at home, using the security settings available on shared devices and regularly checking the web history to see the sites most visited. While accepting that their children's mobile phones are often 'off limits' to parents and they are entitled to a level of privacy in terms of texts and messaging via social media, it is worth taking the opportunity to point out that having pornographic images on a phone is illegal, even if both parties consented or if the subject is unknown, for example downloaded content.

When offering a general guide to assessing if a picture is appropriate or not, parents might like to suggest that their child consider if it is a picture they would be happy sharing with a grandparent or older relative. While this is a light-hearted approach that should raise a smile, the message behind it is clear and might encourage young people to hesitate and think again before uploading pictures. More direct advice is included within some of the lesson plans that look at staying safe online and social media, and a quick guide for parents is provided in Appendix 4.

Encourage parents to keep communication channels open so that they can ask about any noticeable differences in the volume of texts their child sends and/or receives and discuss the risks of photo sharing. Other strategies include offering to help with setting up social media accounts and choosing a profile picture without being seen to pry or ask awkward questions. A genuine interest can encourage openness and contribute to young people believing that they have someone to turn to should things go wrong. Taking the opportunity to discuss issues in an everyday way is likely to be far more effective than sitting down to have a 'big talk' about pornography, which can be embarrassing for all concerned. That way the message received is that children can talk openly to the adults they live with, meaning that if they are worried they are more likely to ask them for help or advice.

Using the media

Parents can create opportunities to check out values and attitudes by looking out for media reports relating to indecency and pornography, for example young couples prosecuted for sending and receiving naked photos of each other, or TV storylines that involve characters vulnerable to abusive or manipulative relationships. These all provide great starting points for parents to talk about choices made and to share concerns about potential consequences. Soap operas in particular often have storylines that mirror current concerns and watching them together at home can make it easier to talk about difficult topics in the third person, while reinforcing positive messages to keep young people safe and happy. Simply keeping open the lines of communication in a non-judgemental and unemotional way demonstrates to young people that their parents understand some of the issues and are willing to listen. Having 'what if?' conversations should make it easier if it becomes necessary to have real ones.

Ultimately what most young people need is the reassurance that if they make a mistake or get into a difficult situation there is an adult they can rely on for advice, information and support at home.

- Useful resource: *Let's work together: A practical guide for schools to involve parents and carers in sex education*, available to download from the Sex Education Forum.[1]

Managing parental concerns

Many parents/carers are concerned about the easy access to porn that the internet and smart phones allow their teenagers, and are horrified if they discover that their child is one of the many thousands who has viewed it.

As well as being a bit of a taboo subject, one issue is that unlike other complex social 'firsts' experienced during the teen years, social media in its current form was not around when many parents were the same age, so they have no personal experience on which to draw. Add to that the barrage of worrying stories in the news and it is unsurprising that

---

1   www.sexeducationforum.org.uk/schools/partnership-with-parents-and-carers.aspx

parents, especially those not confident using digital technology, are left feeling alarmed and a bit helpless.

For young people to participate fully in the lessons contained in this resource it may be necessary to obtain parental consent, especially within an environment that does not have any statutory powers, such as a youth club. In schools this might already be covered by existing consent given for PSHE lessons, but it is good practice to advise parents (and young people) what is going to be covered and the intended learning outcomes, along with a consent form for parents to read, sign and return. An example letter is included in Appendix 1 that can be adapted by schools for use.

Youth services will need to decide if parental consent is required to participate in this area of social education. Although this may not be possible in circumstances where the issue of pornography arises out of an informal discussion, to develop it into a wider project it might be advisable to keep those with parental responsibility informed, even if this is going to take place in a detached setting. An example consent form is included in Appendix 2. Explain to young people that without a signed consent form it will be assumed that consent has been denied and they will be unable to participate.

Hosting an open evening or workshop that offers practical support to parents/carers and an opportunity to see the teaching materials that will be used, plus information and advice on how to broach this complex subject at home, can help to allay any fears they may have. These could include worries that discussing porn might actually encourage young people to use it more, or introduce them to things they don't yet know.

An example invitation to a parental information workshop is provided in Appendix 3.

During the parent/carers information workshop educators should be prepared to answer questions about what will be covered and how. Schools may want to consider preparing a handout that details how this new topic fits into existing schemes of work. This would aim to reassure parents that pornography will be raised in an age-appropriate way that is professional, supportive and ethical as part of a properly planned SRE or PSHE curriculum. Again, reinforce that no pornographic or inappropriate material will be shown at any time, under any circumstances.

Finally, consider offering the contact number of a named person in school or the youth club and a time slot when parents can call for an update on learning or to share any concerns.

Signposting to additional support for parents

All schools should have a PSHE or SRE policy that can be shared with parents on request to have a deeper understanding of the topics within the curriculum. This should describe what the point of it is and how it supports young people to learn social and emotional skills for life. There should also be opportunities scheduled into the school year for parents to be updated about their child's learning.

Consider signposting parents to the additional services listed below, making it clear that no responsibility can be taken for the content or advice given by outside organisations.

- Young Minds Parents Helpline: 0808 802 5544 (free for mobiles and landlines) – offering free, confidential online and telephone support, including information and advice, to any adult worried about the emotional problems, behaviour or mental health of a child or young person up to the age of 25

- Relate: Parenting Troubled Teenagers: 0300 100 1234 – offering free confidential online and telephone support to parents concerned about their teens' substance misuse, relationships or behaviour

- Mermaids: 0208 123 4819 – family and individual support for children and teenagers with gender identity issues

- FPA – the FPA provides an advice sheet for parents on how to talk to their child or teenager about sex and relationships.[2]

---

2   www.fpa.org.uk/help-and-advice/advice-for-parents-carers

Partnership Agencies and Involving the Wider Community

Effective SRE in schools can be enriched not only by working in partnership with young people and their parents, but also with key professionals in health and social care services and members of the community with particular areas of expertise, for example spiritual or community leaders, who can reflect the beliefs and culture of the communities in which they live. These familiar, respected people can help reinforce learning as well as offering a cultural, religious or ethical context to SRE, making it more likely that some young people will engage.

Specific professionals can be invited to contribute to lessons, for example social media experts who can explain how home-shot porn videos can go viral in a matter of hours, or local police officers who can explain the laws regarding the taking and sending of naked selfies or the consequences of being convicted of sexual assault or rape following alcohol- or drug-fuelled non-consensual sex.

Before agreeing a guest speaker it is always important to check that both parties can work together effectively. Make sure they have seen this book and understand how it fits within the SRE curriculum and are comfortable with the boundaries set for engagement. Take time to clarify confidentiality and how it applies within the lesson to ensure mutual understanding and to identify any potential difficulties or conflicts. For example, while all professionals should be clear about their duties regarding reporting a safeguarding issue, if police are invited into class and a young person reveals they have an account with a social media site they are too young to join, will the officer have to act on it? It is far better to consider any potential challenges in advance and agree a joint strategy.

Inform young people in advance that an outside professional will be joining the class and explain their role. Inviting a stranger into a fully formed group without any explanation can damage the learning environment, change group dynamics negatively and be counter-productive to trust built.

Monitor the impact that an outside speaker's contribution has on the learning outcomes for that session and review to plan for the next time.

PART 3

Guide to Using this Resource

Teachers: The lessons in Part 5 (split into five chapters) are designed for teachers to pick and choose activities that fit within their own scheme of work within the curriculum. They can also be delivered as standalone exercises for short blocks of time, for example during registration or class assemblies to look at a specific topic.

Youth workers: The activities in Part 5 (split into five chapters) can be delivered within a wider sex and relationships curriculum. They can also be used as standalone sessions to explore different issues relating to pornography and to consider the potential impact it can have on relationships, self-image and emotional wellbeing.

All of the games, quizzes and exercises included in this book raise awareness in an engaging and age-appropriate way that is sensitive to different levels of ability. Some are intended to spark creativity while others enable young people to explore their own awareness, values and attitudes safely by using case studies, scenarios and examples. Lessons can be chosen from across the five chapters and there is no intention that they should be delivered in any specific order. However, for a holistic view facilitators may choose one from each chapter.

All lessons have been designed to develop the three key skill areas required for effective learning: knowledge, attitudes and skills.

1. *Knowledge:* Offering correct non-biased information about the pornography industry; facts about sex and relationships and the legal context.

2. *Attitudes:* Exploring values and opinions about porn and how watching porn can affect young people's view of sex and relationships. This includes the important issue of consent, body image and the potential impact on expectations of sex and relationships as well as aspirations for the future.

3. *Skills:* Developing good self-esteem, building assertiveness and confidence and enabling young people to make their own informed choices about pornography, as well as how to develop positive relationships and maintain emotional wellbeing.

For more information about teaching SRE and PSHE go to:

- Brook – www.brook.org.uk

- PSHE Association – www.pshe-association.org.uk

- Sex Education Forum – www.sexeducationforum.org.uk

- The National Curriculum – www.gov.uk/national-curriculum/other-compulsory
-subjects

Extension activities

While some extension activities have been suggested for individual lesson plans, it is generally anticipated that most learning will take place within the classroom/ informal learning environment. This is to reduce the likelihood of young people using inappropriate websites for 'research' and acknowledges that most of these lesson plans will be used within a wider SRE curriculum.

However, young people are directed to different campaigns for better, more inclusive SRE and may choose to look into this in more depth. Alternatively, lesson activities may be used as a basis for a peer education or Youth Health Champions project or to inspire individual campaigns on some of the issues raised.

Facilitating Group Learning

This book has been written as a group work resource for educating young people together. The timings given are based on facilitating a group of up to 20 young people, but can be used with greater or smaller numbers with minimal adaptation. As a rough guide, allow more time for a whole class, especially where activities include feedback and presentations, and select some additional tasks for small groups (between 6 and 12) in case they get through planned learning more quickly.

Research shows that pornography creates certain gender bias. Young men say they use it to satisfy curiosity about sex and, in particular, technique, positions and the female anatomy, as well as for arousal purposes.[1] Young women report watching it to find out about sex itself, although not exclusively.

New research by McCormack and Wignall[2] finds that some young men explicitly use pornography as a 'safe place' to explore their sexuality and to help them understand their sexual identity, concluding that this challenges notions that porn is harmful. By comparison, research undertaken by Bridges[3] concludes that as pornography has become more accessible it has increasingly shaped expectations of romantic relationships and created new sexual 'norms', which is cause for concern in terms of decreasing body image satisfaction for young women and altering perceptions of acceptable behaviour.

To facilitate learning, consider delivering some sessions in single gender groups. Both young men and women may find it easier to be honest about concerns and ask questions in this type of environment and it can reduce embarrassment around intimate topics. Having said this, there is value in bringing males and females together to learn from each other, for example discussions about consent and gender stereotypes, so that they have the opportunity for greater awareness and to build empathy about different perspectives.

1 Flood (2009) 'The harms of pornography exposure amongst children and young people.' *Child Abuse Review, 18,* 384–400.
2 McCormack, M. and Wignall, L. (2016) 'Enjoyment, exploration and education: understanding the consumption of pornography among young men with non-exclusive sexual orientations.' Department of Sociology, Durham University.
3 Bridges, A. (2015) 'Pornography's influence on interpersonal relationships.' Department of Psychology, University of Arkansas.

Supporting Different Learning Needs

While sex and pornography are repeatedly mentioned, the main focus of this learning resource is on building healthy, trusting relationships and enabling young people to recognise the difference between real life and the types of sexual encounters often depicted in porn. For under-16s consider running sessions within a wider context, for example the media's influence on body image or the ethics of using images of a sexual nature in music videos, rather than focusing solely on pornography.

Young people learn in different ways so the lesson plans in this book are facilitated to met the needs of audio, visual and kinaesthetic learners through discussion, presentation, quizzes, pair and share activities, media (websites/film/magazines) and interactive group work. For a more creative approach, there are several activities that are art or craft based, meaning that young people learn while they make something.

The lesson plans are deliberately flexible to respond to different levels of existing knowledge and ability. Where appropriate, adaptations have been suggested for a more inclusive approach, such as facilitating 'agree/disagree' activities using red and green cards while seated, rather than by moving to points around the room. There are also suggestions for alternative activities for young people who may feel uncomfortable talking in larger groups and for those who do not enjoy role-play activities.

It is important that facilitators take into consideration that young people may:

- have no experience of porn or alternatively have seen lots of it

- hold existing opinions about pornography and the availability of material with an adult content

- receive mixed messages either from parents or older siblings who openly bring adult material into the home or from family members who refuse to talk about sex and relationships at all

- have values and attitudes influenced by their faith, culture and/or community

- feel uncomfortable talking about intimate issues with anyone.

To address this, consider including a 'time out' system if things get too much, opportunities to 'pass' or ask questions on a one-to-one basis, an anonymous questions box to post questions into at any time, or opportunities after the formal learning has ended to share concerns.

A wider strategy for support will need to be agreed in advance, ready to be put into place when appropriate. Best practice suggests that this should be part of a whole-school approach, so it will be important to inform other school services, such as the pastoral support team, school counsellors or chaplains, when the lessons are taking place. This way they can be prepared for any referrals made or any additional calls on their time for one-to-one support and advice.

Finally, information about local community support services for young people should be made available both in schools and within youth service provision. This includes community health clinics, emotional and spiritual support and confidential sexual health services, dependent on age and maturity.

Assessment and evaluation

Before starting, teachers and youth workers are encouraged to carry out a needs assessment in order to assess existing knowledge and identify the appropriate level for the group. There is a 'reflection and review' activity suggested at the end of each lesson plan. This will enable young people to participate in a facilitator-guided evaluation of the learning within the main lesson and reinforces the key points to check that everyone has understood and processed the information given. Additionally, for use at the end of a block of lessons, project or extended lesson there is an evaluation sheet (Appendix 5) for young people to complete. Facilitators can use this to review learning and identify further educational needs.

Dependent on the young people participating and activities chosen, a risk assessment may be appropriate. This should be undertaken in line with organisational guidelines.

Suggested tools for group assessment include: mind mapping, quizzes and questionnaires and facilitated discussion.

Suggested tools for individual assessment include: one-to-one questionnaires or informal and formal review by teachers.

Suggested tools for evaluation include: individual and group feedback, private reflection and self-evaluation, quizzes to reinforce and check learning.

Creating a Safe Learning Environment

Please note that it is anticipated that ground rules, confidentiality and appropriate behaviour will have been discussed, agreed and put in place before facilitating any learning. There is a reminder to review this at the start of every lesson.

Ground rules

To ensure a safe learning environment it is good practice to negotiate and agree ground rules with young people before starting any learning. These are different to the formal rules already in place within a school or youth centre and focus on how the group will work and learn effectively together, handle differences of opinion, approach questions and clarify confidentiality and boundaries.

Going through this process will help create a space in which all young people can learn, discuss sensitive issues, ask questions and work together safely and with respect for each other.

The following ground rules could be used as a starting point:

- Respect each other's rights, beliefs, values and experience.

- Use the correct anatomical words for body parts during discussions (where known; if not known, ask).

- Listen to one another.

- Ask questions to help learning.

- Respect diversity, faith and culture.

- Nobody has to share anything personal.

- Everyone has the right to an opinion.

- Each person must take responsibility for what they say or share.

- Maintain confidentiality – unless this could put someone at risk of harm or harming others.

The educator is also bound by these ground rules, except in circumstances where a young person discloses something that they are obliged to report under child protection and safeguarding laws or where a criminal act has been committed.

Some schools or faith groups may have agreed guidance about how to answer questions on specific topics so this will need to be taken into account too when planning for the lesson.

Confidentiality and safeguarding

The Department for Education published new statutory safeguarding guidance, *Keeping children safe in education* (2015),[1] with reference to teaching children about how to keep themselves and each other safe and the role of SRE in prevention.

As the issues discussed in SRE, including the potential impact of pornography, can be extremely sensitive, make sure that the need to respect each other's points of view has been fully considered and that young people are clear from the start that personal questions about sex, relationships and sharing direct experiences of watching porn will not be allowed.

Alongside the ground rules, confidentiality, what it means and where the boundaries lie, needs to be clearly detailed before any work begins. Remind young people regularly that confidentiality does not mean keeping secrets and that there are certain circumstances where facilitators cannot maintain it. These include:

- if a young person is at risk of potential harm or is being harmed, for example abuse, sexual exploitation or as a victim of 'revenge porn'

- if a young person is at risk of, or has caused significant harm to someone else, for example sharing intimate photos without permission, being a perpetrator of domestic abuse or relationship bullying.

Finally, the issues of relationship bullying, sexual consent, revenge porn and abuse between couples are raised within some of the lesson plans, encouraging young people to speak out and get help for themselves or a friend if they suspect unacceptable behaviour. Details of local support as well as national organisations should be made available in ways that do not single out particular young people, for example handing out leaflets to everyone.

For details about online safeguarding go to the website of the Child Exploitation and Online Protection Centre (CEOP).[2]

Managing challenging behaviour

Although ground rules, co-produced with young people, provide a basic framework for acceptable behaviour, facilitators should agree in advance strategies for managing challenging behaviour effectively. Young people should be clear about behavioural expectations and aware of any sanctions that will be evoked (if any) should they be broken.

Part of the learning process is to offer safe opportunities to constructively challenge comments and opinions and this should be encouraged. However, it is important to recognise that some young people may object to porn for religious or cultural reasons, or have strong political feelings about it, for example feminist views about the

---

1   www.gov.uk/government/publications/keeping-children-safe-in-education--2
2   http://ceop.police.uk

objectification of women, and the facilitator should be prepared to close down heated challenges before they become personal to prevent anyone feeling isolated or attacked.

Additional support and guidance

How much is too much? Some young people may be concerned that their use of pornography is becoming compulsive or use the term 'porn addict' to describe the amount of porn they watch. Facilitators should be ready to encourage young people to seek professional support and guidance where appropriate. In addition to researching local support services for young people, the following organisations may be helpful in signposting to national services:

- ChildLine – a counselling service for children and young people[3]

- NHS Choices – sex additction and love addiction. NHS website on a variety of aspects of sex and relationships with links to help and support[4]

- The Site – provides information and advice on a range of issues, including sex and relationships, safe sexting and webcam sex, affecting young adults aged 16–25[5]

- *Understanding Sex and Relationships Education, A Sex Education Forum Briefing* (2010).[6]

3   www.childline.org.uk
4   www.nhs.uk/Livewell/addiction/Pages/sexandloveaddiction.aspx
5   www.thesite.org
6   www.sexeducationforum.org.uk/media/2572/understanding_sre_2010.pdf

Key Vocabulary

Below is a table of common terms, acronyms and words used throughout this resource book. It may be helpful for teachers/youth workers to read and become familiar with any unknown vocabulary. It can also be shared with young people, where appropriate, who may want to offer suggestions for local meaning or new additions.

Throughout this book some key vocabulary is highlighted in **bold** text at the start of each activity/lesson plan.

Vocabulary	Meaning
Abstinence	The avoidance of any kind of sexual activity
Adult entertainment industry	Adult entertainment industry (also called the sex industry or sex trade) consists of businesses which either directly or indirectly provide sex-related products and services
Advertising standards	The Advertising Standards Authority (ASA) is the self-regulatory organisation of the advertising industry in the UK
Asexual	Someone who does not experience sexual attraction (or very little) to any person
Assertiveness/ assertive behaviour	Saying what you think, feel, need or want with confidence while respecting the rights and needs of others
Beauty industry	A collective term for anyone involved in the manufacturing, designing, marketing, promotion and sales of products (including cosmetics), which aim to enhance physical appearance and improve the self-image of those who buy and use them
Bisexual	Physically, romantically and sexually attracted to your own and other gender(s)
Body confidence and body image	People with body confidence have positive body image, meaning that their perception of their physical self and their positive feelings as a result of that contribute to emotional health and general wellbeing. Some people are not body confident, meaning that their feelings towards themselves are negative. Body confidence and body image can be influenced by individual, environmental and cultural factors
CAMHS	Child and adolescent mental health service
Celibate	Someone who chooses to refrain from sexual intercourse
Cis gender	Someone whose gender identity, gender expression and biological sex all align
CLA	Children looked after
Collective responsibility	Something that is the responsibility of many people, rather than one person
Consequences	The potential sequence of events that is likely to happen as the result of a choice, decision or action. Before making a decision, potential consequences should be considered and then balanced against the likelihood of it happening. In this way, decisions are likely to be more informed with the potential for better outcomes
CPD	Continuing professional development

Vocabulary	Meaning
Criminal Justice and Immigration Act 2008	An Act of the Parliament of the UK that commenced in July 2008. Section 63 creates a new offence of possessing 'an extreme pornographic image'. Section 69 extends the definition of indecent photographs in the Protection of Children Act 1978 (which creates offences relating to child pornography). Section 72 amends section 72 of the Sexual Offences Act 2003 to extend sexual offences against children overseas. Section 73 and Schedule 15 extend the definition of the offence of child grooming. The complete Act is available to download in PDF form online[1]
Debate	To offer different viewpoints, along with supporting arguments, and then take turns in discussing them
DfE	Department for Education
DH	Department of Health
Diversity	Understanding that each person is a unique individual and recognising and valuing these individual differences
Domestic abuse and relationship bullying	Any type of controlling behaviour, bullying, threats and intimidation or violent behaviour between people in a relationship. This can be emotional or physical
Emotional wellbeing	Defined by the Mental Health Foundation[2] as a 'positive sense of wellbeing which enables an individual to be able to function in society and meet the demands of everyday life; people in good mental health have the ability to recover effectively from illness, change or misfortune'
Film classification	In the UK the British Board of Film Classification classifies films before they can legally be shown in cinemas and other public venues. This determines the age that the film is suitable for
Flirting	Showing someone that you find them sexually attractive without openly saying so. This can be face to face or, for example, by sending flirty texts. Flirting is not always reciprocated so it is important to be responsive to the body language of others so that it is not interpreted as harassment
Gay	A man who is sexually, physically and romantically attracted to the same gender. Often used to describe women attracted to women too
Gender identity	The internal perception someone has of their gender and how they label themselves
GUM clinic	Genito-urinary medicine clinic
Heterosexual	A medical definition for someone who is attracted to someone of the other biological sex
High street	Shops and well-known brands that are typically found on a high street rather than independent shops or boutiques and designer labels
Homemade porn	Also called 'amateur porn' or 'realcore', it generally means pornography made by real people rather than professional actors, directors and film crew, etc., often in their own home. It describes digital images, videos and live steaming as well as printed pictures
Image	How you present yourself to others, also described as 'public image'
Indecent image	As defined by the legislation for England and Wales which deals directly with offences concerning indecent images of children: • The Protection of Children Act 1978 – Section 1 • The Criminal Justice Act 1988 – Section 160

---

1   www.legislation.gov.uk/ukpga/2008/4/pdfs/ukpga_20080004_en.pdf
2   www.mentalhealth.org.uk

Internalise	To accept or absorb an idea, opinion or belief so deeply that it becomes part of your character and can define how you see yourself
LBGT+	An inclusive term for those identifying as lesbian, gay, bisexual or transgender plus any other non-heterosexuals
Lesbian	A woman who is physically, sexually and romantically attracted to another woman
Manga comics	Created in Japan and identifiable by their unique style of drawing characterised by elfin features and big eyes, which was developed in Japan in the late 19th century. Manga comics are popular in the UK, along with Manga (or Manga-style) cartoons. While traditional Manga images are age appropriate for under 18s, animated pornographic films using the same style of characters are not and this is legislated for within the Criminal Justice and Immigration Act 2008
Marketing	The promotion and selling of products and goods
Naked selfie	Sometimes called 'nudes' or 'glampics' this refers to intimate and/or erotic selfies usually taken for the purpose of sexual arousal. They are often sent via text or instant message, but can be kept by the owner. Illegal to take, possess and share if the person is under 18
National curriculum	Sets out the programmes of study and attainment targets in schools for all subjects at all four key stages
NEET	Not in employment, education or training
NHS	National Health Service
Online app/ Mobile app	An online app is a program stored on a remote server that can be downloaded and installed on a computer. A mobile app is designed to run on mobile devices, such as smart phones and tablets
Online dating	Commonly used to describe those engaged in looking for a potential romance or sexual partner online, usually via a dating app
Online safety	Gaining the knowledge and skills to enjoy the internet safely and securely
Overt and covert messages	Overt = what you openly say, see or do; covert = the subtext or underlying message given
Parental responsibility	The legal rights, duties, powers, responsibilities and authority a parent has for a child (under 18) and the child's property. A person who has parental responsibility for a child has the right to make decisions about their care and upbringing. This is can be someone other than the birth mother or father, for example a grandparent or older sibling if assigned by a court. If a child is in the care of the local authority, often referred to as 'in care', then the local authority may have parental authority
PCT	Primary care trust
Peer education	The teaching or sharing of information by people of the same or a similar age
Penis	The male genital organ
Personal boundaries	The internal rules and limits people set about what is and isn't acceptable in the way other people behave towards them. This includes emotional boundaries, which may remain unspoken until someone challenges them
Personal responsibility	Things for which individuals have choices and responsibility for the consequences of their actions
Popular culture	Also 'pop culture', to mean ideas, music, attitudes, images, etc. that are widely popular within mainstream Western culture
Porn actor	An actor who is employed to be filmed having sex in pornographic films
Pornographic image	An image, visual or picture which fits within the description below
Pornography	Sexually explicit material that is for the primary purpose of sexual arousal. Porn is the abbreviation

Vocabulary	Meaning
Positive relationship	A relationship based on mutual feelings, equality, respect and trust. Although this can include friendships the term is popularly used to describe intimate relationships, which may or may not involve penetrative sex
PSHE	Personal, social and health education
Queer	The collective term used to encompass anyone not identifying as straight
Reality TV	A common catch-all term used to mean programmes that purportedly use 'real-life' people instead of professional actors, and film them in a variety of situations, tasks or challenges to entertain the viewer. This genre includes popular TV shows 'Big Brother', 'Gogglebox', 'Made in Chelsea' and 'The Only Way Is Essex'
Revenge porn	The distribution of a private sexual image of someone without their consent and with the intention of causing them distress
Self-esteem	Confidence in your own value, worth and/or abilities
Selfie	A self-portrait taken with a mobile phone, usually to send to someone else or post on social media. These can be taken alone or with others
Sexting	Sending messages, usually by text, of a sexual nature
Sexual attraction	Attraction that someone feels for someone else based on sexual desire
Sexual consent	Currently, the legal definition is that the individual must be over the age of 16 and able to understand the nature of the sex act and its consequences, there must be no pressure used, and they are able to communicate their decision to have sex
Sexual expectations	Used to describe what someone anticipates their experience of sex will be like. These expectations are informed by culture, faith, education, family, peers and experience, as well as things like the media, music industry and watching pornography. Some research suggests that pornography is informing young people with sexual expectations unlikely to be met outside a film and is putting pressure on them or their partners to fulfil these unrealistic expectations
Sexual harassment	Unwelcome sexual advances or behaviour of a sexual nature that makes someone feel uncomfortable, unsafe, bullied or afraid
Sexual innuendo	Something that sounds innocent but has a sexual interpretation too. Some traditional forms of comedy rely on it, for example pantomime dames usually use some form of sexual innuendo
Sexual intimacy	Physical intimacy, or closeness, within a relationship. This can be within a romantic relationship or confined to sexual activity only. Being sexually intimate does not mean that penetrative sex has to take place
Sexualisation of cartoon images	Cartoons that use gender and sexual stereotypes to produce characters that epitomise idealised body shapes and sizes, for example cartoons that depict women with an unrealistic bust to waist ratio, or that have exaggerated 'six packs' drawn on males. Some cartoons take this a step further, intended for an adult audience, where cartoon characters are shown engaging in sexually explicit activities. Some of these cartoons, along with Manga cartoons where childlike characters are depicted having unlawful sex, are illegal to create, have or sell in the UK
Sexualised slogan	Similar to a sexual innuendo but in a written form with the intent to say something that might otherwise be unacceptable or offensive. Arguments about this have included the use of the acronym 'FCUK' by the clothing company French Connection UK
Sexual norms	Most cultures have social norms that extend to sexuality and define 'normal sexuality' as certain acts between certain people. This does vary between cultures and it is accepted that 'normal' means different things to different people. Societal attitudes to those not conforming to 'norms' has relaxed over the last 30 years, providing both people are consenting adults and no laws are broken

Sexual Offences Act 2003	Replaced older laws with updated versions and offered greater protection to children from harm. Specifically it redefined rape and sexual assault from the Sexual Offences Act 1956 and included new offences related to 'sex tourism', which refers to adults travelling overseas specifically to pay for sex[3]
Sexual orientation	The type of sexual, romantic and physical attraction someone feels for another person, usually based on gender
Skin flick/ Adult movie	A pornographic film
SMSC education	Spiritual, moral, social and cultural education
Social media	Websites and applications that enable users to create and share content or to participate in social networking. This includes Facebook, Instagram and Twitter
SRE	Sex and relationships education
STI	Sexually transmitted infection (now used in preference to STD, sexually transmitted disease)
Stereotype	A stereotype is a commonly held belief about a person or group of people based on an assumption or incomplete knowledge, and then widely applied. For example, all women are bad drivers, all men like football. This can lead to prejudice and discrimination
Surgical enhancement	Generally used to describe enhancements to the face or body made through surgical intervention. This is also called 'cosmetic surgery' 'plastic surgery' or 'invasive treatments', for example a breast enlargement or reduction, which requires an anaesthetic and a surgeon, as opposed to 'non-surgical interventions'. These tend to describe things which are less likely to be permanent, for example fillers, skin peels and Botox, which can be done outside an operating theatre in a beauty salon by a trained beauty therapist rather than by a medically qualified professional
Transgender	Someone who feels that their gender identity (their sense of themselves as a boy or girl) is not a complete match with the sex they were assigned at birth[4]
Unclassified porn film	A film that has not been classified by the British Board of Film Classification. Porn films are usually classified as R18, meaning that they are only legally sold to those aged 18 or over
Vagina	The muscular tube leading from the external genitals to the cervix in women and most female mammals[5]
Values and attitudes	A value is the worth or importance a person attaches to something. An attitude is the way someone expresses or applies their values, usually through words and/or behaviour

---

3   To read the Act in full go to www.legislation.gov.uk/ukpga/2003/42/pdfs/ukpga_20030042_en.pdf
4   www.bbc.co.uk/programmes/articles/XZjhcLhQW08Ylw5b0p9xgH/gender-dysphoria-transgender
5   Definition taken from www.oxforddictionaries.com

PART 4

Overview of Each Chapter

In this resource book lesson plans are divided into five chapters:

Chapter 1: What is Porn?
Chapter 2: Shopping, Music and the Media
Chapter 3: Porn and Body Image
Chapter 4: Porn vs. Real-Life Relationships
Chapter 5: Sexting, Revenge Porn and Online Sexual Bullying

Below is a quick guide to each section to help facilitators select activities to put together to meet the needs of young people. These can be delivered as standalone lessons, used to enhance existing SRE materials or fitted together to provide an interesting and varied curriculum.

Chapter 1: What is Porn?

The Collins English Dictionary defines pornography as 'writing, pictures, films, etc. designed to stimulate sexual excitement'. Within this is a very wide continuum from mildly erotic photographs through to exploitative images of abuse and the misuse of sexual images without consent.

This opening chapter aims to explore definitions of 'porn' and support young people in understanding what constitutes pornography, including online films, DVDs, magazines and 'homemade' porn such as 'sexting'.

In addition, there are ideas for opening up discussions about values and attitudes to the legislation that governs much of what is in the public domain, including how films that contain content of a sexual nature are classified for distribution and the laws in place intended to protect exploitation and keep children and young people safe.

Chapter 2: Shopping, Music and the Media

This chapter explores the messages that children and young people pick up from the world around them. This begins with the casual use of sexual images on the high street, from Barbie and Ken to 'mommy porn' books[1] on display in supermarkets, to the messages given about sex from high street shops selling underwear and sex toys.

Ideas here include creative and engaging ways of exploring the impact of sexualised computer games and raunchy music videos on young people's expectations of intimate relationships and how they view each other's emotional needs and wants. Although there are strict regulations for the industry to adhere to, including those that outlaw the

---

1   www.dailymail.co.uk/femail/article-2190829/Poll-ranks-50-Shades-Grey-erotic-mommy-porn-novels.html

inappropriate use of sexuality of both women and men, there is still an argument that says that these rules are not applied strictly enough.

Chapter 3: Porn and Body Image

In a survey for the Channel 4 programme 'Sex Education versus Pornography', 60 per cent of teenagers said that pornography affects their self-esteem and body image negatively. With teenagers bombarded with images of the 'perfect body' and looks traditionally associated with the porn industry crossing over into mainstream, it is easy to understand why some young people are left feeling less than body confident.

To help challenge this, the lesson plans in Chapter 3 include looking at the effect of porn on self-image and the influence it has on appearance, from hair extensions to waxing, and invite young people to consider how notions of perfection change. Activities aim to build self-confidence by reminding young people that happiness comes from within, so be proud of yourself, whatever the shape or size of your body, and celebrate difference and diversity.

Chapter 4: Porn vs. Real-Life Relationships

All activities in this section start from the viewpoint that watching pornography is not the best way for young people to learn about sex and relationships. Topics include the influence that friends, partners and peers can have on decisions to watch or engage in porn, with a focus on the message that desire and sexual feelings are perfectly normal but sexual attraction doesn't have to lead directly to sex, which is only one way to show someone you care.

A Sex Education Forum survey in 2013 found that the majority of young people know the basic legal facts about consent to sex but are much less sure about how to deal with the complexity of real-life relationship situations.[2] This includes different types of sexual bullying, negotiating relationship boundaries and consent as well as how to be assertive and resist unwanted pressure, which are explored in detail in this chapter.

The key messages are for young people to make positive, informed choices to develop safe, healthy relationships.

Chapter 5: Sexting, Revenge Porn and Online Sexual Bullying

Digital communication is an exciting, ever-changing platform that is here to stay, with many young people choosing to be exposed on a 24/7 basis. Amidst celebrity 'sex tape' scandals and reports of hacked social media accounts, mobile technology has brought new ways to send and receive information and pictures, leading to phenomena such as cyber bullying and sexting,[3] which is the general term for using digital media to send self-made sexual images and/or content.

Issues of coercion or peer pressure to take/send intimate images, revenge porn and threatening to share images to control someone are issues explored in this chapter. Activities to build empathy and explore the meaning of trust are included alongside discussions on privacy and the loss of it, as well as considering the other potential consequences of decisions made.

2   Sex Education Forum (2013) Survey with young people about consent and SRE, published in *The Consent Issue*, 2014, National Children's Bureau
3   Terrence Higgins Trust 2014

PART 5

Activities

CHAPTER 1

What is Porn?

Lesson plans in this chapter explain what pornography is, including online porn, and set out the existing UK laws in place to protect children and young people.

ACTIVITY 1.1: WHAT IS PORNOGRAPHY?

(Years 7–13+)

Aim

- To discuss the line between acceptable, provocative and pornographic images, before giving information about the law.

Time: 45 minutes

Learning outcomes

- To learn about the UK legal definition of a pornographic picture.
- To understand the difference between pictures of naked people and pornographic pictures.

Key vocabulary

- **Pornography**
- **Social media**

You will need

- Copies of the *Porn/not porn activity cards*
- Flipchart paper and markers

How to do it

1. Introduction

- Establish/revisit ground rules (see pages 42–43 for guidance).

Explain that this exercise helps explore the fine line between acceptable and unacceptable images, for example paintings of naked frolicking cherubs by the old masters on public display for anyone to see, through to public complaints about over-realistic sex scenes on late night TV.

2. Opening activity

Working in small groups, each with a set of activity cards, the task is to discuss the different scenarios offered and then define them as 'porn' or 'not porn'.

Allow about 15 minutes for discussion and then ask if consensus has been reached. Facilitate a feedback session inviting each group to share which pile they have placed the cards in and their reasons for doing so.

3. Development activity

Then offer this UK definition of porn, taken from the Criminal Justice and Immigration Act 2008, asking young people afterwards if they would like to change any card placements now that they have heard what the law says.

> An image is 'pornographic' if it is of such a nature that it must reasonably be assumed to have been produced solely or principally for the purpose of sexual arousal.[1]

Facilitate a discussion that considers:

- Are all naked pictures pornographic?
- Why are famous paintings containing naked images not considered porn?
- Where does the boundary between sexy/provocative and pornographic lie?
- Can an image that is legally considered pornographic be taken or made unintentionally?

4. Reflection and review

Hand out sticky notes and ask each learner to write down one suggestion as a response to the following question:

> What can be done to help young people understand the difference?

Then ask them to stick their ideas on the wall and invite a couple of volunteers to read them out and review with the wider group, encouraging further debate and questions.

5. Summary

- In the UK a picture is considered pornographic if it can be assumed that its purpose is sexual arousal.
- Not all naked pictures are pornographic.
- A naked photo posted on social media is a pornographic image.

---

1   For full details of this Act go to www.legislation.gov.uk/ukpga/2008/4/part/5/crossheading/pornography-etc

ACTIVITY 1.1: PORN/NOT PORN ACTIVITY CARDS

Choosing a close up of your mouth blowing a kiss for your social media profile.	Sending a topless selfie to your partner to show how much you miss them.
Sharing holiday pictures of you in swimwear on social media.	Buying a postcard of a naked statue from an art gallery.
Posting pictures of sexy costumes at a fancy dress party.	Taking pictures of a drunken friend urinating in a public place.
Consenting partners taking intimate pictures of each other during sex.	Posting pictures of your naked genitals on an online dating site.
Taking headshots of a friend and Photoshopping them on to random naked bodies for a joke.	Drawing a naked person during a life drawing class.
Retweeting naked pictures of celebrities.	Posing in sexy underwear while your boy/girlfriend takes pictures.
Sharing an online naked photo along with comments containing sexual innuendo.	'Liking' online topless pictures of glamour models.
Taking pictures of a sleeping boy/girlfriend and posting them online without permission.	Showing work colleagues holiday photos of you sunbathing topless.

ACTIVITY 1.2: PICTURES NOT PORN, PLEASE

(Years 9–13+)

Aim

- For learners to be able to raise awareness among their peers about the difference between provocative photos and pornography as defined by UK law.

Time: 45–60 minutes (including research time)

Learning outcomes

- To research and discuss the Criminal Justice and Immigration Act 2008 legislation (section 63) and/or the Sexual Offences Act 2003.

- To devise guidelines to share with peers to educate and inform them about the risks of taking and sharing intimate photos.

Key vocabulary

- **Social media**
- **Pornography**
- **Criminal Justice and Immigration Act 2008**
- **Sexual Offences Act 2003**

You will need

- Online access (or to download the key sections of the legislation identified above)
- Paper and pens

How to do it

1. Introduction

- Establish/revisit ground rules (see pages 42–43 for guidance).

Remind young people of the learning from the previous activity about the importance of knowing the difference between taking (or being the subject of) a flirty, fun picture and a pornographic image.

2. Opening activity

In small groups, ask learners to research online more about the Criminal Justice and Immigration Act 2008[2] and the Sexual Offences Act 2003 (see section 45, 'Indecent pictures of persons aged 16 and 17' and section 48, 'Causing or inciting child prostitution or child pornography'[3]) in relation to pornography and make notes.

To make this age appropriate to younger pupils or more accessible for students with additional needs you may choose to select the key facts and put these onto a handout to reduce the level of research and self-directed learning required.

3. Development activity

Using the key points of the legislation, task each group to create a set of 'Pictures not porn, please' guidelines to be shared with their peers via social media. These should be:

---

2   www.legislation.gov.uk/ukpga/2008/4/part/5/crossheading/pornography-etc

3   www.legislation.gov.uk/ukpga/2003/42/pdfs/ukpga_20030042_en.pdf

- factual

- engaging

- easy to understand.

4. Reflection and review

Invite each group to present their guidelines, leading a round of applause after each one. Ask for at least one question from each group in the audience and encourage wider discussion about the law and how each presentation meets the three criteria set.

These guidelines can then be displayed to refer to during future learning.

5. Summary

- The importance of understanding the difference between pictures and pornography.

- The taking and sharing of intimate photos of anyone under the age of 18 is illegal, even with their consent.

Extension

Consider promoting these guidelines more widely to younger adults using social media as part of a peer education project.

ACTIVITY 1.3: LEGAL ATTITUDES

(Years 8–13+)

Aim

- For participants to share and discuss opinions about the laws controlling pornography in the UK as well as gaining a deeper understanding of the principles behind them.

Time: 30 minutes

Learning outcomes

- To consider that people have different opinions about the restriction of pornographic images and the law.

- To recognise that these values and attitudes are shaped by a multitude of things, including family, faith and culture, peers and the media.

Key vocabulary

- **Pornographic image**

- **Society**

You will need

- Large sheets of paper and marker pens

How to do it

1. Introduction

- Establish/revisit ground rules (see pages 42–43 for guidance).

Explain that this is an opportunity to share opinions about the laws that govern pornography, reminding young people about the boundaries to this, for example respecting each other's right to have an opinion, and the meaning of confidentiality.

2. Opening activity

Pose the question: 'Why do we have laws?'

Invite young people to call out suggestions and record these onto flipchart paper so they can be seen. Ideas could include:

- keeping people safe

- enforcing rules

- stopping people from doing wrong things

- governing society.

Take time to discuss ideas and in particular any suggestions that laws are there to stop people enjoying themselves or preventing them doing what they like, by asking about the potential consequences for both society as a whole and for individuals if there were none.

3. Development activity

Explain to the group that you are going to read out a series of statements that describe opinions and attitudes to pornography and the laws that control its making and distribution. Allocate the area to the left as an 'agree' zone, to the right as a 'disagree' zone, and in the middle identify a zone for those who are 'undecided'.

Ask the young people to listen to each statement and then move to the zone that corresponds best with their opinion. Point out that this is not a test but a way of finding out what people think and that there is likely to be some disagreement within the group about different topics.

Leave space between statements to discuss the views and opinions indicated by where young people are placed in the room and invite questions and debate where these differ before moving on to the next statement.

To adapt this exercise for less mobile pupils or to facilitate in a small room use a show of hands to indicate an opinion.

4. Reflection and review

Ask young people to consider in pairs how their opinions of pornography have been formed and to choose the thing or person who they think has influenced them the most.

Allow five to ten minutes for discussion and then write the word 'PORN' inside a circle in the middle of a large sheet of flipchart paper (or on a whiteboard) displayed where everyone can see it. In turn, invite each pair to come forward and write in large letters who and/or what they think has been the biggest influence on their values and attitudes. If there are duplicates then the words should be clustered close together or shown by drawing a large tick next to the appropriate word. Suggestions might include:

- family
- faith
- friends
- partners
- media attitudes
- experience
- culture
- society.

Once each pair has contributed their ideas, add up the words and ticks to see which has influenced their beliefs most.

5. Summary

Conclude that people may have conflicting views about pornography, informed by lots of different things, including their family and peers. They may disagree with the punishments that breaking the law warrants, but ultimately the law is there to protect children and young people from things like exploitation and harm. This includes the age restrictions that are in place that make it illegal for those under the age of 18 to make, view or share pornographic material. The law is not static and it changes to encompass new risks identified from things like the misuse of new technology, for example through social media. Breaking the law, by adults or by those under 18, could lead to charges and/or a criminal record so it is important to have a basic understanding and to factor this into decisions made, regardless of an individual's personal opinion about what is or isn't acceptable.

ACTIVITY 1.3: LEGAL ATTITUDES – STATEMENTS

1. Most people watch porn at some point in their lives.

2. The police should arrest anyone under 18 caught in possession of explicit images to protect their innocence.

3. People are perfectly capable of making up their own minds about what is appropriate to watch without laws.

4. Anyone caught sending explicit images of an under-18-year-old should be put on a sex offender register.

5. Parents should be notified if their child is found watching porn.

6. Anyone under 18 caught taking an intimate 'selfie' should be reported to social services.

7. The laws regarding porn are old fashioned and out of date.

8. Tightening up the porn laws and enforcing them would reduce the number of people watching it.

9. Parents should take legal responsibility if their child has explicit images on their phone.

10. There should be no free online porn. If everyone had to pay then fewer people would watch it.

11. Censorship laws just make pornography seem more interesting to young people.

12. People have a basic human right to see whatever is on the internet, even if it is classified as pornography.

ACTIVITY 1.4: THE GREAT PORN DEBATE

(Years 9–13+)

Aim

- To use this framework for debating the issue of whether pornography should be included in school-based sex and relationships education.

Time: 60–90 minutes (dependent on research time available)

Learning outcomes

- To develop communication and debating skills as the young people consider both sides of this argument.
- To participate in a simple vote.
- To find out about the UK Youth Parliament campaign for better SRE in schools.

Key vocabulary

- **SRE**
- **Emotional wellbeing**

You will need

- Copies of the quotes given to represent both sides of the debate
- Online access
- Paper and pens
- Sticky notes
- A bag to collect votes in
- Two sheets of paper headed 'View one' and 'View two'

How to do it

To prepare for the debate, set up a debate area so that learners can sit facing each other when they speak, for example using to rows of chairs or benches. Additionally, set up paper, pens and online access via a computer or laptop to provide a separate research and planning area for each team. Finally, stick up the two sheets of headed paper on to a wall where they can easily be seen.

1. Introduction

- Establish/revisit ground rules (see pages 42–43 for guidance).

Explain that this debate is based on the arguments for and against the introduction of teaching young people about the potential impact of pornography on self-image, sex, relationships and emotional wellbeing as part of the National Curriculum SRE in schools.

2. Opening activity

Divide the group into two teams, handing one team copies of View one, which sets out the basic argument for not talking about porn in school, and the other View two, which supports the view that SRE must change to include current concerns for young people, including porn.

Explain that both teams will be presenting an argument to support the quote they have been given, which cannot be changed. This must be backed by opinions, facts and evidence found during an allocated 40 minutes' research and planning time. After the teams have presented their initial argument both views will be debated.

Give each team online access and paper to record their findings and plan their argument.

3. Development activity

After the planning process is complete, facilitate a five-minute group presentation from both sides of the debate followed by opportunities for responses from the opposition. Once both sides of the debate have been heard and responded to, allocate another 10–15 minutes for teams to regroup and strengthen any arguments or do additional research before both groups have the opportunity to present a final summary.

The final summary should be a maximum of three minutes long to present the highlights of the argument, plus any supplementary findings, rather than just a quicker repeat of the first presentation.

Lead a round of applause after each summary and thank both teams for their arguments.

Then give out sticky notes and a pen to each person, explaining that there is going to be a secret ballot to discover the majority opinion within the room. To do this everyone should secretly write 1 or 2 on their sticky note and then fold it, before placing it in a bag being passed around.

4. Reflection and review

Invite a volunteer from each team to come and count the votes, asking that they take it in turns to take a sticky note out of the bag, unfold it and then stick it in on the wall in area 'View one' or 'View two' as required.

Once all of the votes have been stuck to the wall the volunteers can count and check the votes to see which side of the argument has been supported most. Congratulate the winning team on their ability to present an argument and back it up with research.

Review the debate, summarising points made on both sides of the argument and asking young people to share what influenced their final vote 'for' or 'against'.

5. Reflection and review

Ask if any of the young people is a member of a youth council, or knows someone who is. Then ask if anyone has voted in the Youth Parliament elections or has any knowledge of the UK Youth Parliament (UKYP). Explain that UKYP 'provides opportunities for 11–18-year-olds to use their elected voice to bring about social change through meaningful representation and campaigning'.[4] Elections for members of the Youth Parliament are held locally in most parts of the UK and those elected represent the views of young people in their area.

UK Youth Parliament, along with many others, support the Sex Education Forum's ongoing campaign 'SRE – It's My Right'[5] This campaigns for all young people to have high quality SRE, regardless of gender identity or sexual orientation, which includes the potential impact that pornography can have on sex, relationships and emotional wellbeing. Ask:

- Is it important that sex and relationships education changes to reflect current issues and concerns for young people? If yes, why; if no, why not?

- Do young people have a right to have a say in what is taught in SRE? If yes, how; if no, why not?

6. Summary

- Opinions differ about what children and young people should learn about SRE and at what age.

---

4   www.ukyouthparliament.org.uk/about-us
5   www.sexeducationforum.org.uk/policy-campaigns/sre-its-my-right.aspx

- There are current campaigns to improve the quality of SRE in schools to better reflect the needs of young people. This includes campaigning for education and better awareness about the potential impact of pornography.

Extension

Suggest that anyone wanting to get more involved in the real-life debate on this subject go to the Sex Education Forum's ongoing campaign 'SRE – It's My Right'[6] which is supported by the UK Youth Parliament.

---

6   www.sexeducationforum.org.uk/policy-campaigns/sre-its-my-right.aspx

ACTIVITY 1.4: THE GREAT PORN DEBATE

View one – against

Bringing pornography into the classroom will introduce sexual images to many children who have not encountered them before and will arouse in some pupils a curiosity to search out more images for themselves. It will not solve anything and will only compound the problem.*

....

View two – for

The rise of sexting, online bullying, porn and young people documenting their entire lives on the web needs to be a core tenet of how we teach sex and relationships to children in secondary schools.**

---

*   Norman Wells, Director, Family and Youth Concern, taken from article www.scotsman.com/news/education/sex-education-to-confront-deluge-of-internet-porn-1-3598922 (accessed 19 January 2015)

**   Claire Perry, Conservative MP for Devizes, taken from article www.telegraph.co.uk/women/sex/10277458/Sex-education-Claire-Perry-MP-Its-time-to-teach-children-the-difference-between-porn-and-healthy-relationships.html (accessed 18 January 2015)

ACTIVITY 1.5: PORN STEREOTYPES
(Years 10–13+)

Aims

- To raise awareness about stereotypes within the porn industry and clarify the legal regulations that govern those who are paid to appear in porn films.

- To consider the differences between adult movie actors and individuals allowing themselves to be filmed in a sexual context.

Time: 30–45 minutes (to include discussion time)

Learning outcomes

- To understand the legal differences between actors paid to produce porn and homemade porn.

- To know the age that a person can legally appear in a porn film.

- To know the laws about 'sexting', 'naked selfies' and homemade porn.

Key vocabulary

- **Sexting**
- **Naked selfies**
- **Stereotypes**
- **Homemade porn**
- **Adult movie**
- **Porn actor**
- **Film classification**

You will need

- Flipchart paper
- Plenty of coloured markers
- Sticky tack

How to do it
1. Introduction

- Establish/revisit ground rules (see pages 42–43 for guidance).

Start by asking for definitions for the following:

- pornographic film
- porn actor
- homemade porn.

Example definitions:

Pornographic film – a pornographic film is one that presents sexually explicit material for the purpose of sexual arousal. They are sometimes referred to as 'skin flicks' or 'blue movies'.

Porn actor – a porn actor is a term used for an actor of any gender or sexual orientation who is paid to perform in a pornographic film.

Homemade porn – a term used to describe amateur pornographic material made by individuals for sexual arousal.

2. Opening activity

Divide learners into three groups with a sheet of flipchart paper and some markers. Explain that you are going to give each group a topic and you want them to draw the first things that come into their head when they see it. Emphasise that this is not a drawing competition and that they can use any style that they like.

Allocate each group with one of the following tasks, Group 1: Draw a female porn star; Group 2: Draw a male porn star; Group 3: Draw someone likely to engage in making homemade porn. Set the following rules:

- Figures drawn should be clothed.
- Figures drawn should not be engaging in any sexual activity.

Allow ten minutes to draw, encouraging them to think about age, body shape/size and ethnicity as well as things like clothes and hairstyles. Ask that they do this without looking at each other's sheets for the moment. Please note that responses to this are likely to vary dependent on age, experience of pornography and knowledge of stereotypes.

At the end of the time ask everyone to stop and then invite each group to show their picture, explaining any particular bits they want to draw attention to before sticking it on the wall. Encourage the group to share how they decided what to draw and what influenced their choices, and record any recurring themes to produce a whole-group profile of a male and female porn star and a person they think likely to engage in homemade porn using the following categories:

- gender
- age
- nationality
- height
- hair colour
- body shape/size
- outward appearance.

Once complete, ask what informed their ideas about actors from the porn industry and people who choose to make homemade porn. Remind learners that it is illegal for anyone under the age of 18 to be filmed in this way and that porn films are censored and classified R18 as only suitable for those aged 18+.

3. Development activity

Introduce the idea of stereotypes. Discuss what it means and offer the following definition: 'A stereotype might be defined as a generalisation and assumption that together portrays the reputation of a group.'

Now, back in their groups, ask learners to discuss the following questions and then record ideas to be shared with the wider group:

1. Can you tell if someone is involved in the adult entertainment industry just by looking at them? If so, how?

2. What assumptions might be made about men and women who choose to act in legally made and distributed porn films?

3. Is this the same for people who take intimate pictures of themselves or who make 'homemade' porn films? Why/why not?

4. Reflection and review

Porn industry films are made with a director and filmed using paid actors aged 18+ who auditioned for the role. The films are then edited and censored before being rated R18 and sold/shown only in licensed premises. Point out that most legal porn film companies insist on actors having regular sexual health checks and do not employ anyone under the age of 18.

Contrastingly a smart phone can be used to make homemade pornographic videos or to take erotic or intimate photos, with or without knowledge and/or consent. These can then be shared with a partner or uploaded onto the internet or via social media. Once they are out there it is very difficult, if not impossible, to restrict viewing or take them back.

What are the differences between actors in licensed adult movies and people who make their own porn?

Answers about professional porn films may include:

- Porn actors audition for the role and are paid.

- Being a porn actor is a job and actors pay tax and national insurance.

- Legal porn actors are over the age of 18.

- Porn films are sold for money.

- Porn films are edited.

- Legal porn films have to meet the quality and standards required by the censorship board before being given a film rating.

- Porn films are legal to make, buy and watch if you are over 18 (subject to content laws).

Answers about homemade porn films may include:

- Homemade porn features ordinary people.

- People who choose to make homemade porn do not usually get paid as it is more of a lifestyle choice.

- Homemade porn may be consensual but once shared it can quickly go viral and potentially be seen by people worldwide.

- If homemade porn does go viral it may impact on things like future relationships or employment prospects.

- Homemade porn is not professionally edited or censored.

- Once uploaded online it is very hard to control who watches or downloads it.

- It is illegal for anyone under the age of 18 to engage in any type of homemade porn or intimate pictures.

5. Summary

- There are strict laws that govern the making and distribution of adult entertainment and the making and distribution of homemade porn.

Legally made and distributed porn	Homemade porn
Actors must be consenting adults over the age of 18. Porn films are given a film classification R18, meaning restricted to over-18s.	It is illegal to take a pornographic image/film of a child under the age of 18 even with his or her consent. It is classified as child porn. This includes intimate 'selfies', filming without consent, revenge porn and the sharing of intimate images online, via Bluetooth or by text.

ACTIVITY 1.6: VIEWING NUMBERS

(Years 9–13+)

Aim

- To explore attitudes towards and values of the current laws in place surrounding film and video game censorship.

Time: 45 minutes

Learning outcome

- Clarity on the laws of censorship in the UK, who decides them and why.

Key vocabulary

- **Film classification**
- **Pornography**

You will need

- Two A4 sheets (one marked 'Most acceptable' the other 'Least acceptable')
- A set of the viewing cards
- Sticky tack (optional)
- Online access

How to do it

1. Introduction

- Establish/revisit ground rules (see pages 42–43 for guidance).

Ask learners what film they last saw at the cinema and if they can remember what classification the film was.

```
U = Suitable for all
PG = Parental guidance
12A = Cinema release suitable for 12 years and over
12 = Video release suitable for 12 years and over
15 = Suitable only for 15 years and over
18 = Suitable only for adults
R18 = Adult works for licensed premises only
```

Ask: Why do you think films are classified in this way?
Use this description from the British Board of Film Classification (BBFC) to explain:

In order to protect children from unsuitable and even harmful content in films and videos and to give consumers information they might need about a particular film or video before deciding whether or not to view it, the BBFC examines and age rates films and videos before they are released. This independent scrutiny prior to release ensures the highest possible level of protection and empowerment.[7]

---

7   www.bbfc.co.uk/what-classification/how-does-classification-work

2. Opening activity

Place the two sheets of pre-labelled paper approximately two metres apart either on the floor or stuck to a wall to form the framework for a continuum.

Once this is done hand each learner a viewing card, face down, asking them not to look at it yet.

The task is for each young person in turn to read aloud what is on their card and then place it on the continuum between the 'Most acceptable' and 'Least acceptable' signs to demonstrate how appropriate, acceptable or OK they think the scenario on the card is. As they do so they should briefly explain why they have put it there. At the moment this exercise is asking for personal opinions and attitudes rather than demonstrating any knowledge of the law, so no comments should be made until all of the cards have been placed.

Once this has been done, give other members of the group the opportunity to move any cards they disagree with, provided that they offer some explanation for doing so. Encourage peer discussion and the sharing of opinions.

3. Development activity

Move on to re-set the task, but this time asking everyone to be involved at once and dividing the space into two areas, 'Legal' and 'Illegal'. Once done, instruct young people to stand back and reflect on the following:

- Has the position of any of the cards changed?

- If so, have any of the cards previously considered 'Most acceptable' been moved to the 'Illegal' area?

- Does this mean that it is OK to ignore censorship law if those responsible for children and young people think something is acceptable viewing?

- Why are films, digital material and mobile content rated by age?

4. Reflection and review

In pairs, set learners the task of going online to see the classification framework.[8] Online activities available include young people being able to watch and then classify a movie trailer to experience the process.

5. Summary

- In the UK films are classified before release by the British Board of Film Classification.

- This is done to protect children and young people from unsuitable, and in some cases harmful, viewing.

- This should empower parents (or those with parental responsibility) and educators to make appropriate choices about which films are suitable to view or purchase for children.

- These should be complied with by everyone and laws are broken if they are not.

---

8   www.bbfc.co.uk

ACTIVITY 1.6: VIEWING CARDS

Parents allowing their 13-year-old son to watch an 18-rated horror movie at home with them.	A youth worker showing a 15-rated rom-com movie to a group of under-13s during a residential.
A group of university friends watching an R18 porn movie.	A teacher using a clip from an 18-rated film during PSHE with Year 9s.
A 16-year-old lying about his age to buy an R18 porn movie online.	An over-18 couple watching online porn together.
A young person using fake ID to get into the cinema to see an R18 movie.	A 12-year-old using his foster parents' online account to download a 15 movie.
A 14-year-old being in the same room as her 18-year-old brother who is streaming legal online porn.	A group of Year 7s watching content rated by the mobile provider as unsuitable for those under 18.
A 15-year-old converting scenes from an 18-rated action movie to MP4 to share via email with friends.	A 19-year-old man downloading an R18 porn movie to show his 17-year-old girlfriend.
A 16-year-old sending a video clip of an 18-rated movie to friends using Bluetooth.	An adult couple watching online porn together on an over-18 website.
A 14-year-old burning and selling copies of her parent's R18 porn movies.	A 13-year-old opening a YouTube account using a fake date of birth to watch porn.

ACTIVITY 1.7: WHO IS RESPONSIBLE?

(Years 7–13+)

Aim

- Learners will consider whose responsibility it is to keep children safe online and away from inappropriate web content.

Time: 45–60 minutes

Learning outcomes

- To gain information and increased knowledge about keeping children safe online.
- To develop listening and reasoning skills.

Key vocabulary

- **Personal responsibility**
- **Parental responsibility**
- **Collective responsibility**
- **Law enforcement**

You will need

- At least one copy of each of the discussion points (to work in groups of four)
- Flipchart paper and marker pens

How to do it

1. Introduction

- Establish/revisit ground rules (see pages 42–43 for guidance).

Introduce the topic by sharing the following information: although the legal age to watch an adult film or webstream is 18 years old, a 2014 BBC3 documentary, 'Porn: What's the Harm?' revealed that children as young as eight are regular viewers of online porn.[9]

If the legal age is 18 but children less than half that age are accessing adult material, who has a responsibility for stopping it and enforcing the law? For example, an 11-year-old cannot go into a licensed sex shop and buy a porn movie, but according to numerous reports they can easily see it online anytime, any place.

2. Opening activity

Use the following questions as the basis for a short discussion:

- Should the porn industry be more responsible about who sees their products?
- Should the government take charge?
- Is it the responsibility of parents, schools or the police?

---

9   'Porn: What's the Harm?' BBC3 (broadcast 16 April 2014) www.bbc.co.uk/programmes/b040n2ph

- Is there a collective responsibility for the protection of children? This could include faith leaders, community, law makers and other bodies and organisations with wider responsibility for health and welfare.

3. Development activity

Divide learners into working groups of four and allocate each a different viewpoint – 'the government', 'the porn industry', 'the parents', 'the schools' and 'the police'. Give each group paper and pens to record their work.

Their task is to discuss and devise arguments to support it and to plan a short presentation to be given in the style of a TV news report that will be presented back to the main group with the intention of gaining the support of others.

This can be done as a straight presentation or role-play dependent on how comfortable learners are participating in drama-based activities.

After all the presentations, facilitate a basic vote using a show of hands to reveal which argument is the most compelling and which group the young people believes is most responsible for keeping children safe from potential harm. Allow two votes each to prevent people simply voting for their own team and count them up before announcing which viewpoint has the most support.

4. Reflection and review

Seat all learners in a circle and then invite each person in turn to share one thing they think is the responsibility of others in protecting under-18s from viewing potentially harmful content, and one thing that is the responsibility of the individual.

Make the point that although as a society we have a responsibility to others, each person has personal responsibility for the choices they make too.

5. Summary

- In the UK the British Board of Film Classification classifies films viewed at the cinema, DVDs released and some online media.

- This takes into account what the general public think is acceptable viewing for each age group and enables adults to make informed viewing choices for under-18s.

- The classifications aim to keep children (and vulnerable adults) safe from potential harmful or inappropriate content.

- Everyone has a responsibility to ensure that these classifications are respected and young people are kept safe.

ACTIVITY 1.7: WHO IS RESPONSIBLE? VIEWPOINTS

The government

The government should take charge and clean up the internet. It is voted into power by the people, so should use that responsibility to include making decisions about what can and cannot be seen online. That way it would be impossible for children to see inappropriate material and the problem would be solved.

....

The porn industry

The porn industry makes millions worldwide every year. Therefore they have a responsibility to re-invest some of that profit into online security measures to ensure that children cannot access adult material. This would enhance their reputation in both the business and home communities.

....

The parents

Parents are responsible for what their children do and need to protect them from accessing online porn. Parents should be stricter about blocking inappropriate sites and allowing their children to have smart phones with easy access to the web. As legal guardians it is for them to decide what their child can and cannot watch, and enforce it.

....

The schools

Schools should educate children to be more responsible. SRE doesn't currently prepare children and young people for the modern world so they don't always know what is right and wrong. Children should be taught to know that adult sites are for over-18s only and keep out!

....

The police

If children are watching online porn then they are breaking the law and it is the responsibility of the police to enforce it. If children under the age of criminal responsibility (ten in England and Wales, eight in Scotland) are caught then their parents should be taken to court and fined. If children and teenagers are over the age of criminal responsibility (but under 18) then they should be arrested and taken to court.

ACTIVITY 1.8: PORN AS SEX EDUCATION

(Years 10–13+)

Aim

- This discussion uses the 'four corner' method to debate the notion of using pornography as part of school sex education.

Time: 45 minutes

Learning outcomes

- To understand it is never appropriate for adults to show under-18s anything classified as unsuitable or inappropriate for viewing.

- To know where to go for additional support and information if required.

Key vocabulary

- **Debate**
- **SRE**
- **Pornography**

You will need

- A copy of the four *Porn as sex education debate points*

- Paper and pens

- Leaflets and information about local and national support services for young people

How to do it

1. Introduction

- Establish/revisit ground rules (see pages 42–43 for guidance).

Start by reading out the following quote:

Data from ChildLine suggests there is a real need for greater discussion of pornography, which was often missing from SRE. Over a quarter of young people surveyed by ChildLine felt that pornography changed the way they thought about relationships. This proportion rose to 70 per cent in responses from the 16 and above age group. 74 per cent of 11–18 year olds said that porn should be discussed in sex education.[10]

One young person told ChildLine:

Things like porn and all the things you can access online isn't really told to you in school which leaves you in the dark. If they did tell you then you wouldn't have to go and find out for yourself. Teaching needs to change.[11]

---

10 NSPCC (2013) Sex education survey 2013 evaluation, www.nspcc.org.uk/preventing-abuse/keeping-children-safe/online-porn

11 Written evidence submitted from NSPCC (June 2014) The Education Committee inquiry into Personal, Social, Health and Economic education (PSHE) and Sex and Relationships Education (SRE) in schools, http://data.parliament.uk/writtenevidence/committeeevidence.svc/evidencedocument/education-committee/pshe-and-sre-in-schools/written/10201.html

2. Opening activity

Divide young people into four small groups and hand each group a different debate point, either in support or arguing against the suggestion of using pornography in school. Point out that this is about exploring different ideas and learning the skills to debate and it is recognised that the view they are allocated may not necessarily correspond with their own.

Send them off with paper and pens to the four corners of the room to spend 15–20 minutes discussing and constructing a short presentation to support the given viewpoint.

3. Development activity

Invite each group to present their argument without questions or further discussion among groups until the last one has spoken. Then facilitate a debate that considers each of the arguments put forward, encouraging young people to answer from their given stance.

Finally hold a simple show of hands vote for young people to demonstrate how they really feel now that they have heard all the different arguments.

4. Reflection and review

Ask these questions to prompt debate and allow young people to say what they really think:

- Who should decide what is right or wrong for young people to watch?

- Why won't watching porn help young people learn about healthy, positive, real-life relationships?

- What would be a better way for young people to learn about sex and relationships?

- Where can young people go if they want to ask more questions or get advice or support with sex and relationships issues?

5. Summary

Ensure that young people receive the message that local and national support is free and confidential. The staff are trained to help answer questions or offer practical advice about a whole range of sex and relationships issues, including sexting, pornography and things like sexual bullying or relationship abuse, so there is no need to be embarrassed or feel awkward about calling, texting or visiting them.

Extension

Give out information and leaflets about local services (as appropriate) and ask young people to read them before the next lesson.

ACTIVITY 1.8: PORN AS SEX EDUCATION DEBATE POINTS

Debate point 1

Most people watch porn so it makes sense to use what is already online to educate young people about sex in schools. This would save money and give young people more up-to-date information than they currently get.

....

Debate point 2

Using porn in schools as part of young people's sex education is a very bad idea. Not only is it morally corrupt, it would also give young people the message that porn is a positive thing, which would encourage them to watch more in their own time.

....

Debate point 3

Using porn in schools to show young people more about sex is a reasonable suggestion as long as it is managed properly. This means teachers screening the material first to ensure that it is appropriate, and parents being informed to give their consent.

....

Debate point 4

No way should porn ever be allowed into a classroom. Schools are places where pupils should be kept safe, not put in danger. Teachers should be warning young people about the dangers, not making them watch it as part of a sex education lesson.

ACTIVITY 1.9: PORNOGRAPHY AND THE CURRICULUM
(Years 7–13+)

Aim

- To provoke discussion about the quality and content of sex and relationships education in schools before voting to see if young people think this should change to reflect current issues.

Time: 45 minutes

Learning outcome

- To be aware of the SRE statutory requirements of the National Curriculum for all UK pupils in maintained schools.

Key vocabulary

- **National Curriculum**
- **SRE**

You will need

- A voting card for each learner
- A blank copy of the voting card enlarged on a photocopier and pasted to the wall
- Paper and pens
- A cardboard box or shoebox painted black and sealed with a slit in the top large enough to post the voting cards into

How to do it
1. Introduction

- Establish/revisit ground rules (see pages 42–43 for guidance).

In pairs, task young people with solving the following anagrams related to SRE in school:

CIT EDSUAXONS = Sex education

POLREATINSHI = Relationship

ALSEEX UHHALT = Sexual health

SECNONT = Consent

MSTOIEON = Emotions

Then ask them to write in full what the following acronym means:

SRE = Sex and relationships education

Ask each pair to imagine that the 'sex' and 'relationships' parts of SRE are an equation and then write the ratio of education they think they currently get on each subject out of 100.

Go through the answers first, ensuring that each term is understood and the reason why it is included within SRE.

Finally, compare and contrast the equations given by each pair:

- Are both sides of equation equal?
- Which carries the greatest weight?
- Which is the most important in a loving relationship?

2. Opening activity

Idea storm opinions about the sex and relationships education they currently receive in schools by asking young people to call out their opinions and recording key points. Prompt suggestions by using some of the following questions:

- Should SRE be compulsory for everybody in school?

- Is it important to teach children and young adults about sex? Why/why not?

- Is the relationship side more important than knowing the biology?

- How should young people learn, and in what lessons (for example, biology, SRE, PSHE or citizenship)?

- Should SRE be taught by existing teachers or by specialist staff/sexual health workers/youth workers bought into school?

- Does SRE tell people enough, or is there more to learn?

- Should awareness about things like pornography, sexting and sexual bullying be added to the SRE curriculum?

Discuss points as issues are raised and read young people the statutory information below:

- SRE is a compulsory subject from age 11 onwards. It involves teaching children about reproduction, sexuality and sexual health. It doesn't promote early sexual activity or any particular sexual orientation.

- Parents have the right to withdraw their children from the non-compulsory parts of SRE.

- PSHE is a non-statutory subject.

- Section 2.5 of the National Curriculum framework document states that: 'All schools should make provision for personal, social, health and economic education (PSHE), drawing on good practice.'[12]

3. Development activity

Hand out a voting card and a pen to each young person. Explain that having discussed the topic there is going to be a democratic election, i.e. one person, one vote. Stress that the votes will be cast privately and remain anonymous. They will then be placed in the ballot box, counted and the results shared.

When all votes have been cast, invite the young people to tally up the number of votes for each motion and record the results onto the large voting sheet on the wall in marker.

4. Reflection and review

Review the results with the group to see what the majority vote is on their current sex and relationships education, plus the motion to update it to include educating young people about the potential risks of pornography.

5. Summary

- Currently SRE is compulsory in schools but parents can take their child out of non-statutory parts.

- There have been complaints nationally that there is too much focus on the biology of sex and not enough on the relationship elements of SRE. Consider how this contrasts with the equations developed on experience in the room earlier.

---

12 For more information see the PSHE Association www.pshe-association.org.uk or for SRE curriculum requirements www.gov.uk/national-curriculum/other-compulsory-subjects

- It has been recommended to the government that pornography should be included in the SRE curriculum.[13]

- If anyone wants to get involved with campaigns for changes to PSHE in schools they can look at the Sex Education Forum's campaign: 'SRE – It's My Right',[14] which is supported by the UK Youth Parliament.[15]

13 www.publications.parliament.uk/pa/cm201415/cmselect/cmeduc/145/145.pdf

14 www.sexeducationforum.org.uk/policy-campaigns/sre-its-my-right.aspx

15 www.ukyouthparliament.org.uk

ACTIVITY 1.9: PORNOGRAPHY AND THE CURRICULUM

Voting card

Place a cross **X** in the box to cast your vote.

	YES	NO
I support the legal requirement for pupils to have high quality SRE taught within PSHE in all schools.		
This should include teaching about e-safety and sexual exploitation.		
It should also include teaching about the potential negative affects of pornography on body image, sexual expectations and relationships.		

ACTIVITY 1.10: WHERE IS THE DANGER?

(Years 9–13+)

Aims

- To use a basic traffic light system to define what constitutes appropriate and inappropriate taking, making and sharing of photos.

- To better understand the emotional, social and legal implications of sharing erotic pictures and/or pornographic material.

Time: 45 minutes

Learning outcomes

- To know the difference between appropriate and inappropriate pictures and messages.

- To discuss the potential negative risks of personal photos becoming public.

- To be clear about the laws regarding the taking, making and sharing of inappropriate content.

Key vocabulary

- **Appropriate content**

- **Inappropriate content**

- **Permission and consent**

You will need

- A copy of the *Traffic light worksheet* (one per group)

- A set of the *Danger cards* (one per group)

How to do it

1. Introduction

- Establish/revisit ground rules (see pages 42–43 for guidance).

Start by asking young people to imagine the following scenario:

> You are taking a new partner home to meet the family. Everything is going really well and you are feeling relaxed, comfortable and happy to be there. This relationship is really important to you and you are pleased to see everyone getting along so well.
>
> Suddenly, a family member produces an old photo album and amidst shrieks of laughter displays your baby photos and pictures taken as a child, some of them very unflattering, without first asking your permission or checking if it is OK.

Ask the following questions:

- How might you feel about your partner seeing the old photos? Why?

  For example, embarrassed or angry, unhappy that you have had no choice about which photos are seen, concerned it may change their perception of you, you don't like the photos, you prefer to choose what is seen and when.

- What should have happened in this scenario?

  For example, permission should have been sought before showing anyone private photos, you should have been given time to select those you wanted to share, you should have been given the opportunity to refuse, more thought should have been given to the appropriateness of sharing family pictures with a new person.

- How can we make sure that photos stay private?

  For example, keeping photos stored in albums that are only shared if everyone in them agrees, storing online photos safely, password protecting photo files, keeping phones containing photos locked, checking if people are happy for photos to go on social media before 'tagging' them.

Explain that this lesson is going to explore the risks involved in sharing inappropriate photos and online content, some of which have laws in place to protect children and young people.

2. Opening activity

Divide young people into small groups and given them paper and pens. Their first task is to define a meaning for 'dangerous behaviour'. This could mean risk of harm to self, harm to others or even harm to society, but in order to undertake the second part of the lesson an agreed definition is required that all members of the group are happy to work to.

At this stage there is no need to share definitions.

3. Development activity

Give each group a *Traffic light worksheet* and a set of the *Danger cards*. Explain that for this activity:

Red = Stop! This is dangerous.

Amber = Caution! This could be dangerous.

Green = Go ahead! This is fine.

In turn, each person must pick up a card from the pile and read it aloud before deciding whereabouts on the traffic lights it should be placed, explaining their reasons for doing so. After this explanation other members of the group can challenge or agree with the placement before moving on to the next card.

Repeat until all of the cards have been discussed.

Once finished, ask each group what criteria they used to define 'dangerous'. This could include a mix of:

- the potential negative effects on a personal relationship

- the potential harm to self (spiritual, cultural)

- the potential harm caused to others

- breaking the law and the potential consequences, for example getting a criminal record, a fine or even a custodial sentence

- the potential harm to society

- the potential harm to a person's mental health and emotional wellbeing.

Using their own definition as a measure, invite feedback from each group starting with cards placed in the green zone before moving on to those in the amber and red. Encourage discussion to ensure that everyone understands the risks they take if they engage in this type of activity, but also reassuring them that things like sending a loving text, taking a romantic picture or reading age-appropriate novels are all perfectly acceptable to do.

Remind the young people that within some of these scenarios the law has been broken and therefore at least one person involved could get into trouble. Point out that if an intimate picture is taken of a person under 18 years of age it is not just the person who takes the picture who is breaking the law, even if it is of themselves, but also anyone viewing it, especially if they in turn forward it. Taking erotic or intimate 'selfies' and keeping them on a phone also breaks the law if the person is under 18.

4. Reflection and review

Emphasise that one of the biggest risks is that an uploaded picture can go 'viral' very quickly and there are no controls to how far it goes or who sees it. Screenshots can be quickly taken, especially on social media like Instagram and Snapchat, so even if the picture is taken down minutes later there is no guarantee that it hasn't been captured and circulated to a wider audience. Ask:

- How might this impact on things like education, employment and future relationships?

- What would you advise a friend who is considering making an intimate film with their partner? Would this differ if they were over 18?

5. Summary

- If you are under 18 it is illegal to take, possess or share intimate pictures of yourself or others.

- If you are found with pornographic or inappropriate content on your phone, tablet or laptop you could be charged and get a criminal record.

- The only way to guarantee that erotic or intimate pictures do not get into the public domain is to not take them.

- Inappropriate private photos can become public very quickly and it is impossible to know how far they have spread.

ACTIVITY 1.10: DANGER CARDS

Sending a text to say you love someone.	Ordering an R18 DVD online using a fake ID.	Streaming online porn to your mobile.
Searching online to find and watch celebrity sex tapes.	Using a sexy emoticon at the end of a text.	Tagging friends in a photo taken at the beach.
Reading an erotic novel in a public place.	Buying a sex toy in a high street lingerie boutique.	Calling 0800 numbers to listen to a sex hotline.
Photoshopping a friend's head onto a naked body and sharing it for a joke.	Sending and receiving naked pictures with your partner.	Asking for someone you fancy to post an intimate picture on social media.
Clicking 'Like' on a steamy picture.	Taking artistic erotic selfies and keeping them on your phone.	Posting a portfolio of topless shots online to try and get into glamour modelling.
Allowing a partner to take intimate photos.	Forwarding a naked photo of someone else to friends.	Watching online porn to learn about sex.
Watching a porn movie with friends.	Posing for photos with friends in nightwear at a sleepover.	Putting pressure on a partner to video intimate moments together.
Accepting friendship requests from people you don't know.	Using a selfie stick to take pictures of you in your underwear.	Taking screenshots of celebrities caught in intimate moments to share.

ACTIVITY 1.10: TRAFFIC LIGHT WORKSHEET

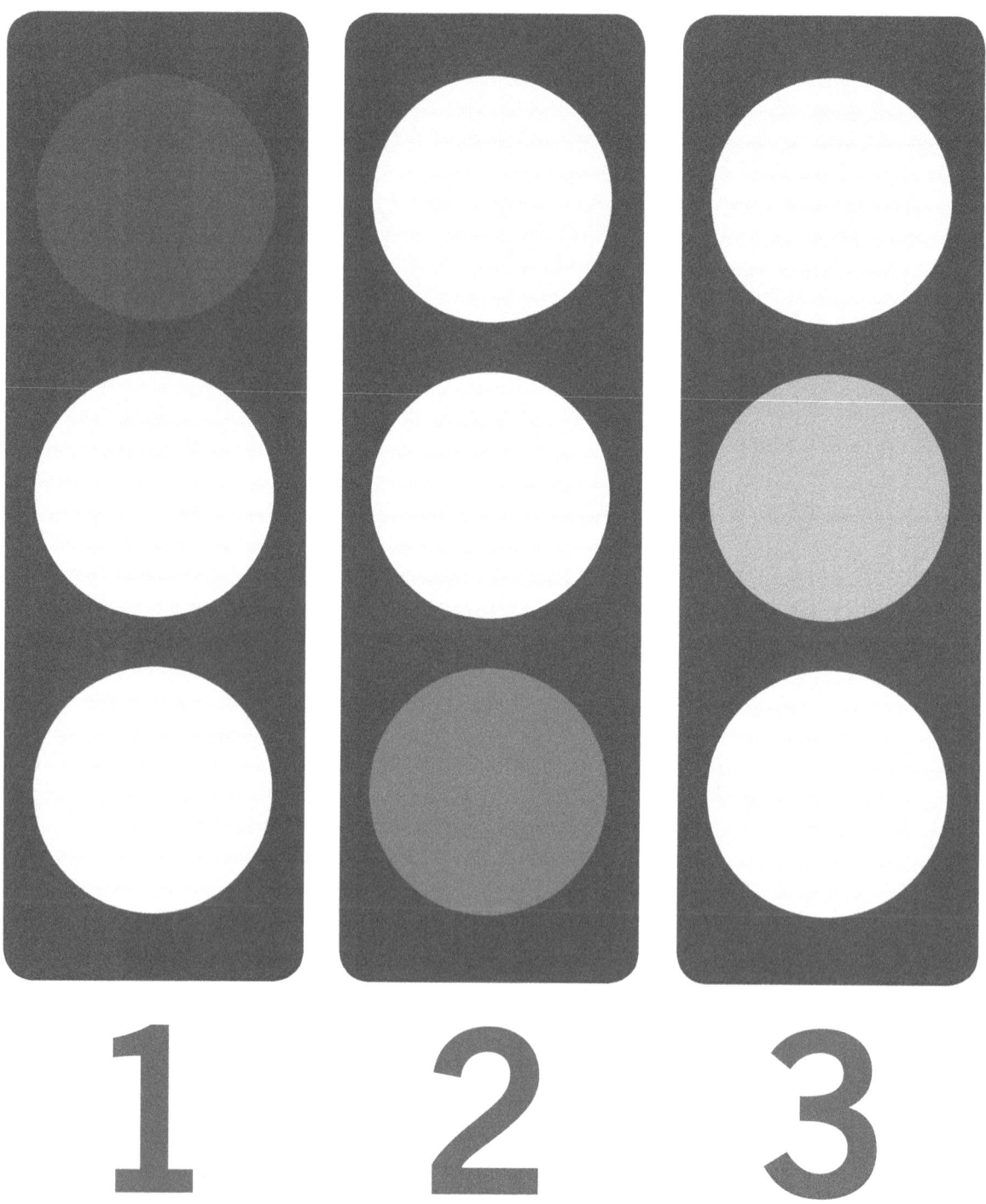

ACTIVITY 1.11: IS THAT EVEN LEGAL?

(Years 10–13+)

Aims

- The quiz helps clarify the law regarding pornography and the taking, sharing and distribution of indecent images.

- Young people will then use this knowledge to design a presentation to educate their peers.

Time: 60 minutes

Learning outcomes

- To have a clear understanding of the laws regulating the distribution of porn and restricting access to pornographic material.

- To consider the best way to share this knowledge with peers.

Key vocabulary

- **Peer education**

- **Pornography**

- **Indecent image**

- **Naked selfies**

- **Sexting**

You will need

- Copies of the *Pornography and the law* quiz

- Paper and pens

- Copies of the *Peer education worksheet*

- Access to a computer with PowerPoint (or a similar package) and facilities to show a presentation

How to do it

1. Introduction

- Establish/revisit ground rules (see pages 42–43 for guidance).

Explain that young people are going to take part in a quiz to see how much they know about the laws that govern the making, sharing and distribution of pornographic material. There is no expectation that anyone will know all of the answers, although someone might. Explain that if they don't know the answer it is fine to make an educated guess based on the topics covered so far.

Remind the group that not all porn is illegal to those over 18 and that the purpose of this quiz is not to pass moral judgement on adults (over the age of 18) who choose to legally buy, watch and enjoy it, but to learn.

2. Opening activity

This quiz can be facilitated by providing a copy of the quiz for each young person and inviting them to complete it alone by choosing from the multiple choice answers given, and then going through the answers to see who has the most correct.

Alternatively, assign young people teams to work in, giving each team a sheet of paper and a pen. Read out the quiz questions one by one, leaving time between each for a quick group discussion before a team volunteer writes down their agreed answers. This method works particularly well with mixed ability groups as only one person needs to write but all can participate.

Go through the answers slowly, encouraging discussion to clarify any points raised and invite questions. A point is awarded for each correct answer and the team with the most points at the end, wins. Lead a round of applause and congratulations.

Quiz answers

1. Which of the following is legal for adults over 18?

a) Own R18 movies or adult pornography.

Legal: Providing it is legal pornography owned by someone over the age of 18.

b) Own pornography featuring children.

Illegal: To take, allow or make any indecent photograph or pseudo photograph of a child (including digital images); possess, distribute or show; publish or cause to be published anything advertising the images.

c) Own pornography showing adults who look like children.

Illegal: It is illegal to make, own or distribute pornography or indecent photographs (including selfies) where younger looking adults over the age of 18 are presented as underage children or young people. This excludes things like buying a dressing up costume to wear to a fancy dress party, for example a school uniform, where it will be obvious that an adult is wearing it and there is no intent to deceive.

d) Own pornography showing adults engaging in 'extreme' sex.

Illegal: The Criminal Justice and Immigration Act 2008 makes it an offence to possess extreme pornographic images. 'Extreme' includes something that threatens a person's life or which results, or is likely to result, in serious injury to a person's anus, breasts or genitals; one which involves sexual interference with a human corpse, or involves a person performing intercourse or oral sex with an animal.

e) Look at online pornographic images of children.

Illegal: The offence is based on the severity (graded 1–5) and number of images downloaded.

2. A 15-year-old can legally buy a magazine that features pictures of naked breasts in a newsagent.

True: There is no law around buying magazines that do not have a classification on them. Retailers may have a policy not to sell them to under-18s but there is no legal requirement. This is different for magazines sold in licensed sex shops, which have a classification R18, meaning that they can only be legally sold to those over the age of 18.

3. It is illegal for a 16-year-old to pose for pornographic pictures.

True: The Sexual Offences Act 2003 stipulates that only people over 18 can legally be filmed or photographed. This includes homemade porn and sexting.

4. It is illegal for two consenting 16-year-olds to take and share intimate sexual pictures.

True: Although the age of consent is 16, the taking and sharing of pornographic images (or films) is illegal for anyone under 18, even with the consent of both parties. This includes naked selfies and sexting.

5. It is illegal for a group of friends to watch a porn movie in the privacy of home.

Maybe: It depends on the age of the friends and the film they are watching. All licensed pornographic films have a classification of R18, so everyone watching must be aged 18 or over. Some pornography is illegal for anyone to make, watch or distribute regardless of age.

6. An adult who shows a child a pornographic image is breaking the law.

True: It is illegal to show pornography to a child under the Sexual Offences Act 2003. The offence is 'causing a child to watch a sexual act'.

7. The law for gay and straight porn is different.

False: Pornography of any kind is subject to the same laws.

8. In England it is not a crime to be naked in public.

True: But a naked person could be arrested and charged with causing harassment, alarm or distress under the Public Order Act 1986 if they do not put some clothes on when a member of the public or a police officer asks them to do so.

3. Development activity

Divide the class into small groups and task each with discussing and agreeing the task set on the *Peer education worksheet*, which asks young people to design a short presentation to give the basic facts about pornography and the law to be shown to peers to distribute learning.

Hand out paper and pens to make notes on. Then give each group access to a computer so they can present their ideas in a short PowerPoint presentation. This should comprise of no more than ten slides.

Make it clear from the outset that as this is an exercise based on information contained in the quiz answers there is no need for young people to undertake any further online research.

Once complete take it in turns for each group to show their presentation.

4. Reflection and review

Facilitate a feedback session to review the presentations. This should include teacher comments and feedback from classmates. Structure comments around the following:

- How well was the information presented?

- Was it easily understood?

- Was it offered in a non-judgemental way that took diversity into account?

- What would make another young person engage with it?

- What else might the presentation need to enhance the learning experience?

Encourage a response from each group after they have received their feedback.

5. Summary

- In the UK there are laws in place to restrict the making, viewing and sharing of pornographic material.

- These laws are different for those over and under 18

- Sexting, the making and sharing of naked selfies and homemade porn is illegal for anyone under the age of 18, even with both party's consent.

- Some pornography is illegal for anyone to make, watch or distribute and conviction could result in imprisonment.

Extension

Consider using the presentations as the starting point for a larger peer education project or to make posters to raise awareness about the law regarding taking explicit photos of someone under the age of 18.

ACTIVITY 1.11: PORNOGRAPHY AND THE LAW QUIZ

1. Which of the following is *legal* for a consenting adult (over 18) to do in the UK?

   a) Own R18 movies or adult pornography?

   b) Own pornography featuring children?

   c) Own pornography showing adults who look like children?

   d) Own pornography showing adults engaging in 'extreme' sex?

   e) Look at online pornographic images of children?

2. A 15-year-old can legally buy a magazine featuring naked breasts in a newsagents.

   True ☐

   False ☐

   Maybe ☐

3. It is illegal for a 16-year-old to pose for pornographic pictures.

   True ☐

   False ☐

   Maybe ☐

4. It is illegal for two consenting 16-year-olds to take and share intimate sexual pictures.

   True ☐

   False ☐

   Maybe ☐

5. It is illegal for a group of friends to watch a porn movie in the privacy of home.

   True ☐

   False ☐

   Maybe ☐

6. An adult who shows a child a pornographic image is breaking the law.

   True ☐

   False ☐

   Maybe ☐

7. The law for gay and straight porn is different.

   True ☐

   False ☐

   Maybe ☐

8. It is not a crime to be naked in public.

   True ☐

   False ☐

   Maybe ☐

ACTIVITY 1.11: PEER EDUCATION WORKSHEET

Task

Your task is to prepare a short presentation to tell other young people what you have learnt about pornography and the law. This should include the taking, making and sharing of naked selfies, sexting, etc.

Remember

The presentation needs to appeal to young people with different levels of knowledge and understanding. Your task is to present the facts, not your opinions.

The rules

- Your presentation will be designed in PowerPoint using no more than ten slides.

- You should design it in a way that will be interesting to your peers and keep their attention.

- You will also need to agree what is going to be said while presenting the slides.

- One or more of the group can share the verbal presentation.

- You will need to assign tasks within the group but everyone must work together.

- At the end of the presentation you will receive constructive feedback from the other groups, which can be discussed but not argued.

Restrictions

- You can only use the information given to you in the quiz.

- You may not use any pictures that could be considered sexual in any way.

- The usual rules about confidentiality and boundaries apply.

ACTIVITY 1.12: REVENGE PORN AND THE LAW
(Years 9–13+)

Aim

- To clarify what the term 'revenge porn' means, and encourage young people to discuss the moral rights and wrongs of betraying relationship trust in this way.

Time: 60 minutes

Learning outcomes

- To understand what is meant by 'revenge porn'.
- To know that blackmailing, threatening to use or actually using photos, films or other material given within the context of a private personal relationship are all illegal and can lead to prosecution.

Key vocabulary

- **Revenge porn**
- **Positive relationship**
- **Trust**

You will need

- Copies of *News article 1 worksheet*, which is based on a news article which can be found online[16]
- Paper and pens
- A smart phone (optional)

How to do it

1. Introduction

- Establish/revisit ground rules (see pages 42–43 for guidance).

Read aloud the mock 'fairytale' of love and betrayal on page 94. Then, in pairs, ask young people to discuss:

- Who is to blame for what happened?
- Did the handsome prince get his 'just deserts' for betraying the princess?
- Is paying someone back for something bad done to you ever justified?

Conclude that the story is about revenge.

2. Opening activity

Suggest that a twist on the previous story is the relatively new phenomenon, 'revenge porn', a name developed by the media to describe someone who uses photos or films taken in private to shame, humiliate or embarrass an ex-partner, sometimes in retaliation for something they have done, or to profit financially.

---

16 www.telegraph.co.uk/news/uknews/crime/11927345/Top-actor-wins-legal-ban-on-revenge-porn-material.html

Divide the class into groups of four and give each group a copy of the *News article 1 worksheet*, paper and pens. Point out that this story involves consenting adults and that it is illegal for those under 18 to take, keep or share similar images.

3. Development activity

After reading the worksheet article, each group should discuss the following areas, which should be written on flipchart paper and displayed to help focus the conversations.

In the article a 'Top Actor' won a High Court ruling preventing sexually explicit material and 'revenge porn' from being published.

- Why do you think a famous person agreed to the photos being taken in the first place?

- Why do you think the other person decided to share them?

- What do you think they were hoping to achieve by it?

- Do you think justice was done?

- How do you think a) the actor and b) his ex-partner feel now?

Listen to feedback from each group, encouraging questions and further discussion as points are made.

Ask the young people if they think that the impact of revenge porn would be the same or different for a non-famous person, and consider the different areas of life that may be affected if private pictures are made public.

4. Reflection and review

In 2015 the act of posting adult 'revenge porn' on the web became a specific offence in the UK under new legislation. If someone is found guilty of revenge porn they can be sentenced to up to two years in prison.

Review this information by asking young people if they think this is fair, if the penalty should be higher or lower and what else a person found guilty could do to make things better, or show they are sorry.

5. Summary

- Positive relationships are built on trust.

- Revenge is not the best way to resolve a dispute, no matter what the other person has done.

- Adult revenge porn generally involves someone posting photos of an ex-lover on specific websites or social media sites where the images can go viral. The photos are not illegal (as long as everyone in them is consenting and 18+) but the law is broken if they are shared without the full knowledge and consent of everyone in them.

- Revenge porn is illegal for anyone under the age of 18 and the perpetrator could be charged with publishing or distributing child pornography, which is a very serious offence.

ACTIVITY 1.12: A FAIRYTALE OF LOVE AND BETRAYAL

Once upon a time a handsome prince married a beautiful princess and they were meant to live happily ever after but they didn't, and here's why.

On their wedding day the princess sighed, 'I am the luckiest girl in the world. I have everything I ever dreamt of – a handsome prince to love and cherish me, a lovely home and a happy life together to look forward to.'

But it can get a bit boring stuck at home while your beloved is out all day slaying dragons and all night showing off to other princes in the local tavern. Before too long the princess began to feel lonely and told the prince she was going to get a job.

'What?' said the prince in amazement, 'A job? You have a job! You are my princess and your job is to make me happy. How can I go out ridding the land of dragons if you are not at home looking lovely and waiting for me? I absolutely forbid it.'

The princess was shocked; surely this wasn't the man she married? She realised that in her haste she hadn't got to know him very well. Trembling a little at the stern look on her husband's face she replied bravely, 'I can do anything I choose, just watch me!'

The prince decided to teach his wife a lesson and ordered a tall wall to be built around the castle, with a huge gate and one key, which he kept with him at all times. 'I will show her who is boss,' he thought, 'She can't get a job now!'

But the princess was not only beautiful she was clever and resourceful too. Determined to get her own back on the prince she vowed never to let anyone bully her again and set to work on a business plan. Within six months the princess had created a successful online business and with every penny earned she worked her way towards freedom.

Having saved enough cash, the princess hired a helicopter and flew out of the palace grounds to find a good divorce lawyer. She bought a penthouse apartment with a view of the city, leaving her ignorant husband to rattle around in the castle alone with his chauvinistic views.

Independent and happy at last she wrote her ex a note, 'Love is sweet, but respect is even sweeter. I will never be fooled by a handsome face again.'

But the prince, who by now missed his lovely wife and was truly sorry for his bullish ways, couldn't reply. He was too busy looking for his lost key.

ACTIVITY 1.12: NEWS ARTICLE 1 WORKSHEET

A famous actor wins a legal ban on 'revenge porn'

The judge said the incident was motivated by revenge and possibly blackmail

A famous actor won a High Court ruling preventing sexually explicit material, often called 'revenge porn', from being published after a bitter break up with an ex-partner.

The couple had been in a relationship for several months and during that time the actor had allowed his partner to take nude photographs and video them having sex together. The actor trusted his partner and did not expect the pictures and films to be seen by anyone apart from them.

After they split up, the now ex-partner contacted the actor threatening to post their private images on social media or to sell them to a magazine if they didn't get back together. When that didn't work, some of the photos were posted on a website and the actor was informed that locked files with copies of the images had been placed with two unidentified friends who would be authorised to get them published if the police became involved.

The judge ruled that there was clear evidence that if the photos were made public they could damage the actor both emotionally and financially. He said that it was not in the public interest to see the photos and that they should remain private as no laws had been broken.

He concluded that the motive for making the threats and posting the photos was revenge for the actor ending the relationship.

The actor managed to get the images removed from the website and a legal ban placed on further publication, but still fears that some photos have been missed and could go viral at any time.*

---

* Based on an article by Lexi Finnigan, first published in the Daily Telegraph on 12 October 2015. To read in full go to www.telegraph.co.uk/news/uknews/crime/11927345/Top-actor-wins-legal-ban-on-revenge-porn-material.html

CHAPTER 2

Shopping, Music and the Media

This chapter explores the messages that children and young people pick up about sex and relationships from the world around them and how these inform personal values.

ACTIVITY 2.1: WHERE DO YOU STAND?
(Years 9–13+)

Aim

- To question the impact of provocative images seen in high street shops on children's thinking and behaviour.

Time: 30 minutes

Learning outcomes

- To understand that we internalise the things we see around us.
- To know that this can impact on what children and young adults aspire to be and look like.

Key vocabulary

- **Internalise**
- **Marketing**
- **Gender stereotypes**

You will need

- Three A3 sheets of paper
- Marker pens and sticky tack
- A copy of the *Where do you stand? statements*

How to do it

Before the young people arrive prepare the room. Use the three A3 sheets to divide the room into three zones. On one sheet write in large letters 'Yes, I agree' and place it on one wall. On the next sheet write 'No, I disagree' and stick it to the opposite wall. Finally place a sheet in the middle of the room, which says, 'I am not sure'.

1. Introduction

- Establish/revisit ground rules (see pages 42–43 for guidance).

Explain that pupils will be sharing experiences of shopping on the high street and considering how window displays, merchandising and product marketing can influence children's attitudes and thinking as they grow up.

2. Opening activity

Ask learners to turn to the person next to them and spend three minutes telling each other about the last purchase they made in a high street shop that cost over £20. Focus discussions by asking them to consider if this was a planned purchase or a spur of the moment purchase, and the things that influenced their decision to buy.

Answers may include: seeing a TV advert, a discounted price or sale, recommendations from friends or family, seeing it in a shop window, point of sales advertising or seeing clothes displayed on a dummy in the shop.

Share highlights from each pair with the wider group, recording suggestions made about both overt and covert influences.

3. Development activity

Bring the whole class together and show them the areas you previously set up. Ask the young people to listen to the statements you read out from the activity sheet before moving to the area that corresponds best with their own opinion. If they are undecided explain that they should stand in the 'I am not sure' zone.

Alternatively, if moving about is not possible, provide each person with a red, amber and green coloured piece of paper and use a traffic light system to indicate opinions.

After each round, stop to discuss different points of view. If there is disagreement, ask the 'Yes, I agree' people to explain to the 'No, I disagree' people what they think. Then provide and opportunity for those who disagree to respond. If anyone from the 'I am not sure' area wants to change places at any stage they can, but encourage them to share their reasons for doing so before physically moving zones.

4. Reflection and review

Finish the activity by facilitating a discussion using these questions:

- How can what we see around us influence our expectations of sex and relationships?
- How can we as individuals challenge this?
- What could society do?

5. Summary

- As consumers we are affected by what we see on the high street.
- Children learn through osmosis, absorbing the images they see around them to create their reality of the world and how it works.
- This can influence their worldview of sex and relationships as well as body image and emotional wellbeing.

Extension

Consider having young people take home and read an extract on 'Influences on children's clothing choices'[1] by David Marshall of Edinburgh University.

---

1   Marshall, D. (2010) 'Influences on children's clothing choices' in *Understanding Children As Consumers*. Sage Publications: London.

ACTIVITY 2.1: WHERE DO YOU STAND? STATEMENTS

1	Magazine articles about how to have good sex influence people's sexual behaviour.
2	Having sex aids (e.g. lubricant and flavoured condoms) on sale in supermarkets makes them more acceptable to the public.
3	Media stories about the size and shape of male genitals affects boys' confidence going through puberty.
4	Seeing sexy underwear displayed in shops on the high street makes teenage girls want to wear it.
5	Having condoms openly on display in shops encourages people to have more sex.
6	Shops reinforce gender colour stereotypes of pink for little girls and blue for little boys.
7	Children grow up thinking thin is beautiful because this is the body shape they see most in advertising.
8	Erotic novels should not be out on public display in a supermarket.
9	R18 Adult films should be sold in supermarkets to anyone with ID.
10	High street sex shops make it more acceptable to watch porn.
11	There is high street pressure on young girls to look sexy from a young age.
12	Most mass produced greetings cards perpetuate male and female stereotypes.

ACTIVITY 2.2: SEX ON THE HIGH STREET

(Years 10–13+)

Aim

- For young people to consider the possible impact of shops on the high street that sell underwear, lingerie, and sex toys on their expectations of sex and relationships.

Time: 45 minutes

Learning outcomes

- To consider how seeing sexual images openly on display in the high street could affect children and young adults' values and attitudes to sex.

- To better understand how a person's environment can shape their perception of what is and isn't acceptable or appropriate.

Key vocabulary

- **Values and attitudes**

- **Sexual images**

- **High street**

You will need

- A copy of the *Diamond nine worksheet* for each group (enlarged and printed on A3 paper if possible)

- A set of *Sex on the high street cards* for each group

- Internet access

How to do it

The point of this lesson is not to debate whether shops like this have a place in the high street, but rather to consider any overt or covert messages picked up by children as they walk past and absorb the images as part of everyday life.

1. Introduction

- Establish/revisit ground rules (see pages 42–43 for guidance).

Set the scene by suggesting that if you walk through a shopping centre or town centre in the UK among the well-lit traditional stores is often a shop with windows displaying models in saucy underwear placed in provocative poses. From budget to high end, there are plenty of places for to buy (and be bought) 'sexy' underwear. Step inside these emporiums, past the welcoming staff and racks of underwear, and there is often a section filled with handcuffs, whips and sex toys along with advice on how to use them. While these may only be legally sold to those over the age of 18, younger people can certainly see the displays and (depending on the diligence of the retail assistants) even browse what is on offer.

2. Opening activity

The question for young people is:

> What messages are received by young people about sex and relationships from specialist shops on the high street selling underwear, lingerie and adult toys?

Divide the young people into small groups, allocating each group a set of *Sex on the high street cards* and an enlarged photocopy of the *Diamond nine worksheet*. Introduce the cards by explaining that just like on the TV show 'Family Fortunes', the author asked 100 young people the same question and the cards are based on the most popular answers given.

Each group should discuss the point of view given on each card before ranking them to form a diamond nine, between the views they believe to be most popular and the least. This can be based on their own opinions, those they have heard peers, family or others expressing, as well as any media influences.

3. Development activity

Once the whole diamond nine has been filled, ask each group to add one more diamond of their own. This should contain any other comment they want to make about sexualised images on the high street and can be on either side of the debate.

Facilitate a feedback session where groups share where in the ratings they have placed each card, discussing the reasons behind their decisions and suggesting potential ways that children and young people could be influenced by what they see, for example 'adverts saying that sexy underwear is a good present to buy your partner for Christmas/Valentines', 'It is important to wear nice knickers' or '"tightie whities" (fitted white underpants for men, usually a designer brand) = being sexually attractive'.

Invite each group in turn to read out their own diamond card to share the additional point that they would like to make.

4. Reflection and review

Ask:

- Are these messages positive or negative?

- Do you think they can influence people's expectations of real-life sex and relationships? If so, how, if not, why not?

- Is it easy to separate out what is real and what is fantasy in these shop windows?

5. Summary

- Children and young people can be influenced, as can adults, by the things they see around them.

- Constant exposure to something can result in it becoming normal and commonplace.

- Decisions can be made on the strength of these assumptions and so perpetuate them.

Extension

Display the *Diamond nine worksheets* to prompt discussion among other young people, or expand it by adding pictures and photos of relevant shops to make a large display and raise awareness to encourage further debate.

Diamond nine

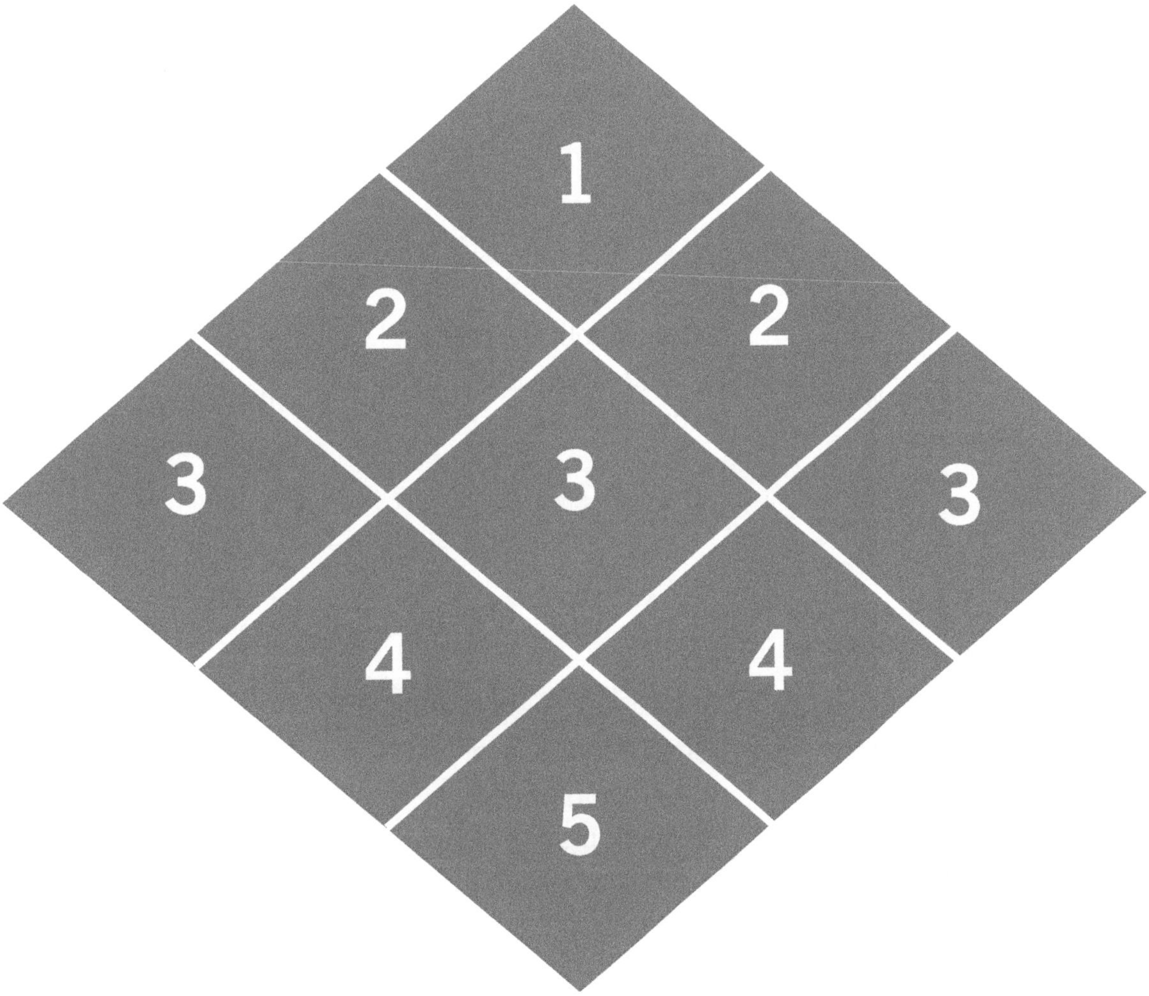

ACTIVITY 2.2: SEX ON THE HIGH STREET CARDS

Stockings, suspenders and high heels are worn to look sexy.	For women to look sexy in underwear they need to be thin with large breasts.	St Valentine's Day is about sex as well as romance.
For males to look good in underwear they need to have a body with well-defined muscles.	Buying your partner underwear is a romantic thing to do.	Adults have underwear for different purposes: the everyday and the sexy.
Adults think school uniforms, nurses outfits and so on are sexy to dress up in.	It is important for women to have matching bra, knickers and suspenders.	Sex is fun and to be enjoyed.
The whips, paddles, love eggs and so on described in bestselling erotic novels are everyday items.	Underwear can be erotic and not just functional.	You don't need a partner to enjoy a good sex life.

ACTIVITY 2.3: SHOPS AND MARKETING

(Years 7–13+)

Aim

- To encourage young people to explore branding and marketing ideas in the high street to see how this can influence assumptions made about people.

Time: 60 minutes

Learning outcomes

- To understand that clothing companies spend time and huge amounts of money marketing and branding high street fashions to appeal to their intended target audience, which consumers then buy into.

- To realise this can lead to assumptions and stereotypes being applied to individuals, based on what they wear or where they shop.

Key vocabulary

- **Branding and marketing**

- **Gender stereotypes**

- **Image**

- **First impressions**

You will need

- A selection of magazines (including those aimed at the LGBT+ community)

- Information about different high street fashion shops (including logos which are available to print from the internet)

- Glue/scissors/craft materials

- A3 stiff paper or card and marker pens

- Flipchart paper

How to do it

To prepare for the session go online and download information, advertising and pictures for various high street clothes shops. Choose some that are clearly aimed at younger people and some that are targeting other sectors of the community.

1. Introduction

- Establish/revisit ground rules (see pages 42–43 for guidance).

Ask young people to call out the names of as many high street clothes shops as they can think of in two minutes.

Record these on flipchart paper, call time and then place a tick next to the names of stores that have been visited and a purchase made by at least one person in the class.

2. Opening activity

Give each group the name of a store, some magazines, a large sheet of modelling card (or stiff paper), pens and a selection of craft materials. Their task is to create a poster that shows who they think the shop targets as a potential customer. Encourage learners to consider the target age, gender and size as well as other factors like ethnicity and sexuality.

Invite each group to present their poster of the 'typical' customer for the store allocated to them, inviting discussion and questions as you go along. Then hand each group the research previously prepared to compare what the young people thought with the different clothing companies' marketing and branding strategies.

Facilitate a discussion that includes feedback about their perceptions, and how correct they were, to consider:

- Where did your perceptions about this store come from?

- How important is the image of a shop in your decision to buy from it?

- Which of these stores specifically target young people? How do they target them?

- How do the clothes and accessories available to young people in-store influence the image they present to the world?

Conclude that marketing and branding experts work very hard to develop an image for clothing companies that will appeal to their target market. Often people will not even go into a shop if they do not perceive it as 'for them'. At the same time, some people will travel further and pay more for an item just because it has a particular label, as they are 'buying into' the whole image or lifestyle a brand represents.

3. Development activity

Select some well-known brands that appeal to young people and write them as headers on different sheets of paper. Examples might include:

- Sports brands – e.g. Nike, Adidas, Puma, Fred Perry

- British brands – e.g. Jack Wills, Burberry, Ann Summers, Topman

- American brands – e.g. Playboy, Victoria's Secret, Ralph Lauren Polo, Juicy Couture

- European brands – e.g. Chanel, Versace, Mango, Zara.

Divide the young people back into small groups and hand each a different headed sheet and pens. Ask them to discuss their allocated brand and suggest what image this label portrays, any assumptions that might be attached to young people who choose to wear the clothes/accessories and finally any messages that might be conveyed about sexual identity or sexual behaviour. Ideas can be recorded onto paper. Invite each group to present their findings, encouraging questions and further discussion between presentations.

4. Reflection and review

Conclude that often the first thing we see when we meet someone new is how they choose to present themselves, including the clothes they wear, which rightly or wrongly can speak volumes. This perception can lead to assumptions being made that may or may not be true, and help to perpetuate stereotypes about lifestyle, relationships, attitudes and behaviour. Stress the importance of looking beyond first impressions and getting to know people, while asking young people to quietly reflect on what their clothes might say about them to make sure they are happy with that.

5. Summary

- Marketing targets specific groups of people to encourage them to buy certain goods, clothes, etc.

- What you wear is the first thing someone sees and it can speak loudly, but not always correctly, so be certain what you say.

ACTIVITY 2.4: WHAT DID YOU SAY?

(Years 7–13+)

Aims

- To explore the use of slogans on t-shirts and the implied messages given when wearing them.
- To discuss how others might receive these.

Time: 60–90 minutes

Learning outcomes

- To consider the meaning behind slogans on popular t-shirts, widely available to buy and worn by children, young people and adults.
- To look behind the words to the meaning to learn how they can contribute towards perpetuating sexual gender stereotypes.

Key vocabulary

- **Sexual and gender stereotypes**
- **Overt and covert messages**

You will need

- Flipchart paper and markers
- Copies of the *What did you say? worksheet*

How to do it

If this session is being delivered in a non-formal education setting then ask young people to wear their favourite t-shirt with words on it. This could be a favourite band t-shirt, one with the name of a place on it or one with a humorous message. If in school, ask young people to either take a picture of their t-shirt, or simply bring it in to show during the lesson.

1. Introduction

- Establish/revisit ground rules (see pages 42–43 for guidance).

2. Opening activity

In small groups, ask young people to review their t-shirts for ten minutes using the following questions:

- What does it say?
- Why did you choose it?
- What does it say about you?

Ask that they make notes on a sheet of flipchart paper as they go along, using the question numbers as a guide. The first question should prompt a list of what is on the t-shirts. Questions 2 and 3 ask young people to look a bit deeper into the reasons for wearing it and what it shows the outside world. This could include:

- Chosen – because I like it, because it is funny, because it looks good, because it shows the t-shirt is expensive, because it says in words what I think, etc.

- Meaning – that I am a supporter of this band, lifestyle, etc., that I belong to this group of people, for example sci-fi geeks, that I am rich enough to be able to wear a designer label, that I agree with the political statement made, etc.

Call time and invite some feedback, recording the main points on a sheet of flipchart paper and discussing issues as they arise. Suggest that wearing a t-shirt with a slogan tells the world in general something about you, your beliefs, likes and attitudes. These messages are both over, i.e. open, and covert, i.e. unspoken. Ask this question of the whole group:

> Would you wear a t-shirt with a slogan that promotes something you do not understand, agree with or like?

3. Development activity

Still working in small groups, hand out copies of the *What did you say? worksheet*. This time ask them to discuss:

- What is the meaning behind the slogan?
- What conclusions could be drawn about the person wearing it?
- How might this contribute towards sexual gender stereotypes?

Again, they have ten minutes to record their impressions. Facilitate another feedback session adding the prompt questions below to generate further discussion:

- These t-shirts all have sexual connotations, about performance, behaviour, etc.
- What messages do they send?
- Many of these t-shirts are available in child sizes. Is it appropriate for children to wear them? Why/why not?
- What impressions might they give about the wearer?

Spend time considering the different messages given about males and females and their attitudes to sex, for example if a female wears a t-shirt sporting the slogan 'Porn Star' does this mean she is up for porn-style sex, or thinks she looks like a porn star? If a male wears a t-shirt with the slogan 'Stud' on it, does it mean that he has a lot of sexual partners or would like to? How does this impact on gender stereotypes about sex? For example, does it perpetuate the myth that women who have a lot of sexual partners are 'easy' or that men are only looking for sex?

4. Reflection and review

Finally, ask the group this question:

> Who is responsible for any messages received, positive or negative, from the producing, selling, buying and wearing of t-shirts with a sexual slogan?

Consider this from the point of view of the designer, manufacturer, seller and consumer as well as the person reading the slogan worn on someone's chest.

5. Summary

- It is important to consider what the slogan on a t-shirt may say about you before choosing to buy it.
- Some t-shirts use deliberately provocative words to provoke a reaction.
- Parents and carers need to think carefully about how appropriate it is to dress a young child in slogan t-shirts more suited to an adult.

Extension

Continue by teaching Activity 2.5 in this chapter next.

ACTIVITY 2.4: WHAT DID YOU SAY? WORKSHEET

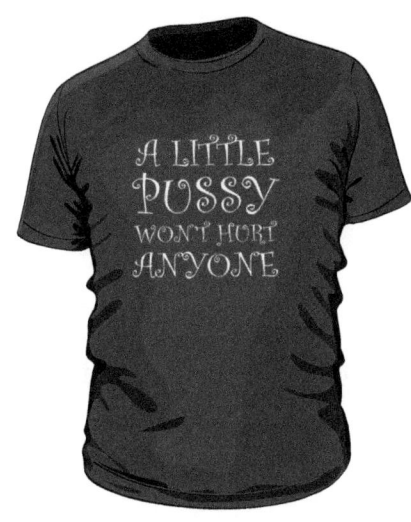

ACTIVITY 2.5: MESSAGE MUGS
(Years 7–13+)

Aims

- To explore the messages contained in slogans that refer to sex or the sex industry.

- For young people to consider the impact that wearing clothing bearing a sexualised slogan or picture might have on other people around them.

Time: 45 minutes (plus additional drying time)

Learning outcomes

- To understand the conclusions that may be drawn about a person who chooses to promote sexual activity or the sex industry on their clothing.

- To recognise the personal responsibility involved in making appropriate choices.

- To understand what your choices say about you.

Key vocabulary

- **Personal responsibility**

- **Sexualised slogan**

- **Sexual innuendo**

- **Making appropriate choices**

You will need

- A plain mug for each young person

- Chinagraph pencils

- Gold and silver permanent paint pens (these come in a range of nib sizes)

- Enamel paints or specialist ceramic paints

- White spirit or brush cleaner

- Fine brushes

- Paper and pens/pencils

How to do it
1. Introduction

- Establish/revisit ground rules (see pages 42–43 for guidance).

Remind the class about slogans on clothing previously discussed in Activity 2.4, some of which have caused public outcry when large high street names have produced them in children's sizes too.[2]

2. Opening activity
Ask:

- What message does wearing a t-shirt containing sexual innuendo or explicit language give to others?

---

2   www.oddee.com/item_99244.aspx

For example, that the wearer is sexually available, aspires to be paid for sex or that the wearer is inviting members of the public to look at a part of their body that is usually kept private, regardless of their age or gender identity, etc.

- How might these messages conflict with other people's values and moral code?

Consider faith, culture and diversity issues.

Suggest that although slogans used on clothing may reflect popular culture or be intended as a joke, they can lead to assumptions being made that may well be incorrect. They can also invite comparisons or hurtful criticism, for example wearing a t-shirt that boasts about the size of body parts or levels of sexual attractiveness. Remind young people that first impressions count and that these are made in the first few seconds of meeting someone.

3. Development activity

The main task for this lesson is to challenge these inappropriate designs by creating a new type of slogan, one that is self-affirming and positive. This can challenge some of the gender stereotypes discussed during Activity 2.4, but should not contain any sexual language.

Hand out paper and pencils to start practising designs and planning the slogan, which must:

- have meaning to the designer

- be something the designer is happy for others to see

- promote a positive message.

Encourage the sharing of ideas and feedback until everyone has a design they are happy with.

Hand out the plain mugs and chinagraph pencils. Chinagraph pencils are the pencils that are used to mark plates and glass – often seen on market stalls or factory outlets where the price is written onto the china. This produces a clear outline to work with, but washes off once the design is finished. If you cannot source a Chinagraph pencil try using a whiteboard marker for a similar effect.

Next, use the gold and silver pens to draw the outlines of the design and to block in any areas required in these colours. These contain oil-based paint, which creates a line that is raised slightly from the surface of the china. This is useful for containing the enamel or ceramic paint later. Leave to dry thoroughly to reduce the risk of paint bleeding through the outline or colours mixing.

Using a thin paintbrush fill in the design with paint. Do this part in stages, leaving the paint to dry in between if required.

4. Reflection and review

Leave the newly designed mugs to dry out fully and then display together to create a gallery of positive slogans that challenge the overly sexualised messages seen on the previous merchandise.

Take a photo of each mug with its owner and invite everyone to create a personal social media message to raise peer awareness about the project, before posting both on Instagram, Twitter, Facebook, etc.

5. Summary

- Always consider the message behind any slogan with a sexual connotation before choosing to wear it.

- Some t-shirts/clothing carry a deliberately provocative message that may offend people.

- Choosing to wear a sexualised message on clothing could provoke an inappropriate response from others who may try to accept any implied invitation or it could draw unwelcome attention.

ACTIVITY 2.6: SELLING THE SONG
(Years 7–13+)

Aim

- To consider the messages received by children and young people through popular songs and music videos and discuss how this might shape understanding and expectations of sex and relationships.

Time: 45 minutes

Learning outcomes

- To explore the lifestyle and values promoted through some music videos.
- To consider the overt and covert messages behind the music and the impact this can have on fans.

You will need

- Flipchart paper and felt pens
- Online access and speakers

Key vocabulary

- **Expectations of sex and relationships**
- **Stereotypes**
- **Popular culture**

How to do it

Prepare by selecting a music video that will promote discussion. An example of a song where both the lyrics and the accompanying video caused national controversy and wide discussion is 'Blurred Lines' by Robin Thicke. This can be found easily on YouTube.

1. Introduction

- Establish/revisit ground rules (see pages 42–43 for guidance).

Have a selection of music clips from different genres playing as young people come into class.

Give everyone a small piece of paper and a pen and ask them to quickly write down a response to each of the following:

- All rap artists are…
- Women in R&B videos look…
- All rock bands are…
- Boy bands appeal to young fans because…
- Classical singers are…

Once done invite everyone to call out the answers before asking where these ideas come from and whether they are true or stereotypes. If they are stereotypes, where do they come from? For example, popular culture, music videos, newspaper articles, 'kiss and tell stories' and rock and roll legends of excess, etc.

2. Opening activity

In pairs, task young people with going online to find and watch their favourite music videos. This could be a current song or an old favourite. Encourage debate and ask for feedback about the reason for selecting these particular songs, the meaning they have for individuals and any feelings associated with hearing them.

Point out that music videos are an extremely powerful way of advertising and marketing recording artists. Suggest that they don't just sell the song but also the singer/band and in some cases promote or showcase a whole lifestyle too.

3. Development activity

Divide the young people into small groups and give out paper and pens. Ask the young people in their groups to first watch the music video you have selected and then make notes in response to the following:

- Do the lyrics of this song have a sexual content?

- If so, what messages are given? To young men? To young women?

- How are these messages reflected in the video?

- How might this impact on children and young people's understanding of sex and male/female roles within a relationship?

4. Refection and review

Allow up to 20 minutes before bringing the whole group together to compare notes and present their findings, asking the young people to comment on how they think music videos generally reflect or influence popular culture, particularly the impact they may have on intimate relationships and gender expectations.

5. Summary

- Music is an important and powerful part of life for many people and affiliation with a musical genre, such as hip-hop, punk or rockabilly, can define some people's lifestyle, politics and values.

- Music videos are crucial in creating the public image of a performing artist or band to showcase their talent and present them in the way they want to be seen.

- The lyrics of some songs are sexual and arguably perpetuate sexist attitudes, reinforced by the accompanying video. There are examples of music videos that have been classified as 18, meaning that viewing is restricted to over-18s.[3]

---

3   Example: *Couple of Stack* by Dizzee Rascal

ACTIVITY 2.7: CARTOON MESSAGES
(Years 7–13+)

Aim

- To consider the differences between male and female characters in old newspaper cartoon strips and now in terms of gender roles and sexual stereotypes.

Time: 60 minutes

Learning outcome

- To know how men and women were depicted in cartoons from the past and compare them with those of today.

Key vocabulary

- **Gender stereotypes**
- **Sexualisation of cartoon images**

You will need

- A selection of newspaper cartoon strips featuring relationships (these can be vintage, up to date or a mixture of both)
- Flipchart paper
- Marker pens
- Paper and pens

How to do it

1. Introduction

- Establish/revisit ground rules (see pages 42–43 for guidance).

Research and print some traditional old-style newspaper cartoon strips. You don't need the whole cartoon, but enough to show how the female and male characters interact. Examples could include Andy Capp[4] or George and Lynne.[5]

Explain that this lesson is going to focus on how men and women are depicted in cartoons through different generations.

2. Opening activity

Divide young people into small teams, give out paper and pens, and facilitate this short quiz. There are three rounds and each round will be timed for three minutes:

Round one: Name as many male cartoon characters as you can.

Round two: Name as many female cartoon characters as you can.

Round three: Name as many cartoon couples/partners as you can.

Call time after each round and ask for examples from each team. The team with the longest list of valid characters wins the round. The overall winner is the team with the most names across all

---

4   www.mirror.co.uk/lifestyle/cartoons/andy-capp
5   Originally a comic strip in *The Sun* until 2010, www.georgeandlynne.com

three categories. Move on to discuss the way that relationships are depicted in these cartoons, for example Popeye and Olive Oil or Mickey and Minnie Mouse.

3. Development activity

Distribute the pre-selected cartoon strips, paper and markers among the teams. Explain that these cartoons, which date from the 1950s onwards, are from daily family newspapers, so are likely to have been read by men, women and children.

Underneath two headings, 'Male' and 'Female', ask learners to discuss the cartoon characters and then record the differences between how they are depicted under the appropriate heading. This can include how they look, how they behave, their role in the cartoon, their relationship with each other, etc.

On a flipchart draw two columns and write up the same headings as before inviting feedback from each group:

- How are female cartoon characters shown?

  For example, younger females often wear less clothing or clothing that could be considered sexually provocative, such as Betty Boop or Tinkerbell. They tend to have big eyes, long hair, large breasts, small waists and long legs. Some (see George and Lynne) are drawn topless or naked. Wives are usually shown as sexually unattractive older women who nag their male partners (see Flo in the Andy Capp series). Women are either out looking for a man, or at home in the kitchen once they have one!

- How are males drawn?

  For example, young males are tall, strong and capable with well-defined muscles. The alternative type of man shown is a 'regular bloke' (see Andy Capp) trying to cope with his wife's demands, but always with his eyes on the 'dolly birds' (younger women). In this version, men are often seen trying to escape from their wives to go to the pub with their friends.

4. Reflection and review

Conclude with a short discussion to reinforce learning:

- What messages do these cartoons give about sex and relationships?

- Are the couples shown relevant to the couples of today? If not, what has changed?

- How are issues of faith, ethnicity or sexuality portrayed in these cartoons? For example, how are LGBT+ couples represented?

5. Summary

- In older cartoons gender roles tend to be set and fixed; women and men behave in traditional ways.

- Gender stereotypes about sexual attractiveness can be perpetuated through the sexualised images of cartoon characters, for example 'strong' men being physically attractive and 'weak' men being dominated by large women.

- In today's cartoons, characters are not so defined by gender, although this is not so true for video games.

Extension

Set young people the group work task of designing a six-frame cartoon strip featuring a couple of their own design to represent a modern relationship.

ACTIVITY 2.8: CREATE YOUR OWN SUPERHERO
(Years 7–13+)

Aims

- To consider the differences between male and female superheroes and to identify gender roles and stereotypes.

- To challenge these preconceptions.

Time: 60 minutes

Learning outcomes

- To acknowledge that female superheroes are often drawn in a way that is highly sexualised, compared with men who are often covered from head to toe and masked.

- To recognise that these have little or nothing to do with real life but can affect expectations and social norms.

Key vocabulary

- **Challenging gender stereotypes**
- **Social norms**
- **Pornography**

You will need

- Pictures of male and female superheroes
- A3 paper
- Marker pens
- Sticky tack

How to do it

1. Introduction

- Establish/revisit ground rules (see pages 42–43 for guidance).

Hold up some pictures of traditional male superheroes, such as Superman or Batman. Suggest that although cartoons featuring male superheroes have been around for over 50 years, often starting life as a strip in a newspaper or comic, female action heroes are a much newer concept. Show some pictures of females, for example Lara Croft (Tomb Raider), Catwoman or Black Widow (Marvel).

2. Opening activity

Divide the young people into small groups and distribute the superhero pictures, paper and markers. On a large sheet of paper their task is to write a long stream of words, using three full stops as punctuation between each one, first to describe females and their male superheroes. These should start 'Male superheroes are...' and 'Female superheroes are...'

For example:

Female superheroes are slim...with big breasts...small waists...have long legs...wear high heeled boots...have extra long hair...dress in revealing clothes...wear make-up...have long eyelashes...are super sexy...etc.

Male superheroes are strong...have big calf and thigh muscles...look like they work out...have small waists...have broad shoulders...wear a mask...carry weapons and gadgets...have super powers...etc.

Invite each group to take turns in reading out their long sentences, and then ask:

- Which are more important to most storylines, male or female characters?

- How does the colour of a female character's hair relate to her personality?

  For example, are blondes depicted as more feminine and sexy, brunettes more intelligent and redheads more feisty?

- How do female characters compare to porn star stereotypes?

  Probably they share many of the same characteristics as well as having a similar taste in clothes.

3. Development activity
Hand out more paper to each group. Their task now is to draw a new female superhero that challenges traditional female roles and represents one for the modern age. As well as designing her look and costume, she needs a name and a character profile, including her super powers and/or special skills.

4. Reflection and review
Facilitate gallery time, where each group presents their new superhero and explains what she can do. Display the new female superheroes for other young people to see and to promote further discussion.

5. Summary

- Most female superheroes perpetuate female stereotypes in terms of looks, powers and behaviour. This includes characters, for example Catwoman and Poison Ivy, who use their sexuality to seduce and get what they want, rather than having proper super powers like their male counterparts.

- Some female comic characters look very similar to male fantasy pictures associated with the porn industry, with skimpy outfits and exaggerated body curves.

- Arguably this doesn't provide a positive role model for little girls growing up.

ACTIVITY 2.9: THE ONLY WAY IS REALITY
(Years 7–13+)

Aim

- To open up discussions about reality TV and the messages viewers may internalise about sexual attraction, desire, appropriate behaviour and relationships from the lifestyles portrayed.

Time: 30 minutes

Learning outcomes

- To consider the difference between the easy wealth and fantasy lifestyle promoted by reality TV and achievable life goals.

- To recognise that the relationships shown on reality TV shows are created to entertain and are not necessarily reflective of real-life ones.

- To understand that the relationships depicted in reality TV and through celebrity culture can affect how people perceive sexual norms.

Key vocabulary

- **Reality TV**
- **Celebrity culture**
- **Sexual norms**
- **Relationships**

You will need

- Copies of the *Reality TV review sheets*
- Pens

How to do it
1. Introduction

- Establish/revisit ground rules (see pages 42–43 for guidance).

Start by making sure that everyone has a common understanding of reality TV (based on the one given below) and asking the young people to call out some of the TV programmes that they have watched. This could include programmes like 'The Only Way Is Essex', 'Geordie Shore' and 'Made in Chelsea' or game shows including 'Love Island' and 'Big Brother'.

Reality television is a genre of television programming that presents purportedly unscripted dramatic or humorous situations, documents actual events, and usually features ordinary people instead of professional actors.

2. Opening activity

Hand out a reality TV review sheet and a pen to each young person. Their task is to read the statements and then place a tick next to the ones they agree with and a cross next to those they don't. If you know you have young people who struggle with reading and writing, do the activity in pairs so that only one person needs to write. Stress that it is a personal opinion that you want so there are no right or wrong answers.

Allow a few minutes for everyone to complete the task and then go through the responses, inviting people to share where they agreed or disagreed with statements and encouraging discussion where opinions differ.

3. Development activity

Facilitate a discussion that considers the following questions:

- Why do people volunteer for reality TV shows? What do they get out of it?

- Is it ethical to be watching random people embarrass/upset/argue/become romantically involved with each other as 'entertainment'?

- What do you think about reality 'stars' having sex or claiming to have sex, during the show? What messages does this give the viewers?

- Do you think that relationships that start in the public eye like this are likely to last? Why/ why not?

- How can reality TV and celebrity culture impact on what society considers 'normal' sexual behaviour to be? For example, desensitising viewers to public nudity, dysfunctional relationships and casual sex.

4. Reflection and review

Ask young people to imagine a spectrum with real life on one end and fantasy on the other. Explain that you are going to call out a few statements that reflect the discussions that have just taken place. What you want young people to do is listen and then rate each statement on the spectrum by lifting between one and five fingers above their heads. One finger = pure fantasy; five fingers = real life. Encourage explanations and comments between votes.

If this is not possible, ask young people to demonstrate their view by verbally voting between one and five.

- People on reality TV shows are paid to be themselves.

- The relationships developed between people on reality TV shows are natural and true to life.

- The intimate relationships shown are based on mutual affection, respect and trust.

- People on reality TV shows are more provocative and sexier on camera than in real life to ensure that the public supports them.

- Some reality shows encourage people to do things that they would not usually do.

5. Summary

- Reality TV shows should be enjoyed as entertainment rather than viewed as a blueprint for life to aspire to.

- Often the relationships we watch are created or enhanced by the creators of the show to increase viewing figures.

- In real life behaviour like having sex in public is illegal and could result in a criminal record.

ACTIVITY 2.9: REALITY TV REVIEW SHEET

1. Reality TV companies encourage the people featured to get together. ☐

2. Viewers expect people to be sexy for the cameras. ☐

3. People want to be on a reality show to become a celebrity. ☐

4. Real people don't live like they do in reality shows. ☐

5. TV companies will show anything to get high viewing figures. ☐

6. Reality TV stars are role models for children and young people. ☐

7. A relationship started on a reality TV show won't last. ☐

8. People watch reality TV to see beautiful people behave badly. ☐

9. If a couple have sex during a reality show they should be sacked. ☐

10. Nudity and anything of a sexual nature should not be shown on TV. ☐

11. Reality TV shows a celebrity lifestyle that most young people aspire to. ☐

12. If I had the chance I would appear in a reality TV show. ☐

ACTIVITY 2.10: REALITY SEX

(Years 10–13+)

Aim

- To analyse the number of times sex is mentioned or discussed in an average episode of a reality TV show and consider how this could influence younger viewers.

Time: 60–90 minutes

Learning outcomes

- To understand that reality TV shows use sex and relationships as the basis for many of the plotlines.
- To question if this is a fair representation of real life.
- To consider how lifestyle choices shown on reality TV shows can influence viewers.

Key vocabulary

- **Reality TV**
- **Sex and relationships**

You will need

- Young people to pre-view an episode of a reality TV show
- Three sheets of flipchart paper headed, 'Untrue', 'Real life and 'Reality TV'
- Sticky notes and pens
- A bag or bowl to collect notes in

How to do it

Set young people the task of watching one episode of a reality TV show of their choice. This should feature young adults, for example 'Made in Chelsea' (MIC), The Only Way Is Essex' (TOWIE) or 'Geordie Shore'. While viewing they must keep a tally of how many times sex is mentioned, joked about or becomes a topic of conversation. This information should be brought to this lesson.

1. Introduction

- Establish/revisit ground rules (see pages 42–43 for guidance).

Explain that the genre of TV shows you are going to be discussing in this lesson are generally shown after 9pm, because they are likely to include adult themes and/or some scenes of near nudity. Read out this description of reality TV:

Reality TV features real people put into planned situations to see how they react or cope. Some of what you see is real life, but other things have been devised to entertain the viewer.

Ask young people what they think of this – is it a fair description?

2. Opening activity

Ask everyone to give the name of the reality TV show they watched and how many times they counted sex being mentioned or becoming a topic of conversation on the show. This should include jokes made or innuendo as well as other conversations. Write each number up, using a tally system for ease, onto a sheet of flipchart paper or a whiteboard and then combine all the numbers to give a grand total. Then use the following formula to work out the average times that sex is mentioned in an episode of a reality TV show:

Number of times sex is mentioned: _____

Number of episodes watched: _____

Ask young people:

- Is this a higher, or lower number than expected?

- Who spoke most about sex in the episodes watched, males or females?

- Were openly LGBT+ cast members represented in the same way?

- What type of language was used to describe sex and relationship?

3. Development activity

Next, hand each person three sticky notes and a pen. On each note they should write something they saw, heard or learnt about sex and relationships from watching the show, before folding the note in half.

Collect in the sticky notes and mix up.

Introduce the three pre-prepared headed sheets of paper and lay them out on the floor. Explain that the 'Reality TV' sheet is for capturing situations and ideas most likely to be seen in a reality TV show, the 'Real life' sheet is for those more likely to happen in the context of a real life sex and relationships. The 'Untrue' sheet is for misinformation about sex and relationships identified within the show.

Hand the randomly shuffled sticky notes out one at a time. They should be read out aloud and then stuck on to the corresponding 'Real life', 'Reality TV' or 'Untrue' sheet on the floor. There are likely to be the fewest notes in the 'Untrue' zone, but it is important to capture any myths or incorrect information to challenge later.

Encourage discussion as each card is placed, which can be moved after hearing more information. For example:

If you get drunk you may have sex you later regret = Real life

If you get drunk and have sex you are not responsible for your actions = Untrue – in law you are responsible

If you get drunk you may have sex, regret it, tell all your friends and then be disrespectful about your lover on national television = Reality TV

4. Reflection and review

Once all of the cards are placed, review the learning from the activity using these prompt questions to explore young people's attitudes to reality TV and the impact they can have on real life:

- What do you enjoy or not enjoy watching on reality shows about the life and loves of different groups of young adults?

- Do you think people who watch reality TV shows know that it isn't the same as real life?

- Do you think that reality TV relationships can influence or change viewers' sexual behaviour and/or attitudes? If so, how?

- Do they change perceptions of what is and isn't acceptable behaviour?

As these questions ask about attitudes and opinions there are no right or wrong answers. The following information may be useful to support the idea that watching reality TV can influence real-life aspirations, choices and behaviour:

Fans of 'The Only Way Is Essex' have led a £1.4 billion high street bonanza.

False nails and lashes, fake tans, vajazzles, white stilettos and watches have boomed as shoppers copy Amy Childs and her TOWIE pals.[6]

It has been revealed that MIC's supposedly rich and well-connected cast is actually positioned nearer the TOWIE end of the wannabe spectrum, after it came to light that scenes filmed in an exclusive Chelsea nightclub were all staged.[7]

Geordie Shore Series 10: 'I argue a lot and have a lot of fights,' said Charlotte (Cosby), proudly. 'I get involved in everyone's business. Five people I have actual rows with and some of them turn into fist fights.'[8]

Point out that although these programmes are called 'reality TV' they do explain at some point that while the people are real some of the situations have been contrived to provide a storyline or add to the plot. They also tend to be scheduled later in the evening because of their adult content. However, with catch-up TV and devices like tablets and mobiles, younger teens or even children can watch them.

How might this affect their perceptions of what it is like to be a young adult, both positively and negatively?

Finally, invite young people to demonstrate with a show of hands whether they think reality shows should be given an age rating, similar to films with adult content.

5. Summary

- Reality TV shows like TOWIE and MIC are supposed to allow us a good look into the lives of a group of young adults living and socialising in different parts of Britain.

- Even though they are tagged 'reality' they usually include a warning in the opening titles about the truthfulness of what we see, for example 'The people in this programme are real, but some of what they do has been staged for your entertainment.'

- The target audience is adults, which is why they are screened after 9pm, but many young people watch on catch-up TV or live streaming via a mobile device.

- There are concerns about the types of sexual behaviour and intimate relationships depicted in some shows.

- Reality TV can normalise bad behaviour and glamorise potentially harmful sexual choices, such as cheating, drunken one-night-stands and choosing a partner based on their looks rather than their personality.

---

6   www.thesun.co.uk/sol/homepage/news/4095425/TOWIE-news-The-Only-Way-Is-Essex-boosts-economy-by-14bn.html

7   http://metro.co.uk/2011/05/15/made-in-chelsea-revealed-to-be-fake-as-club-admits-cast-arent-members-10713/#ixzz3od1qWvso

8   www.mirror.co.uk/tv/tv-news/geordie-shore-series-10-secrets-5472184

ACTIVITY 2.11: MEDIA SEX SCANDALS
(Years 9–13+)

Aim

- This activity focuses on two media stories that both feature a couple having sex in an inappropriate place. Young people are asked to consider any potential emotional and social consequences for the individuals involved, as well as the wider impact stories like these could have on what is and isn't considered acceptable public behaviour.

Time: 45 minutes

Learning outcomes

- That it is an offence to have sex in a public place.

- That publicity isn't always a positive thing and can have short- and long-term repercussions.

- That the media contributes towards a shared understanding of what constitutes acceptable public behaviour.

Key vocabulary

- **Media**
- **Reality TV**
- **Newspapers**
- **Pornography**

You will need

- Copies of the two news reports provided
- Flipchart paper and marker pens

How to do it
1. Introduction

- Establish/revisit ground rules (see pages 42–43 for guidance).

Start by asking who has heard the old saying, 'There is no such thing as bad publicity.'

Basically, in this context, it means that any way of bringing public attention to yourself is a good thing, no matter what you have to do to capture the interest of the media.

Then ask if the young people think there is any truth in it and invite examples of where they have seen this type of exposure – for example, contestants entering talent shows on TV as a singer when they can't sing or people uploading videos onto YouTube that show them doing dangerous or silly things to get noticed. Suggest that this sort of fame hunting can work as long as the public like what they see and approve of it; however if the opposite happens, and the publicity is negative, it can lead to a pubic shaming or a media storm of negative comments. Again, ask for examples before concluding that sometimes publicity can be so bad it becomes a form of public bullying, especially online where it is easy for everyone to have a say without much censorship.

2. Opening activity

Explain that this session is based on two media reports that have allegedly been featured on TV, online and in the national newspapers. Although they are based on real-life stories, they have been deliberately altered to include elements from more than one article and do not intend to represent a particular incident.

Split the class in two and then ask them to work in groups of four. Give groups in the first half the *News report 1 worksheet* and those in the second half the *News report 2 worksheet* to focus on. Once you have done this, ask a volunteer from each foursome to carefully read the story to the rest of their group before addressing the following questions:

- Do you think the 'journalist' has reported this story in a non-judgemental way? If yes, how? If not, what judgements' have been made?

- Why do you think the couple featured chose to have sex where they did?

- How did other people around them react?

- How might their families and friends feel when they hear / see the story?

- Do you think that what they did was acceptable? Why/why not?

- Do you think this is good or bad publicity for the couples featured?

Give out flipchart paper and pens to each group to make notes on.

3. Development activity

To facilitate feedback from the discussions, pair a group studying News report 1 with a group considering News report 2 and invite them to take it in turns to firstly tell their story and then share their findings. Encourage additional debate after each group has spoken.

Remaining together, pose the following questions for wider discussion to reach an answer they all agree on:

- In both stories, the couples having sex were filmed and this film was distributed to a wide audience, some without their knowledge or consent. Are these films pornography?

   ◦ If yes, explain why.

   ◦ If no, explain why not.

- Remind everyone of the UK definition of porn, taken from the Criminal Justice and Immigration Act 2008:

   > An image is 'pornographic' if it is of such a nature that it must reasonably be assumed to have been produced solely or principally for the purpose of sexual arousal.[9]

- What are the potential consequences of being filmed having sex for these people? *(E.g. at work, home, socially and/or within their community. How might a new partner react? Or children/siblings/parents/etc.?)*

- What type of publicity might they receive? *(E.g. the film could go viral, screenshots may be taken, people they know might be interviewed, the audience could make nasty comments about personal things, etc.)*

   ◦ How might this differ for: a) the young couple b) the older couple c) females d) males? *(E.g. the words that are used to describe the different people and the size/shape of their bodies, sexual stereotypes about men and women, etc.)*

   ◦ How might it affect them longer term? *(E.g. it may be hard to shake off the publicity, people may judge them for it, they may grow to wish they hadn't done it and worry that the story will always be out there, the younger couple could have children later in life or new partners who could find out about this and feel ashamed/angry/etc.)*

---

9   For full details of this Act go to www.legislation.gov.uk/ukpga/2008/4/part/5/crossheading/pornography-etc

4. Reflection and review

Call the whole group back together and go through the questions together inviting each joint group to feedback the key points from their discussions.

5. Summary

- People have different personal opinions about what is acceptable in public, but the law says that it is an offence to have sex in a public place.

- While the film itself may not be classified as pornography, any stills or screenshots taken could be.

- This story could keep re-appearing, meaning that it could be hard to shrug off any negative impact.

- TV, the internet and news media all contribute towards a shared understanding of what is acceptable public behaviour.

ACTIVITY 2.11: NEWS REPORT 1 WORKSHEET

**Middle-aged couple filmed having sex naked on
car bonnet in middle of residential street***

Last night a young woman was amazed to discover a naked couple having sex on the bonnet of a parked car as she walked home from work.

'I was shocked,' said the young woman who prefers not to be named. 'It's not the sort of thing you expect to see happening in the street, especially not at their age.

It was disgusting. They didn't even try to hide what they were doing and didn't stop as I walked past, even though I know they saw me. I took a sneaky film on my phone and put it on social media when I got home.'

The social media site got over 10,000 hits before the explicit film was taken down following complaints of indecency.

The lovers, who are both in their fifties, hotly denied any wrongdoing when police officers arrived.

'We are both consenting adults and it's my car. Why not? I may not be young but I'm not ashamed of my body and think that people are making a fuss over nothing! Why should I confine sex to the bedroom? Sure, children may have seen us, but we weren't doing anything they can't see on primetime TV.'

Meanwhile a spokesperson for the police had this advice to give to anyone else considering a bit of al fresco loving:

'Having sex in a public place is an offence and is classed as outraging public decency. We take any reports of this nature seriously and prosecutions have been made in similar cases.'

'If anyone sees people engaging in sexual activity in a public place they should report it straightaway by calling 101.'

---

*   Story based on a feature on 29 July 2016 by Rachel Bishop: www.mirror.co.uk/news/uk-news/randy-middle-aged-couple-filmed-8513247

ACTIVITY 2.11: NEWS REPORT 2 WORKSHEET

Contestants and viewers stunned as couple have sex live on TV show*

Contestants last night on the hit TV show of the summer are left reeling after two of their fellow housemates had sex live on air.

'To be honest I was amazed,' said one 19-year-old housemate. 'This is a show full of beautiful boys and girls looking for love, but I never dreamt anyone would go this far.'

'It's disgusting,' said another. 'Why couldn't they have waited until the lights were off? We saw everything, as we were only a few meters away. Secretly I think they only did it for the publicity and to get more people at home to vote for them, they are not even a proper couple.'

Viewers immediately took to social media, with many upset that the intimate scenes were screened without warning.

'My teenage daughter watches this,' complained one mother. 'What message does it give? That sex is something you do in front of your friends? I am outraged.'

TV officials are waiting to hear if the show can continue after Ofcom** was deluged with complaints about the raunchy scenes.

The two housemates whose raunchy behaviour sparked the storm have refused to say if their 'dream summer' will continue or if they will have to leave the house, possibly to face legal charges of gross indecency.

A spokesperson for the police had this advice to give: 'In real life having sex in a public place is an offence we take seriously and prosecutions have been made in similar cases.'

'If anyone sees people engaging in sexual activity in a public place they should report it straightaway by calling 101.'

---

* Story based on a feature on 23 June 2016 by Emily Sheridan for the Mailonline: www.dailymail.co.uk/tvshowbiz/article-3656069/Love-Island-viewers-horrified-Malin-Anderson-Terry-Walsh-sex-house.html

** www.ofcom.org.uk

ACTIVITY 2.12: GUESS THE PRODUCT

(Years 7–13+)

Aim

- To understand the power of media advertising and the subliminal messages given about sex and sexual attraction.

Time: 60 minutes

Learning outcomes

- To learn how sexualised images, or images that hint at seduction, sexual attraction and relationships are used to sell a wide range of products.

- To learn about the advertising standards that govern the industry and protect consumers.

Key vocabulary

- **Sex and relationships**

- **Sexual attraction**

- **Media and advertising**

- **Advertising standards**

You will need

- 12 x A5 cards (prepared in advance as shown below and laminated where possible for re-use)

- Scissors and glue

- A selection of lifestyle magazines (including gossip weeklies and monthly glossies)

- A4 paper and pens

- Online access to check advertising standards and laws (optional)

How to do it

Prepare for this exercise by looking through a wide selection of magazines to find adverts that could be considered to have a sexual connotation. This can be through words or pictures used to sell anything from cars to food to beauty products.

To make the activity cards, cut off (or use a permanent marker to block out) anything that identifies the product being sold, such as the name of the product, the logo, etc., and crop the picture ready to stick onto a piece of A5 card. On the back write the product being sold, the magazine it was taken from and the year of publication. This will be hidden during the game, but means that anyone can facilitate it, including young people, in the future.

1. Introduction

- Establish/revisit ground rules (see pages 42–43 for guidance).

Explain that when a large company wants to sell a product to a target audience it can spend millions on marketing and advertising. Marketing finds out more about the potential buyer, for example how old they are, their social status, what 'look' they go for, which accessories they use and why – in fact, all about the target groups' lifestyle and aspirations.

This information is then given to advertising agencies that compete against each other to come up with the most creative ways of selling the product and so win the contract. Advertising agencies employ creative directors, writers, photographers, researchers and designers, as well as models, to ensure they come up with the most innovative campaigns for their clients to sell everything from toilet rolls to high-end designer fashion.

Ask the class to suggest clothing brands with a clear 'look' that represents the lifestyle that the people who wear it 'buy into' or aspire to. For example:

Jack Wills = classic British look based on public schools and vintage upper class pursuits like hunting and fishing.

Topshop/Topman = high street fashion with a twist. This British brand has its finger on the pulse of youth culture, mixing street fashion with catwalk looks to produce affordable fashionable clothes, shoes and accessories.

2. Opening activity

Start the activity in a wide-seated circle, with the facilitator seated mid-point and in easy view of everyone. In turn hold up a card and invite learners to ask questions before guessing what it is the advert is selling. The rules are:

- One question at a time

- The facilitator can only answer 'yes' or 'no'

- One guess at a time

- If someone guesses correctly they take the role of facilitator for the next round

- If after three guesses the right answer has still not been given the facilitator tells everyone and moves on to the next card.

3. Development activity

Divide the class into small groups and allocate each at least one advert to work on. Their task is to produce an in-depth profile of the person or people they think that this advertisement is targeting.

To do this they should consider the relationship between the images or words used and the products sold and then idea storm, for example:

- Who is this advert aimed at?

- What age are they?

- What gender identity and/or sexual orientation?

- What kind of interests might they have?

- What are their life aspirations?

- Are they likely to be political, fashionistas, hip or sporty?

- What is their area of work or study?

- Will this advert appeal to a specific faith or ethnic group?

The profile can be recorded on paper in any chosen style or design.

Invite each group to present their advert and profile, displaying them next to each other, and explaining the thought process that they went through to draw these conclusions.

When everyone has presented their ideas ask the whole class:

- What messages are given about sex, relationships or sexuality in these adverts?

- Will buying this product make you more (or less) sexually attractive?

- How might it affect self-image?

Discuss how true these messages are and how representative they are of real-life sexual attraction between people. For example, can any fragrance or body spray *really* make you more sexually attractive?

In the UK strict laws govern advertisements. The basic framework for this says that:

'All marketing and advertising must be:

- An accurate description of the product or service

- Legal

- Decent

- Truthful

- Honest

- Socially responsible (not encouraging illegal, unsafe or anti-social behaviour).'[10]

4. Reflection and review

Recap on the techniques used in the adverts discussed and reflect on overt and covert messages received. For example, the overt message in this advert is that using this specific beauty product will make you look younger and sexier, the covert message from the accompanying picture of a mature woman smiling over the shoulder of a young, handsome man is that you will find a younger, sexier partner to enjoy your re-found youth with. No laws are broken as no specific claims are made, but the message is implicitly understood.

5. Summary

- Branded goods are designed with a target market in mind, which includes children and young people as well as adults.

- Adverts invite people to 'buy in' to the lifestyle promoted, as well as purchase the product.

- Some have sub-messages that relate to sex, physical attraction and relationships. The images used do not always include the actual product being sold.

- Adverts often show extremely attractive young men and women using the product, or have celebrity endorsement. The idea is that if you, as the potential buyer, like the celebrity you are more likely to buy what they are selling.

Extension

Set learners the task of finding out more details about the laws that govern UK advertising and what happens if these laws are infringed, or what you can do if you believe that an advert does not meet the set standards.

---

10 www.gov.uk/marketing-advertising-law/overview

ACTIVITY 2.13: ADVERTISING – FACTS AND OPINIONS
(Years 7–13+)

Aim

- To consider the use of facts and opinions in advertisements and the influences these can have on consumer behaviour.

Time: 45 minutes

Learning outcomes

- To be able to assess advertisements and separate out facts, i.e. something proven, from opinions, i.e. what someone thinks.

- To be able to use this knowledge to inform future buying habits.

Key vocabulary

- **Facts and opinions**

- **Advertising and the power of the media**

- **Sexual behaviour**

You will need

- Highlighter pens (of different colours)

- A selection of magazines

- Sets of *Opinion cards* (one set per three students)

How to do it

1. Introduction

- Establish/revisit ground rules (see pages 42–43 for guidance).

Explain that information used to sell products in advertisements tends to fall into two categories: facts and opinions. Remind young people that, as discussed in Activity 2.12, advertising is strictly regulated by law, so any facts offered must be true. Define a fact as a statement that can be proved true or false, for example, '199 people tried this product'. Alternatively, an opinion is a statement based on a belief or value, for example, '199 people said they thought this product made them feel more sexually attractive'.

2. Opening activity

Divide the young people into pairs and distribute a magazine and two marker pens to each couple. Their task is to go through the magazine to find and pull out adverts or promotional features for beauty products for men and women. This can include products like toothpaste, deodorant, shower gel and shampoo, as well as fragrances and aftershave. They should then assess their findings to determine which phrases are facts about a product, and which are opinions. They should use the pens to highlight facts in one colour and opinions in another.

3. Development activity

Ask each group to present the facts and opinions they found, allowing time for questions and discussion. Facilitate a discussion that considers the following:

- Which occurred more frequently in the advertisements studied, facts or opinions? (This is likely to be opinion.)

- Which are most useful to consumers, facts or opinions?

- Which are more likely to make consumers buy a product, opinion or fact?

4. Reflection and review

This part of the lesson can be facilitated as a conversation or a role-play, depending on how comfortable learners are with acting out a scenario.

Working in threes, give out sets of opinion cards. Invite each person in the trio to randomly select a card without showing the other two people. On each card is an opinion or fact that the young person should use as the basis for persuading the other two to buy a new wonder fragrance that claims to make you more sexually attractive.

Taking it in turns, people have two minutes to use their powers of persuasion to confirm a sale. At the end of each two-minute round call time and ask those being sold to if they are more or less likely to buy the product now.

Review the selling techniques used:

- How were claims made that this product will make you look/feel better and become more sexually attractive?

- Which argument was most effective?

- Were any lies told that in real life would mean that this advertising strategy would not pass the Advertising Standards Authority?

5. Summary

- No matter how clever, creative or beautiful an advertisement is, it is always wise to consider the facts and make decisions based on these, rather than be swayed by opinions which may or may not be true.

ACTIVITY 2.13: OPINION CARDS

Opinion 1 – buy this product because:

- 85 per cent of the people who took part in our clinical trials said that they felt more confident and sexually attractive while wearing this fragrance.

- It contains 100 per cent natural ingredients, ethically sourced.

- We can trace the history of this fragrance back to Roman times, when men and women used it in its purest form on their wedding night as an aphrodisiac.

- There is currently a 25 per cent discount promotion on this fragrance, which ends next week.

Opinion 2 – buy this fragrance because:

- Legend has it that Roman courtesans used it to lure their spellbound lovers into marriage.

- The secret recipe was lost and presumed gone forever, until it was magically recreated in our fragrance house last year.

- Scientists have worked day and night to recreate the magic that fills the senses with the power of natural pheromones, making you irresistible to the partner of your choice.

- Increasing your powers of sexual attraction is priceless.

Opinion 3 – buy this product because:

- This fragrance is all over social media at the moment and everyone is talking about how great it is.

- It smells so good that several big name celebrities are endorsing it.

- One person reported getting five dates the first night he/she wore it.

- You can send off for a free sample from the fragrance website, which is filled with recommendations from people who have found true love while wearing it.

CHAPTER 3

Porn and Body Image

The lesson plans in Chapter 3 consider the potential effect of porn on children and young people's self-esteem and body image, aiming to challenge stereotypes and build personal confidence levels.

ACTIVITY 3.1: PORNOGRAPHY AND BODY IMAGE

(Years 9–13+)

Aims

- To consider the outside influences that affect how we feel about our body.

- To discuss how watching pornography may contribute to body size and shape ideals, which may not be achievable in real life, leading to negative body image.

Time: 45 minutes

Learning outcomes

- To understand that the body size and shapes featured in most adult material, some of which are surgically enhanced, can inform notions of body perfection.

- To know that these bodies may be unrealistic and unachievable in real life due to a number of factors, including age and maturity.

Key vocabulary

- **Surgical enhancement**
- **Gender stereotypes**
- **Pornography**
- **Body image**

You will need

- Sticky notes and pens

How to do it

1. Introduction

- Establish/revisit ground rules (see pages 42–43 for guidance).

Define 'body image' as the way you see yourself and imagine you look. It is something that comes from within and someone can't 'give you' positive or negative body image. However, some external things do affect it.

2. Introductory activity

Ask young people to listen to the following three statements and then rate them on a sticky note in order of importance:

a) Loving your own body, the way it is.

b) Your partner considering you beautiful in every way.

c) Being considered physically attractive by your friends and peers.

3. Development activity

Explain that you are going to read out a series of statements that relate to the impact watching pornography could have on body image and that influence what size and shape of bodies are considered sexually attractive.

Allocate the area to the left as the 'Agree' zone; the area to the right as a 'Disagree' zone, and in the middle identify a zone for those who are 'Undecided'.

Ask the young people to listen to each statement that you read out and then move to the zone that corresponds best with their opinion. Point out that this is not a test, but rather an exercise to find out what people think and that it is likely that there will be some disagreement within the group.

Leave space between statements to discuss the views and opinions indicated by placement in the room and make sure that there is an opportunity for young people to ask questions and debate any issues raised before moving on to the next statement.

4. Reflection and review

Ask young people to suggest where else they may see images of nudity or people in underwear in a legal context, outside the home or changing room. For example:

- on TV
- on music videos
- at the movies
- in the underwear department of a chain store
- in magazines.

Acknowledge suggestions and reinforce by pointing out that even shows intended for a Sunday night family audience can feature topless male dancers and celebrities in figure-hugging costumes, and 15-rated films often feature semi-nudity and simulated sex scenes.

In pairs, ask them to now consider if they think these images reinforce or challenge those statements previously discussed. Allow a couple of minutes for discussion and agreement before inviting each pair to give their verdict and a quick summary of why.

5. Summary

- Conclude that people have different views on porn and the way it does or doesn't affect body image by idealising the size and shape of male and female bodies.

- There are laws in place to protect children and young people from harm that make it illegal for those under the age of 18 to make, view or share pornography.

- However, some nudity can be seen on mainstream TV and in 15-rated movies, which arguably can reinforce stereotypes of what is sexually attractive.

ACTIVITY 3.1: PORN STATEMENTS

1. Porn films often use actors with unrealistic bodies.

2. The shape and size of actors' bodies in porn films can affect the body image of those watching it.

3. Porn films typically focus on male pleasure.

4. Pornography degrades women by showing their bodies as sex objects.

5. You need a porn-star body to feel sexually confident.

6. Watching porn as a couple can make you feel less satisfied with each other's shape and/or size.

7. Pornography teaches you the bits about your body that sex education leaves out.

8. The size and shape of female porn stars' breasts has contributed to an increase in surgical breast enlargements.

9. Watching porn before having a real-life lover can make people feel dissatisfied with their partner.

10. Watching porn creates unrealistic expectations about the shape and size of male genitals.

11. Stereotypes about the 'perfect' body are reinforced by porn.

12. Watching porn is just a bit of fun that boosts your body image and makes you feel sexually confident.

ACTIVITY 3.2: PERFECT PEOPLE

(Years 7–13+)

Aim

- To use real-life data to compare ideas about the 'perfect' female/male shape with the reality.

Time: 45 minutes

Learning outcomes

- To understand the differences between stereotypes of 'perfect' bodies and real-life ones.
- To consider how pornography might contribute to notions of the perfect body.

Key vocabulary

- **Pornography**
- **Stereotypes**
- **Idealised body images**
- **Self-esteem**
- **Body confidence**

You will need

- Flipchart and markers
- Sticky notes and pens

How to do it

1. Introduction

- Establish/revisit ground rules (see pages 42–43 for guidance).

2. Opening activity

Divide the young people into gender-based groups, before giving out pens and three sheets of paper to each group.

Set them a three-minute task of discussing and agreeing five celebrity women that they think are sexually attractive and then five men and recording this on the first sheet of paper.

Call time and invite groups to share their list by gender. Compare and contrast to provoke a discussion that considers:

- Are male and female notions of sexually attractive celebrities the same?

3. Development activity

Set young men the task of creating the 'perfect' woman on one sheet of paper, and a picture titled 'the ideal man' on the other. This should be based on assumptions held about what they think women are looking for in a man. Young women have the same task but with the gender reversed, so creating the 'perfect' man and 'the ideal woman' based on what they think young men look for.

Invite the young people to show each other their pictures in turn. How do ideals of beauty and perfection differ? For example, does the 'perfect' woman have the same body shape when drawn by both genders? Have the young women assumed that much of what the young men look for in a girl is based on her outward appearance? Is this true, or have things to do with personality been mentioned too? Which gender is the most body conscious? Draw particular attention to what young men and women think the other looks for, compared with the realities.

- How do the women suggested by the female groups compare in terms of hair colour, body shape and so on to those selected by the young men?

- How do the men suggested by the male groups compare to those selected by the young women?

- Are there any generalisations that make either gender attractive? *For example, slim, tall, narrow waists, toned muscles or symmetrical features.*

4. Reflection and review

Facilitate a discussion that asks:

- Where do ideals about what is and is not sexually attractive come from?

- How does this impact on body confidence?

- How might pornography contribute to this?

5. Summary

- No one person is 'perfect' for everyone.

- What is and isn't attractive is down to personal taste and preference.

- A beautiful face or body does not guarantee a person that you can get on with, or even fall in love with, because human desire and sexuality are much more complex than simply someone's outward appearance.

ACTIVITY 3.3: INDUSTRY INFLUENCES
(Years 10–13+)

Aims

- To consider what pressures, if any, are put on men and women to conform to an idealised or stereotypical standard of beauty.

- To look behind these to the industries that potentially inform them.

Time: 45 minutes

Leaning outcome

- To enable young people to draw conclusions about where notions of the 'perfect' body come from and so develop a wider understanding.

Key vocabulary

- **Body confidence**

- **Self image**

- **Beauty industry**

- **Pornography**

You will need

- Four large sheets of paper

- Sticky notes (in two different colours)

- Pens

How to do it

1. Introduction

- Establish/revisit ground rules (see pages 42–43 for guidance).

To prepare for the session, stick four large sheets of paper up on a wall. Write the title 'Porn industry' on one sheet, 'The media' on another, 'Fashion industry' on a third and then 'Real world' on the fourth. The fourth should be displayed slightly apart from the other three, as it will not be used until later in the activity.

Start by asking:

- Who defines what the 'perfect' body is?

- What things are considered sexually attractive in a woman?

- What things are considered sexually attractive in a man?

- Are these attributes the same, regardless of sexuality?

Acknowledge and discuss ideas before introducing the first three boards on the wall. Then distribute blocks of sticky notes among the young people, with a pen each.

2. Opening activity

Explain that they are going to create a word storm by writing on each note something to describe how they think that the porn industry, the media and the fashion industry contribute to the notion of a perfect body.

For example:

Large breasts, a 'designer vagina', a large penis = the porn industry

Long legs, perfect skin and well-defined muscles = the media

High cheekbones, ultra-skinny, tall = the fashion industry.

Allow five minutes, encouraging young people to quickly write down and post all of their ideas without censorship.

Call time and ask everyone to step back and review what has been created, using these prompt questions:

- Do some things feature on more than one wall?

- Does this mean that some sexual/body ideals cross over from one industry to another?

Once this has been discussed, turn to the fourth sheet, which represents the 'real world', i.e. the general public and everyday life. Invite volunteers to read out stickers from the other three sheets to see if any of them apply to the 'Real world'. If so, mark them with a 'P' for porn, 'M' for media or 'F' for fashion so everyone can see which board they originated from, before re-sticking them on the fourth sheet. When all of the stickers have been assessed, count up those that have been re-stuck on the real-life board to see which industry most affects real-life notions of perfection and the ideal body.

Are there any surprises about where ideals, trends and body fashions originate? For example, some young people may have adopted a mainstream body trend, such as body hair removal, without realising this originates from the porn industry, especially if they have never seen any porn.

3. Development activity

Distribute a second wad of notes in the second colour. This time ask young people to write a message to stick on top of those already on the 'Real world' board to describe how they feel when they see these images. This can be a positive or negative message, for example:

- I feel body confident

- I feel envious

- I feel less confident about my body

- I feel anxious

- I feel motivated to go to the gym

- I feel proud of how I look.

Ask:

- Do you feel more, or less attractive?

- Are you more, or less happy with your own body?

4. Reflection and review

Point out that very few people in the world have the perfect body, including models, actors or celebrities as photos are often digitally enhanced. Many of the images that are seen every day, including things like celebrity selfies on social media, are carefully constructed using filters and concealed lighting to get the 'perfect' photo, which is not the same thing as naturally having a 'perfect' body.

5. Summary

- Ideals originating from the porn, media and fashion industry seep into real life, including idealised body shapes and trends like the removal of body hair.

- These can result in stereotypes of largely unachievable or unhealthy body shapes and sizes being perpetuated in the media, for example size zero models and overly muscled torsos.

- There is no such thing as 'perfect' so it is better to aim for the healthiest, happiest version of you, which is more achievable.

ACTIVITY 3.4: UNDER THE KNIFE
(Years 10–13+)

Aims

- To open up discussions about the 'perfect body' and where these notions come from.

- To look at cosmetic plastic surgery and the reasons people might, or might not, choose to have it.

Time: 60 minutes

Learning outcomes

- To be aware of how ideals of body size and shape perpetuated through the celebrity, glamour and adult entertainment industries compare with the realities of the average sized person in the UK.

- To consider if these ideals have influenced the increasing trend towards cosmetic surgery and non-surgical procedures.

Key vocabulary

- **Cosmetic surgery**
- **Surgical enhancement**
- **Non-invasive beauty treatments**
- **Body image**
- **Porn industry**

You will need

- Flipchart paper
- Marker pens
- Sticky tack

How to do it

1. Introduction

- Establish/revisit ground rules (see pages 42–43 for guidance).

Explain that no value judgements will be placed on the choice to have (or not have) surgical enhancements during this lesson. The information about average sizes may vary but are based on information about the UK available at the time of publishing from the Office of National Statistics.[1]

2. Opening activity

Divide the young people into small groups and hand out large sheets of flipchart paper and a selection of markers. Task half of the groups with drawing a large outline of the 'average female body' and the other half with drawing the 'average male body'.

Ask each group to give the drawing a name and then create a personality for him/her that they think personifies a typical young woman or man. Ask them to consider:

---

1   www.ons.gov.uk

- What things are most important to this person?

- What are their hopes, dreams and aspirations for the future?

- Who are the people closest to them?

- What makes this person laugh/feel sad?

These should be written inside the outline of the character to reflect the fact that these are the things that cannot be seen. Invite each group to present their version of the average male or female. Stick the pictures up so that everyone in the group can see.

Facilitate a whole-group discussion based on the pictures to find out what the young people believe are.

For young men:

- the average height

- the average shoe size

- the average chest size

- the average waist size.

For young women:

- the average height

- the average shoe size

- the average bra size

- the average clothes size.

Add these suggestions to the pictures with a marker pen. Then repeat the questions, this time asking for suggestions about what the 'ideal size' is for both young men and women. Write these on the pictures in a different colour pen.

Once done, point out the following:

- The average height for women in the UK is 5ft 5" (162cm).[2]

- The average shoe size of UK women is size 5.[3]

- The average bra size is 34D.[4]

- The average clothes size for UK women is size 16.

- The average height for men in the UK is 5ft 9.5" (176.5cm).

- The average shoe size for UK men is size 10.

- The average chest size for men is 40".

- The average waist size for men is 35".

Review, comparing idealised notions of size and shape with the statistics for the average size.

3. Development activity
Ask young people what they think informs the idealised sizes. This could include:

- glamour models

- male and female celebrities

- comparisons with bodies seen in adult or porn films

---

2   www.ons.gov.uk
3   Source: UK National Sizing Survey 2004
4   Experts say the rise from the UK average of 34B to 34DD is partly because of our diet or women going under the surgeon's knife for a boob job. www.mirror.co.uk/news/uk-news/average-bra-size-has-swelled-by-three-1370021

- catwalk models

- bodybuilders.

Take down and return the labelled pictures to the relevant group, asking them to go back to discuss and then identify the parts men and women might choose to alter with cosmetic plastic surgery. These could include:

- breast size

- penis size

- body fat (liposuction).

Point out that some things, like feet size and height cannot be altered.

Move on to consider why some people choose to have plastic surgery. Encourage learners to think of as many reasons as possible, including medical reasons (such as having a breast reconstruction after surviving breast cancer), gender re-assignment, to enhance low self-esteem, to look younger, self-improvement, to please a partner or to fit stereotypical ideals. Are some reasons better than others? How can you be sure you are doing it for yourself and not others? How do you know that you won't regret it? What will change after cosmetic surgery?

Setting aside the surgery done for medical purposes, reconstruction and gender re-assignment, encourage young people to explore what might impact on decisions made to have cosmetic surgery or non-invasive treatments such as lip fillers and Botox. This could include peer pressure, how the media reports young men and women's bodies, fashion and other sources of pressure or expectations, and then balance these with the right to make a personal choice.

4. Reflection and review

Finally, invite the young people to consider all of the things that they have written inside the body and agreed are the essence of a person and then ask what they think will change after surgery. For example, after cosmetic surgery will the qualities that make someone unique differ? Will their self-confidence and self-esteem improve? Will they be more sexually attractive? Will they have more friends or be a nicer person?

5. Summary

- Comparisons to idealised body shapes and sizes may influence some people's decision to have cosmetic surgery or a non-medical procedure, for example hair extensions to achieve long, thick hair.

- Cosmetic surgery might be the right choice for some people but it is the person you are inside that counts most.

- Having surgery is not a decision to be taken lightly and if you are considering it you need to do lots of research before reaching a decision.

- If you do decide to have plastic surgery then you should only ever use reputable surgeons who can demonstrate a good health and safety record.

Extension

Task young people to look online to find campaigns that promote natural beauty and positive body image. This information can be bought back to share and discuss.

ACTIVITY 3.5: 100 YEARS OF GLAMOUR

(Years 7–13+)

Aim

- To create a photo timeline that demonstrates the changing notions of female beauty over the last 100 years.

Time: 45 minutes

Learning outcomes

- To understand that idealised images of female beauty and what is considered sexually attractive have changed down the decades, and are likely to change again.

- To consider that ideals about body shape and size are likely to change again.

- To know that there is no blueprint for how people perceive beauty.

Key vocabulary

- **Glamour**

- **Beauty**

- **Body confidence**

- **Self-esteem**

You will need

- To research and print off pictures of women considered glamorous or attractive for each decade (see suggestions below)

- Access to YouTube to show 'Women's ideal body shapes through the ages'[5]

How to do it

Although this activity works in a mixed gender environment it can be empowering for young women to reflect on different notions of beauty and sexual attractiveness and understand that these vary.

The film suggested for this lesson plan was made by Buzz Films in January 2015 and uses a diverse cast of models to show how the standard of beauty for women has changed dramatically over time. Please watch in advance.

Go online to find pictures of women from pin up girls to actresses, and catwalk to glamour models. Download and print these to create glamour cards for the timeline activity. Some suggestions for this include (in date order)

- Louise Brooks (American dancer and actress, famous for popularising the first 'bob' haircuts. 1920s)

- Josephine Baker (American-born French dancer, singer, and actress, sometimes called the 'Black Pearl'. 1930s)

- Marlene Dietrich (German-American actress and singer, known for her deep, sexy singing voice. 1930s)

- Jane Russell (American film actress who was one of Hollywood's leading sex symbols. 1940s)

---

5   www.youtube.com/watch?v=Xrp0zJZu0a4

- Marilyn Monroe (American actress, model, singer and worldwide sex symbol. 1950s)

- Twiggy (English model, actress and singer who was one of the main faces of 'swinging sixties' London. 1960s)

- Sophia Loren (Italian-French film star and international sex symbol. 1960s)

- Barbara Windsor (English actress who played sexy roles in the Carry On films. 1970s)

- Farrah Fawcett (American actress and original Charlie's Angel. Her iconic red swimsuit poster sold more the 20 million copies worldwide and a Barbie doll was modelled on her. 1970s)

- Cindy Crawford (American model. She is one of the original Big Six supermodels. The term had not been used before. 1980s)

- Naomi Campbell (English model. Was spotted at age 15 and is still a supermodel. 1990s)

- Kate Moss (English model. Spotted in Topshop aged 15 and still a supermodel. 1990s)

- Jordan (English model, real name Katie Price. Has posed for page 3 and 'lads mags'. 2000s)

- Tyra Banks (African American model, now TV presenter. Was commissioned to model the most expensive bra in the world made of diamonds. 2000s)

- Karlie Kloss (American model. Current campaign for Topshop invites customers to 'Be more Karlie in 2016')

1. Introduction

- Establish/revisit ground rules (see pages 42–43 for guidance).

Start by reading out the following and then asking young people to comment on what they think it means:

Beauty is in the eye of the beholder.[6]

Explain that this is a phrase that can be traced back to 3BC in Greece, which is over 2000 years ago.

2. Opening activity

Introduce the exercise, explaining that the aim is to create a timeline that shows different notions of glamour and female beauty over the last 100 years. Allocate space, such as a long table or the floor, for the timeline. Place a sticky note with '1920' written on it at one end and 'Today' at the other.

Give each person a Glamour card asking that they initially keep it private. The task is for young people to look at the card they have been given and then place it along the time continuum between 1920 and today. This should be the decision of the cardholder, although once all the cards have been placed the rest of the group can make comments and/or move anything they think has been wrongly positioned.

3. Development activity

Encourage and support debate as the activity progresses, comparing the more naturally achievable shapes previously admired with those arguably influenced by the adult entertainment industry, promoted today.

- What differences can they see between the size and ratio of things like breasts to waists and hips?

- How do some of these long-ago recognised beauties compare with modern celebrities?

- How have notions of femininity changed?

- What are the modern day ideals of a sexually attractive woman?

---

6   www.phrases.org.uk/meanings/beauty-is-in-the-eye-of-the-beholder.html

4. Reflection and review

Conclude that ideas about the 'perfect' female body type have changed, from the voluptuous curves of the Renaissance paintings to 90s' heroin-chic, the rise of the term 'lollipop head' and the size zero model, to the ultra-large, surgically enhanced breasts arguably popularised through the porn industry and 'lads mags' in the 2000s. Suggest that this means that they are likely to change again, which is another consideration for any woman contemplating cosmetic surgery, as reversals for things like breast implants are expensive, can be painful and all surgery carries health risks.

5. Summary

- Popular notions of beauty and female sexiness have changed over the last 100 years, and will no doubt change again.

- Being attractive is subjective; what one person considers beauty isn't automatically the same as another.

- Women should love the body they have and keep it healthy and happy, rather than being miserable over an unrealistic ideal that cannot be achieved.

ACTIVITY 3.6: CURVY BOTTLES
(Years 7–13+)

Aim

- To discuss body image through a recycled art project to explore notions of the 'perfect' female body silhouette from the 1950s era of Hollywood glamour.

Time: variable

Please note: this activity uses papier-mâché so it cannot be delivered in one block, as the pulp needs to dry out before decorating.

Learning outcomes

- To consider that there are different ideals of female body beauty.

- To believe that differences should be embraced and celebrated.

Key vocabulary

- **Hollywood glamour**

- **Body image**

- **Diversity**

- **Stereotypes**

You will need

- A full length picture of Marilyn Monroe, Jayne Mansfield, Diana Doors and Jane Russell and information about their careers

- Assorted empty plastic drinks bottles with lids (two for each person)

- Old newspaper and wallpaper paste (non-fungicide)

- A bucket and stick for stirring

- Vaseline

- Paint brushes

- White paint

- Permanent pens

- Craft items (glitter, sequins, gems, etc.)

- Craft knife and PVA glue

- Rice or dried peas (for filling the bottles)

How to do it

1. Introduction

- Establish/revisit ground rules (see pages 42–43 for guidance).

Start by informing the group that it has been said that the iconic coca-cola bottle was designed to represent the ideal female body. This ideal was a woman with large breasts, a small waist and curvy hips, like the 'hourglass' figures of the movie stars of the 1940s and 50s, for example Marilyn Monroe, Jayne Mansfield, Diana Doors, all considered 'blonde bombshells', and the sultry brunette, Jane Russell (show the pictures to illustrate). Explain that all of these women were considered extremely beautiful and sexually attractive by the standards of their day. Give more information as appropriate, for example Jayne Mansfield as well as being a Hollywood actress was also one of the first Playboy Playmates, and Marilyn Monroe did a naked calendar before she became famous, which could be compared to 'sex tapes' that have made celebrities like Kim Kardashian world famous.[7]

Ask if the young people can think of any modern-day celebrities who have adopted a similar pin-up look, such as Paloma Faith and Dita Von Teese, before talking about vintage-inspired fashion from that era.

Explain that this activity is going to take this idea and create bottle bookends that promote and celebrate diversity in body shape both then and now.

2. Opening activity

Make the papier-mâché by tearing small strips of old newspaper and placing it into buckets. Soak with warm water and drain off any excess once all the paper is wet. Mix up wallpaper paste as per the instructions in a separate bucket. Pour this into the newspaper mix, stirring gently with your hands to make sure that all the paper is covered. You can use rubber gloves, but as long as the paste is fungicide free there is no need. Cover the bucket and leave the newspaper to absorb all the paste.

Take the lid off the bottle and discard. Coat the bottle in a thick layer of Vaseline, which will help when you come to get the plastic bottle out later.

Begin to build up layers of papier-mâché. Take time to do this so that you create a thick 'skin' without losing the desired shape. Remember the bookend is going to represent the pin-up girls of yesteryear so curves are fine and the middle of the bottle should dip in to recreate that hourglass figure. Once happy with the shape of the bottles it is important to smooth a final layer of paste over the bottle to flatten any last shreds of newspaper down before leaving it somewhere cool to dry.

Do not be tempted to try and speed up the drying process, for example by putting it on a radiator, as the shape is likely to split.

3. Development activity

Once it has dried, take a sharp craft knife and score along one side of the bottle. Carefully separate and pop the plastic bottle out, resealing the edges with PVA glue (or similar). Carefully fill the dry bottle with rice and seal the end with a few more layers of wet papier-mâché. Again leave to dry thoroughly.

The bottle now is ready to be decorated with paint and/or craft materials. They can be decorated to look as though they are dressed in Hollywood vintage clothes on one side and clothes to represent today's female glamour on the other.

4. Reflection and review

Set the bottles up in a row where both sides can be seen. Facilitate gallery time that walks down one side to look at the vintage fashions and notions of beauty while young people present their ideas, and then the other to look at today's fashions. Ask:

- What has changed?
- Would the women from the 'golden age of glamour' still be judged attractive by today's standards? Why/why not?
- Does a coke bottle represent the 'perfect' female form now? How, how not?

5. Summary

- Notions of female body shape have changed over the last 50 years and are likely to change again.
- Beauty is in the eye of the beholder – even when it comes to sex symbols and glamour starlets.
- Beauty is more than skin deep.

---

7   www.dailymail.co.uk/tvshowbiz/article-3251805/How-Kim-4-5million-sex-tape-thanks-Joe-Francis.html

ACTIVITY 3.7: BODY IMAGE GAME
(Years 8–13+)

Aims

- To build empathy between genders by raising awareness about the body image concerns of both young men and women.

- To explore how outside influences can impact negatively on body image.

Time: 30 minutes

Learning outcomes

- To understand that males and females can have body image concerns.

- To realise that having a negative body image can impact on confidence and self-esteem.

- To discuss what influences body image.

Key vocabulary

- **Body image**

- **Gender**

You will need

- Copies of the *Body image game cards*

- A sheet of flipchart paper and a marker for each group

How to do it

1. Introduction

- Establish/revisit ground rules (see pages 42–43 for guidance).

Explain that this lesson is going to explore body image concerns and discuss where they come from.

2. Opening activity

Demonstrate drawing a Venn diagram, (two overlapping circles), and label one circle 'Male', one circle 'Female' and the bit where they cross in the middle, 'Equally'.

Divide the main group into fours and hand each group a pack of body image game cards and a flipchart sheet and marker.

The first group task is to copy the Venn diagram on to the sheet of paper and then discuss each card, deciding if this is an issue for 'mainly males', 'mainly females' or 'exactly the same for both'. So, for example, if they think that it is mainly women who worry about being too skinny they should place the card in the 'Female' zone, if they think it is mainly men, then it goes in the 'Male' zone. If they think it is of equal concern to both genders then it goes in the 'Equally' section.

3. Development activity

Once done they should then consider who decides how males and females should look, what influences any pressure to conform to these ideals and how it might feel to not fit in. This could include:

- seeing images of models in magazines

- celebrity selfies

- online porn

- advertisements and TV reinforcing who is 'beautiful' and who isn't.

Allow about 30 minutes for discussion and then rotate around the groups asking each for one for their decisions and reasons. Spend time discussing cards that have been placed in different areas and conclude that problems with body image affect men and women and that most people face it at some stage of their life. Reinforce the point that young men have concerns about their body image too and that research has suggested a worrying rise in eating disorders among males. Ask:

- Where do the images that reinforce these messages come from?

  Compare real-life women, who come in lots of different shapes and sizes, with those promoted in the media, TV, porn, etc.

- How much should we trust that the images we see are a truthful representation?

  Discuss the digital manipulation of pictures and the use of filters on cameras to reduce imperfections.

- How might exposure to idealised images impact on someone?

  For example, making negative comparisons, struggling to look like a celebrity or achieve and unrealistic body shape, becoming obsessed with exercise or the gym.

4. Reflection and review

Conclude that although people are bombarded daily with messages about how they 'should' look, the truth is that bodies come in all shapes and sizes. Suggest that instead of striving for perceived physical perfection it is much better for young people to be healthy. This involves eating a balanced diet and exercising regularly, as well as learning to accept and love yourself as you are.

5. Summary

- Being bombarded daily with images of physical perfection can impact negatively on body image.

- This can be reinforced by peers struggling to achieve the idealised shape or size.

- No one is perfect, and health is more important.

- Many images seen are enhanced or Photoshopped, meaning that even those admired do not really look that that.

ACTIVITY 3.7: BODY IMAGE GAME CARDS

Weight concerns	Worry they have too much body hair
Worry about the size/ shape of their bottom	Worry that they are too tall
Worry that they are too short	Worry about the size and shape of their genitals
Want well-defined abdominal muscles	Worry about the thickness of their hair
Want a tanned body	Want a flat stomach
Worry about the size of their thighs	Want perfectly shaped eyebrows
Want a smaller waist	Want toned arms
Want flawless skin	Worry about the size of their hips
Want larger breasts	Want fuller lips
Worry about facial hair	Choose to have a non-surgical procedure to reduce facial lines
Compare the size and shape of their genitals to others	Choose to have surgical procedures to enhance their looks

ACTIVITY 3.8: THE MUFF MARCH
(Years 10–13+)

Aim

- To open up discussions about the impact pornography has had on the fashion to remove pubic hair and the increase in the number of women undergoing vaginal surgery.

Time: 30 minutes

Learning outcome

- To learn about a recent campaign that challenges fashions in the removal of pubic hair and claims that the porn industry is influencing an increase in vaginal surgery.

Key vocabulary

- **Vagina**
- **Plastic surgery**
- **Gender**
- **Diversity**
- **Body image**
- **Pornography**

You will need

- Access to an online article about a 2011 protest and march[8]
- Paper and pens

How to do it

1. Introduction

- Establish/revisit ground rules (see pages 42–43 for guidance).

Ensure that young people know and understand the terms used in the activity and know the correct anatomical names for female genitals.

2. Opening activity

Set the scene by explaining that in 2011 a protest march was organised by a group called UK Feminista. Many women attended and walked with protest banners alongside performance artists The Muffia, who dressed up in nude bodysuits decorated with lots of pubic hair. The aim of the march was to raise awareness about the increase in gynecological cosmetic surgery (including the trimming of the labia and vaginal rejuvenation, called 'tightening'), and to protest about the pressures on girls and women to conform to an ideal 'designer vagina' that they think has been set by the pornography industry.

They also claim that this has sparked the fashion for removing all pubic hair, which in porn is done to enable the photographer or film director to film more explicit shots of female genitals.

Read aloud the first few paragraphs of the article to inform young people further.

---

8   www.theguardian.com/lifeandstyle/the-womens-blog-with-jane-martinson/2011/dec/08/muff-march-designer-vagina-surgery

3. Development activity

Divide learners into small groups with paper and pens to discuss the following questions:

- Do you think pornography influences the decision to remove pubic hair?

- How might this impact on body image and self-confidence?

- Is this a gender issue or is it the same for males who choose to wax or shave their pubic hair?

- Do you think these women are right to protest?

4. Reflection and review

Facilitate a whole-group discussion, based on the small-group feedback, debating points as they arise. Encourage young people to consider how much they think the porn industry has contributed to the rise in waxing and shaving and to consider the practical side of this decision, for example the maintaining and upkeep of it, as well as the moral issue of women buying in to what is essentially a male-dominated adult industry.

5. Summary

- Female campaigners claim that pornography has influenced women, especially younger women, to remove their pubic hair, returning their pubic area to pre-pubescent baldness.

- They also claim a rise in vaginal plastic surgery for women who want a perfect vagina, based on a trend started in the porn industry.

- They want to give the message to all women that vaginas come in all shapes and sizes and that all are perfect.

ACTIVITY 3.9: CHANGING BODY IMAGE THROUGH ART
(Years 10–13+)

Aims

- To raise awareness and celebrate body diversity and make the point that there is no such thing as 'normal'.

- To discuss the differences between art and pornography.

Time: 60–90 minutes

Learning outcomes

- To make simple plaster sculptures.

- To understand that there is no right and wrong shape when it comes to female genitals; every one is unique and that is perfectly normal.

- To learn about The Great Wall of Vagina sculpture, which aims to raise awareness about body image and challenge the idea that genitals can only be seen within pornography.

Key vocabulary

- **Vagina**

- **Body image**

- **Pornography**

- **Art**

You will need

- A large sheet of paper

- A single tube of paint (one colour)

- Paint trays (pre-loaded with paint)

- Pens

- Handwashing facilities

- Mod-roc (strips of bandage pre-soaked in plaster of Paris) – cut into 5cm long strips

- Vaseline

- Scissors

- Warm water

- Plastic bowl

- Gold/silver spray paint (optional)

- Newspaper

- Sequins (optional)

- Glitter (optional)

- Online access to view The Great Wall of Vagina by Jamie McCartney[9]

---

9   www.greatwallofvagina.co.uk/home

How to do it

1. Introduction

- Establish/revisit ground rules (see pages 42–43 for guidance).

Lay out a large sheet of paper and the paint in trays. Invite the young people to create a hand storm by placing their hands in the paint and then making handprints all over the paper.

Deliberately place the hand storm out of sight to dry for a moment, outline the aim of the lesson and then, placing the sheet of handprints back down at a different angle, ask everyone to come and sign their handprint. Learning points from this to make include:

- They are all handprints, but no two are the same.

- While it is easy to make the print it is not always so easy to identify them without looking closely.

- No handprint is better than another.

2. Opening activity

Ask for a volunteer to demonstrate the art of mod-roc sculptures, asking them to choose a hand or foot that they are prepared to have 'sculpted'. Cover the hand or foot thickly with Vaseline. This helps to prevent the mod-roc sticking to any hairs or skin.

Pour the water into a plastic bowl and slowly soak a strip of plaster in the water. Immediately place this onto the volunteer's hand – it is best to start with the largest area first. Slowly cover the hand completely, including the fingers. Once the hand is covered in at least six layers of mod-roc, wet your finger and go over the bandage, smoothing it until the surface is flat.

Leave to dry. This will take at least ten minutes, but longer if you have a lot of layers. You can tell when it is dry as it starts to peel away from the hand, usually from the fingers first.

The result should be a perfect cast or 'sculpture' of the young person's hand or foot. Once demonstrated, invite the young people to work in pairs to take turns in creating their own mod-roc hand sculpture. These look really good sprayed gold or silver and decorated with sequins and glitter. Alternatively they can be painted or covered in collage materials.

Display the decorated casts together, using a drawing pin to fix them to the wall. Facilitate gallery time, encouraging the young people to notice how different each one is and suggesting that rather like a fingerprint they are unique.

3. Development activity

Move on to tell the young people about a sculpture made by English artist, Jamie McCartney. He claims to be 'changing female body image through art'.

Show learners The Great Wall of Vagina, which is a sculpture created using plaster casts of over 400 women's vulvas. Similar to the hand and feet casts, each one is different and perfectly normal.

Facilitate a discussion that asks:

- Why do you think the artist chose to make this sculpture?

- Why do you think women agreed to be a part of it?

- Is it possible to change body image through art?

- What is the difference between this sculpture and a pornographic film showing women's vulvas?

4. Reflection and review

Direct young people in pairs to look online at the sculpture and a wide range of comments and opinions, including those from plastic surgeons, artists and women from around the world.[10]

Ask them to find a comment that reflects their opinion and share it with the whole group.

---

10   www.greatwallofvagina.co.uk/comments

5. Summary

- There is a difference between a labia and a vagina. The art installation features labias, which are the inner and outer folds of the vulva, at either side of the vagina. A vagina is the muscular tube leading from a woman's external genitals to the cervix of the uterus. However, the term 'vagina' is often used to encompass all female genitals.

- Sex organs can be used in art in a way that is not pornographic, but instead makes a social comment on popular culture.

- The main difference is that pornography is made to sexually arouse and this instillation is a celebration of diversity with no sexual intent.

- Pornography often presents one type of vagina as normal, but the reality is that, like handprints, they come in all different shapes and sizes, all of which are perfectly normal.

- Things like childbirth, age and weight can affect the shape, size and colour of a woman's labia and vagina, but this is normal.

- If anyone is truly worried that there is something wrong or unhealthy about their genitals they can visit a GP who can check things out with complete confidentiality.

ACTIVITY 3.10: BEHIND THE MASK
(Years 7–13+)

Aims

- To explore the differences between the face that young people show to the world and the person they really are inside.

- To raise awareness about the 'real' people behind the onscreen characters in adult entertainment.

Time: 60 minutes

Learning outcomes

- To understand that everyone has a public and private side.

- To recognise that the actors in porn films are real people with feelings and emotions.

Key vocabulary

- **Adult entertainment**

- **Pornography**

- **Body image**

- **Self-confidence**

You will need

- A plain face mask for each learner

- Paint and markers

- Craft materials (optional)

- Magazines (including sports, graphic novels and celebrity magazines)

- Glue and scissors

How to do it
1. Introduction

- Establish/revisit ground rules (see pages 42–43 for guidance).

Start by suggesting that sometimes the face we show the world is not really how we feel, for example smiling when we feel sad or crying when we feel angry. It is also the first impression that people get of us, which can be a good or bad thing.

2. Opening activity

Hand out the plain masks. The task for each person is to use the art equipment to literally paint on the 'face' they usually show to the world. Young women may choose to replicate how they make-up their face with cosmetics. Once this is done, hang the masks up to dry and facilitate a discussion about first impressions, asking for examples of assumptions that have been wrongly made about others, as well as personal experiences of being judged at face value.

3. Development activity

Explain that the second part of this activity is to explore the person behind the mask by creating a collage on the inside of the mask, using the scissors, glue and magazines as well as the markers (if required). This should represent all of the things that make each person unique, which could include things like feelings, skills, qualities, aspirations and personal goals.

Allow time to build up the collages, encouraging the young people to literally fill all the space inside their heads and then invite each learner to present the inside of their mask.

4. Reflection and review

Move on to ask how many people have heard of the old saying: 'You should never judge a book by its cover.' Ask:

- What does this mean?

- How true is it in today's world?

- Does this apply to the male and female actors in the adult entertainment business?

Suggest that porn stars (or adult actors) are also people. The porn industry is their day job but behind what is seen on the screen are lives, just the same as everyone else. Suggest that the fact that porn features real people should be remembered, especially by anyone who chooses to watch it.

5. Summary

Conclude by returning to the finished masks and explaining that although there is nothing wrong with caring for your outward appearance, it is really important to nurture and look after the inner you too: your values, beliefs, hopes and dreams as well as your goals and ambitions for a happy, healthy life.

ACTIVITY 3.11: SEXUAL STEREOTYPES

(Years 10–13+)

Aim

- To explore sexual stereotypes, where they come from and how they are perpetuated through TV, the media and movies.

Time: 30 minutes

Learning outcomes

- To learn how constant exposure to stereotypes related to what is and isn't sexually attractive can reinforce prejudicial behaviour and inform our beliefs.

- To increase understanding of how sexual stereotypes can be formed and perpetuated by reinforcement on TV, the media and movies.

Key vocabulary

- **Sexual stereotypes**
- **Media influence**
- **Self-image**

You will need

- Large sheets of paper
- Pens

How to do it

1. Introduction

- Establish/revisit ground rules (see pages 42–43 for guidance).

Outline the basic aim of the lesson without giving details.

2. Opening activity

Divide young people into small groups and give each a vertical sheet of paper and a pen. Warn them that when the activity starts they will need to restrict their writing to the top 10cm of the sheet to ensure that they can fit everything on.

Once this has been made clear, explain that you are going to call out a brief description of someone and then set each group 90 seconds to write down all of the stereotypes they have ever heard relating to it. Point out that the people described are not real to prevent distractions while people try to guess whom it might be.

Call time and swiftly instruct each group to fold their paper over to cover what they have just written. Repeat reading, writing and covering until the whole list has been called out and the paper is folded up.

3. Development activity

Collect and swap the paper sheets among groups, ensuring that no group is left with their own. Then instruct a volunteer from each group to open the fan of paper and read aloud the suggestions one at a time, inviting the whole group to review how true they believe them to be after each one.

Remarks, questions and agreements can be written on in pen and they should also consider how similar the suggestions made are to those they wrote on their sheet, which is being reviewed by another group doing the same thing.

4. Reflection and review

Return the paper to their original owners to review what has been written or queried on the sheet. Invite the groups to pose questions Ask:

- Do you need to have experience of meeting people who fit these descriptions to have an opinion?

- If not, are your descriptions based on stereotypes?

  A stereotype is a widely held assumption or over-simplified belief that is applied to all, which may or may not reflect reality, for example all blondes are dumb, all redheads have a fiery temper.

- If you have never met someone, where do your assumptions about them come from?

  In particular, ask young people to reflect on the messages absorbed about what is and isn't sexually attractive through TV, the movies and newspapers.

- How can this lead to, or perpetuate existing, stereotypes?

  For example, you overhear someone being called a lazy, fat cow during an argument. You watch TV and the characters on the show reinforce that all larger people are lazy, which in turn endorses what you heard and subconsciously triggers you to make assumptions about the energy levels or commitment to hard work of the next larger person you meet.

Conclude that assumptions + stereotypes can = prejudice. This is prejudice meaning actions triggered by opinions based on preconceived judgements rather than facts.

5. Summary

- Opinions should be based on facts and not assumptions made about a whole group of people, without knowing one.

- Stereotypes about those who work in the adult entertainment industry can lead to prejudice and discrimination.

- Prejudice can lead to hate crime, for example being sexually abusive or disrespectful to women whose personal appearance fits with a stereotype held about what a female porn star looks like and how she behaves within the context of a porn film.

- Hate crime is illegal.

- Each person is an individual with their own story and should be respected as such.

ACTIVITY 3.11: SEXUAL STEREOTYPES LIST

1. Someone who works in a massage parlour

2. A pole dancer

3. Older women who date younger men

4. A gay male escort

5. Girls who have lots of different sexual partners

6. Someone who works in a sex shop

7. Middle-aged men who drive expensive sports cars

8. Blonde women

9. Male porn stars

10. Glamour models

11. Single women over the age of 40 who try online dating

12. Middle-aged men who pay for sex

ACTIVITY 3.12: BODY IMAGE POT SHOTS

(Years 10–13+)

Aims

- To explore the negative impact that outside influences can have on internalised body image.

- To promote self-confidence and self-respect and explore the differences between having positive body image and being vain.

Time: 60 minutes

Learning outcomes

- To understand how negative experiences, comments and ridicule can impact on body image.

- To learn how media and porn messages about the size and shapes of bodies can have a negative influence on body image.

Key vocabulary

- **Media influence**

- **Pornography**

- **Self-confidence**

- **Body image**

You will need

- Copies of the *Body image quotes* (these are well-known quotes attributed to the people whose name is beside them)

- Copies of the *Body shots worksheet*

- Paper and pens

How to do it

1. Introduction

- Establish/revisit ground rules (see pages 42–43 for guidance).

Introduce the topic by asking:

- What is the difference between loving yourself and vanity?

Suggest this definition encapsulates it well: 'The difference between loving yourself and vanity is when you love yourself you love your imperfections, but when you're vain, you don't even know you have them.'[11]

2. Opening activity

Divide the young people into small groups, handing each group one of the body image quotes, paper and pens. Explain that the men and women quoted are talking about what motivates them to feel confident and love the person they are.

The group task is to read the quote and then discuss answers to these questions. Point out this will be based on opinions so there are no right or wrong answers:

---

11   Popularly attributed to Marilyn vos Savant (b.1946) who has an IQ of 228, the highest ever recorded

- What do you think the quote means?

- Do you agree with what has been said? If yes, why/if no, why?

- Does it reflect how you feel about yourself? If yes, why/if no, why?

Facilitate a short feedback session to hear the key points from each group. Conclude that self-love includes having positive body image, regardless of your shape and size.

3. Development activity

Suggest that we are all born with a full quota of body image that is undamaged or affected in any way by outside influences, likening it to a bucket filled with water.

Divide the class into pairs, handing each couple a sheet of paper and a pen and asking them to draw a big bucket in the middle of the page. When they hear something likely to damage someone's body image they should draw a hole in the bucket. Read out the following questions, followed by the scenarios listed on the *Body shots worksheet*:

- Which scenarios might impact negatively on a person's body image?

- How might they make someone feel?

- How might someone act?

Allow time for discussion and for ideas to be written on the bucket between scenarios. Invite feedback after working through them all.

4. Reflection and review

Ask:

- How can loving yourself improve body image?

  Loving yourself is about accepting who you are and having self-respect, confidence and self-worth, while accepting that no one (including you) is perfect. If you only see the imperfections and negatives it can make you lose confidence and feel worthless, depressed, envious or jealous.

5. Summary

- Self-love is built on personal accomplishments, values and self-respect and respect for others.

- Self-love encompasses having good body image, i.e. being able to accept yourself as you are and having a healthy view of your body, shape and size.

- Negative body image can be based on fears of not being good enough and can result in constant unfavourable comparisons with the bodies of others. This includes people you know and women/men employed to show off their bodies, such as models, on TV and in pornography.

Extension

Task each group with making up their own quote to remind others to be confident in who they are and to celebrate difference.

ACTIVITY 3.12: BODY SHOTS WORKSHEET

1. Seeing pictures of near naked bodybuilders preparing for a competition.

2. Being told by a relative that you've got 'a great personality to make up for what's lacking in the looks department'.

3. A parent repeatedly turning down cakes and puddings for you, explaining that you have to 'watch your weight'.

4. Being constantly bombarded on social media by pictures of friends you believe to be better looking than you in swimwear.

5. Flicking through celebrity magazines and comparing yourself harshly to the sexualised pictures of models featured.

6. Feeling fat compared to catwalk models.

7. Watching pornography with a boyfriend who makes jokes about the size of your breasts compared with the women in the film.

8. Overhearing a peer making a nasty joke about the size of your backside when you are wearing your new jeans.

9. Reading online that the average size of a penis is nine inches.*

10. Constantly telling yourself that you are fat, ugly and need cosmetic surgery, hair extensions and Botox to be even in with a chance of getting a boy/girlfriend.

---

* To clarify, it isn't. The average adult penis size is about 14–16cm (5.5–6.3 inches) when erect. The average girth for an erect penis is 12–13cm (4.7–5.1 inches).

ACTIVITY 3.12: BODY IMAGE QUOTES

Quote 1

'Imperfection is beauty, madness is genius and it's better to be absolutely ridiculous than absolutely boring.' Marilyn Monroe (actress)

Quote 2

'Be yourself; everyone else is already taken.' Oscar Wilde (author and poet)

Quote 3

'Success is liking yourself, liking what you do, and liking how you do it.' Maya Angelou (author and poet)

Quote 4

'You've got to love yourself first. You've got to be okay on your own before you can be okay with somebody else.' Jennifer Lopez (actress and singer)

CHAPTER 4

Porn vs. Real-Life Relationships

All lessons in this section start from the viewpoint that watching pornography is not the best way for young people to learn about sex and relationships. Topics include issues of consent, negotiating relationship boundaries and tools and techniques to resist unwanted pressure. This includes the influence that friends, partners and peers can have on decisions to watch or engage in porn.

ACTIVITY 4.1: FOUR WORDS
(Years 7–13+)

Aim

- To explore values, attitudes and understanding of four words: flirting, love, pornography and intimacy.

Time: 30 minutes

Learning outcomes

- To be aware that people have a different understanding about what is meant by the terms flirting, love, pornography and intimacy.

- To consider factors that inform these differences.

Key vocabulary

- **Sexual intimacy**
- **Relationships**
- **Pornography**
- **Flirting**

You will need

- Flip chart paper
- Coloured marker pens
- Online access and printing facilities
- Sticky tack
- Facilities to play music

How to do it

1. Introduction

- Establish/revisit ground rules (see pages 42–43 for guidance).

2. Opening activity

Prepare four sheets of flipchart paper by heading them:

1. Flirting is...

2. Love is...

3. Pornography is...

4. Intimacy is...

Stick the sheets of paper to the floor to reduce the chances of them slipping about and leave as much space as possible in between each one. Place a pile of different colour markers by each sheet.

Play the music and then, similar to the well-known children's party game, stop it without any warning. Each young person should then quickly go the nearest piece of paper, grab a marker and write down as many comments and words or opinions as they can think of to finish the sentence. There is no need for people to add their names alongside what they write, but do remind everyone about previous agreements to respect each other's right to have an opinion, even if it is not one they share.

For the first few rounds leave only a short gap between turning off the music and resuming it. This should encourage participation, as there will only be time to write a few words at most. As the game picks up speed, confidence should increase, making young people more likely to be honest about what they really think.

Repeat until there is a good selection of comments and words on all four sheets, and then call time. Review what has been written, asking for clarification where required, inviting questions and encouraging discussion. As you go through the four sheets look for, and make young people aware of:

- words used on more than one sheet

- terminology used

- comments that reflect shared or diverse opinions.

3. Development activity

Divide the main group into four and allocate each group one of the sheets. The next task for each group is to review all of the words written on it, removing any swear words or inappropriate language and choosing words that convey the same message to replace them.

Once this has been done direct young people online[1] where they can design a poster using Wordle. This is a free online design package that takes the words of song lyrics, poetry and so on and transforms them into word art. The words most used in the text will appear in bigger, bolder type and those used only a few times or just once will be much smaller. The site has a gallery of posters, which shows examples of how fonts and colours available have been previously used to inspire new users.

Suggest that the young people try out different styles until they are happy with their designs, which can then be saved, printed off and displayed.

4. Reflection and review

Stick up the word clouds and review them as a whole class. Ask:

- Where do these definitions come from?

- Who and what influence our understanding?

    This could include family, friends, TV, the media, education, etc.

---

1   www.wordle.net

Conclude that words have meaning gathered from different sources. This includes what we know and what we see; education: for example, reading about love and romance, societal norms, faith and community culture and things like popular culture. This is why one person's definition can appear pretty much the same as another's on the surface but underneath have different strands that come together informed by many outside influences.

5. Summary

- Words have different meaning to different people.

- Meaning is informed by many things accumulated over time, both externally and internally.

Extension

This exercise could be used as an effective assessment and review tool to record young people's thoughts, knowledge levels and opinions at the start of the curriculum and then again at the end to measure learning and/or change.

ACTIVITY 4.2: PORN VS. REALITY

(Years 10–13+)

Aims

- To consider different points of view about the effects of watching porn and to consider the ethics of trying to encourage or putting pressure a partner to watch with you.
- To compare porn with real-life relationships to better understand the differences.

Time: 30–45 minutes

Learning outcomes

- To ackowledge that people have different values and attitudes to sex, relationships and pornography.
- To understand the relationships shown in porn are very different to those in real life.
- To know it is morally not acceptable to coerce or emotionally bully a partner into watching adult material, and the law is broken if they are under 18.

Key vocabulary

- **Personal attitudes and values**
- **Sex and relationships**
- **Pornography**

You will need

- Paper and pens

How to do it

The opening agree/disagree activity can be facilitated with young people remaining seated and raising their hand to indicate if they agree with a statement or not, or by moving between two designated points in the room.

1. Introduction

- Establish/revisit ground rules (see pages 42–43 for guidance).

Explain that you are going to read out a series of statements related to values and ethics. These are intended to provoke debate and contain opinions from both ends of the anti- and pro-porn scale, aiming to offer a balanced argument and a vehicle for exploring difference.

2. Opening activity

Introduce two points in the room and designate one to mean 'agree' and the other to mean 'disagree'. For the moment do not offer a mid-point for those unsure of where they stand on the debate, although this can be negotiated as the exercise progresses.

Read out the *Porn vs. reality statements* one at a time and allow time for learners to move. Encourage challenge in a way that is constructive and respectful, but be prepared to move on if things become too heated. Individual issues that arise can always be the topic of deeper discussion at another time.

3. Development activity

Read out the following scenario and then, working in groups of three, ask young people to discuss and then write down the advice they would give to a friend in this situation. This should be written in the form of an email or letter so thought should be given to make sure the advice given is clear, responds to the anxieties shared and is supportive.

> Help! I am 18 and experiencing relationship difficulties. I love my partner but I don't want us to watch online porn together. My partner finds it exciting and says that lots of couples enjoy it but to be honest I find it all a bit embarrassing and intimidating. I hadn't really seen any proper porn before this relationship, just a few screenshots, but last night I felt I couldn't say no. Now I worry my partner might expect me to do some of the things we saw. What can I do? This relationship is precious to me and I don't want us to break up, but I also don't want to be pressured into something I am not happy with.

Ask each trio in turn to read out their response, inviting comment after each suggestion. Ask supplementary questions as required to consider:

- How easy is it to say 'no' to someone you really care about?

- What are the worst fears?

- What could be a positive result?

- In this scenario, what is likely to happen if nothing is said?

4. Reflection and review

There are lots of different opinions about pornography and the adult entertainment business. Apart from the legalities, much of this is subjective and a matter of personal taste and preferences. However, it is never right to try and coerce someone into doing something they are not comfortable with or do not want to do. In a positive relationship both partners should be in agreement before making decisions and anything related to sex must be consensual.

5. Summary

- Pornography is not the best way to learn about real-life sex and relationships.

- Trying to emotionally blackmail or bully someone into watching something they are uncomfortable with, or don't want to see, is never acceptable. If the person being bullied is under the age of 18, laws may be broken as it is illegal to show sexual images to a child.

- What consenting adults choose to do or watch legally once they are over 18 is a matter for them to decide.

ACTIVITY 4.2: PORN VS. REALITY – AGREE/DISAGREE

1. Watching porn is a good way to learn about sex.

2. Only perverts watch porn.

3. Watching porn as a couple can enhance your sex life.

4. More males than females watch porn.

5. Everyone watches porn.

6. Pornography degrades women by showing them as sex objects.

7. Sex in porn films is very different to real-life sex.

8. Watching porn teaches you about relationships.

9. Everyone knows that porn isn't real.

10. Watching porn is just a bit of fun and doesn't mean anything.

ACTIVITY 4.3: WHY DO PEOPLE HAVE SEX?

(Years 9–13+)

Aim

- To explore why people choose to have sex, and other ways to achieve intimacy without it.
- To consider how porn sex potentially impacts on expectations about real-life sex.

Time: 30 minutes

Learning outcomes

- To recognise that having penetrative sex is only one way to show a partner that you find them physically attractive or love them.
- To understand that pornography sex focuses on the sex act rather than the emotional aspects of a relationship.

Key vocabulary

- **Sexual relationships**
- **Pornography**
- **Sexual expectations**

You will need

- Flipchart paper
- Marker pens

How to do it

1. Introduction

- Establish/revisit ground rules (see pages 42–43 for guidance).

Agree a shared definition for the term 'having sex'. For example, although 'having sex' could include masturbation, for the purposes of this lesson it means two people engaging in consensual sexual activity, which is likely to include penetrative sex. Remind everyone that 16 is the age of consent in the UK, but many people choose to wait until they are older.

2. Opening activity

Divide the class into small groups, giving each group flipchart paper and two different coloured markers. Then write the following question up on a whiteboard or sheet of flipchart paper:

- Why do people choose to have sex?

Explain that this includes casual sex, sex within a relationship, sex within marriage, etc. Allow five minutes for groups to discuss the question and idea storm as many reasons as they can think of, for example because it's fun, it feels good, to show love, to get pregnant. Call time and invite feedback from each group, allowing time for discussion and congratulating the group with the most suggestions.

3. Development activity

Now, ask:

- Is this the same for sex and sexual acts shown in pornography?

  This provides opportunities to discuss the differences between real-life sex, which should be consensual and pleasurable for both partners, and porn sex.

- Are men and women show as equal participants in pornography sex?

  This provides an opportunity to talk about how female porn actors often cater to the males with little regard for their own pleasure and explore how this can look imbalanced in terms of satisfaction, which could inform the expectations of young men and women watching it.

Move on to ask each group to go back to their sheet and with another coloured marker circle all the things that can only be achieved through having penetrative sex and not in any other way within a relationship. Conclude that on balance there are very few things that can only be got from having sex alone. Many of the things listed as important previously, such as feeling loved, mutual trust and respect, can be shown in different ways too.

4. Reflection and review

Set the groups another five-minute task, this time to come up with as many ways as they can think of to show they love someone, without having sex. Again, call time and invite ideas from each group, discussing suggestions and before awarding the group with the most ideas the title, 'The Kings/ Queens of Love'.

5. Summary

- Having sex is only one way of demonstrating your feelings and there are lots of other ways to have fun, be intimate and enjoy spending time with someone.

- Pornography is not reflective of real-life sex as the emotional aspects of caring for someone and doing intimate, but non-sexual, things for each other are generally not shown.

- Everyone has the right to make their own decisions about sex and nobody should ever feel pressured into having sex until they are ready.

ACTIVITY 4.4: FANTASY OR TRUTH?

(Years 9–13+)

Aim

- To explore the similarities and differences between real-life relationships and those shown in pornography.

Time: 30 minutes

Learning outcomes

- To acknowledge that the sex depicted in porn is acted and directed, and in some cases scripted, meaning that it bears little or no relation to real-life sex within a mutually positive relationship.
- To know real-life sex must always be consensual.

Key vocabulary

- **Sex and relationships**
- **Sexual consent**
- **Pornography**

You will need

- Sets of *Fantasy or truth cards*
- Two A4 cards marked 'Fantasy' and 'Truth' (placed at opposing poles)

How to do it
1. Introduction

- Establish/revisit ground rules (see pages 42–43 for guidance).

2. Opening activity

Facilitate this as a whole-group activity. The task is to discuss each of the *Fantasy or truth cards* in turn and then decide if they are 'Fantasy', meaning that the information is usually associated with pornography or 'Truth', meaning it is something likely to be true of a real-life relationship. Any cards that young people believe fall into both categories can be placed in the middle for wider discussion.

3. Development activity

Once all of the cards have been placed encourage constructive and respectful debate, allowing cards to be moved where appropriate. Use the following questions to prompt further debate:

- What impact might these fantasies have on young people's sexual expectations of each other?
- How might they feel if their real-life relationships are different to the fantasy stuff?
- How might they behave?

4. Reflection and review

Facilitate a circle time activity that invites each person to share one thing they think contributes to a healthy, positive real-life relationship.

5. Summary

- The relationships depicted in pornography bear little or no resemblance to real-life ones.

- As with other film genres, reality is distorted to fit a plotline and a director tells the actors what to do and how to act.

- In real life, lasting relationships develop at a much slower pace and sex, if and when it happens, is always consensual.

ACTIVITY 4.4: FANTASY OR TRUTH CARDS

Most people have doubts and anxieties about sex at some point.	Most couples have sex the first time they meet.
Most people try a threesome at some point.	It is sexually exciting to be filmed having sex.
It is normal to have sexual fantasies.	Being sexually attractive means always being in the mood for sex.
If one partner does not want sex the other should not put pressure on to make them change their mind.	During sex both partners should orgasm at the same time.
To be sexually attractive you must be good in bed.	If your partner doesn't want sex it means they don't fancy you.
Both partners should give and receive pleasure from sex.	You can kiss and cuddle without it leading to sex.
Males should be able to maintain an erection for up to an hour.	It is important to use condoms and practice safe sex.
Men have sexual needs that have to be fulfilled.	Women have sexual needs that have to be fulfilled.
Girls have sex with other girls to sexually arouse men.	Girls wear revealing clothes to show they are looking for sex.
When it comes to sex there should be no boundaries.	In heterosexual relationships women should be sexually submissive to men.
Lots of happy couples choose not to have sex.	Romance and sex are two very different things.
Most couples use whips, gags and restraints to enhance their sex lives.	Masturbating is normal for both men and women.

ACTIVITY 4.5: AT WHAT AGE ARE YOU READY?

(Years 9–13+)

Aim

- For young people to consider the ages that they think people are ready for different elements of real-life relationships, based on personal values and experience.

Time: 30 minutes

Learning outcomes

- To realise that personal values differ based on culture, gender and experience.

- To acknowledge that personal opinions and the law can differ.

- To be aware that people can feel ready for information, relationships and intimacy at different ages, and that this is normal.

Key vocabulary

- **Consent**

- **Sex and relationships**

- **Values and attitudes**

You will need

- A copy of the *At what age are you ready? worksheet* for each person and a pen

- Flipchart paper and markers

How to do it

1. Introduction

- Establish/revisit ground rules (see pages 42–43 for guidance).

Start by explaining that 'values' are the principles that people believe in and that guide behaviour. A value is something that is of worth, interest or importance to an individual, which may vary between people. These are different to laws discussed in previous activities, which are set up to protect people and are applicable to everyone, regardless of opinions or values.

2. Opening activity

Ask young people to call out how they think personal values might be shaped and formed through childhood into adolescence and record ideas, for example parents, faith, friends, etc. Go on to explain that values inform how we feel about all aspects of life, including what we think is right or wrong.

3. Development activity

Hand each person a copy of the *At what age are you ready? worksheet* and a pen and ask them to complete it. After ten minutes, invite the young people to choose a partner and work through the second part of the sheet together.

Collect in all the worksheets, shuffle them, and then distribute them randomly.

Go through the list and ask young people to call out the ages suggested. Tally these up onto flipchart paper so that everyone can see.

4. Reflection and review

Reflect on the answers given, particularly any areas of difference, and facilitate a discussion that considers:

- Which statements were hardest to assign an age to? Why?

- Does gender make a difference?

- The legal age for consent to sex is 16, but to watch pornography it is 18. Does this seem odd? How does the law affect people's beliefs and behaviour?

5. Summary

- People mature at different ages. The age of consent is 16 but many people are not ready to have sex until they are older.

- A wide range of internal and external factors, including family, peers, faith and community, informs personal values.

- You can be in a loving relationship without having penetrative sex. Abstinence is always a valid choice.

- Any sexual activity must be consensual.

ACTIVITY 4.5: AT WHAT AGE ARE YOU READY? WORKSHEET

Part 1

The legal age in the UK for sexual consent is 16 and 18 for marriage (without parental consent). Have a look at the list below, which is in no particular order, and write what age you think people are ready to:

- understand that male and female bodies look different _____

- receive sex and relationships education _____

- develop close friendships _____

- experience physical attraction _____

- know their sexual orientation _____

- spend time alone with someone they fancy _____

- have a boy or girlfriend _____

- share a kiss on the lips _____

- see or watch TV/films with an adult content _____

- watch or see pornographic images _____

- enter into a committed relationship _____

- become engaged _____

- live with someone _____

- marry or enter into a civil partnership _____

- have children _____

Part 2

Choose a partner to discuss answers with, remembering that this exercise has asked for individual opinions and to be respectful of different views and avoid being critical or judgemental.

ACTIVITY 4.6: BACKWARDS FAIRYTALES

(Years 7–13+)

Aim

- To compare the type of love stories and relationships depicted in fairytales with those shown in porn films and those experienced in real life.

Time: 45 minutes

Learning outcomes

- To explore expectations about sex and relationships.

- To understand that romantic love does not have to include sex.

- To understand the main differences between real-life relationships and porn.

Key vocabulary

- **Romance**

- **Positive relationships**

- **Pornography**

You will need

- Paper and pens

- Sticky notes pre-prepared with 'Adapt to a musical', 'Adapt to an 18+ movie', 'Adapt to a real-life documentary', 'Adapt to a soap opera', 'Adapt to a rom-com' (romantic comedy) written on them.

How to do it

This lesson is shown as a storyboard exercise but can be easily adapted to include role-play or acted out, making sure that you clarify at the start that there should be no inappropriate touching or any behaviour that could be perceived as being of a sexual nature (especially in the scenario where the fairytale is adapted into an 18+ movie).

1. Introduction

- Establish/revisit ground rules (see pages 42–43 for guidance).

Introduce the topic by asking learners to choose their favourite childhood fairytale or film from the following list:

- Snow White

- Sleeping Beauty

- Cinderella

- Aladdin

- Beauty and the Beast

- The Little Mermaid.

Summarise that these are all essentially romantic love stories then ask:

- How do we know that the characters are in love?

- What obstacles are there along the path to happiness?

- How do they show each other how much they care?

- How true to life are the plotlines?

Conclude that central to all these love stories is a massive challenge that has to be overcome before the couple can live happily ever after. Although we know they are in love, nothing more intimate than a kiss ever happens, which is romantic and usually signals the end of the story. The stories are not true but we can learn from some of the positive points made, for example the importance of trust, honesty and caring for each other in a romantic relationship.

2. Opening activity

Divide the young people into small groups and give each group pens and paper. Explain that the 20-minute task for each group is to create a storyboard that tells a new romantic love story in the same genre as the traditional fairytales. They will be given the first and last line but it will be up to them to decide what happens in between.

Read out the first line and last line, which are:

'Once upon a time...'

'...and they lived happily ever after.'

Encourage everyone to be as creative as possible when telling their tale of romance, using pictures, words or a mixture of both. The only rules are that it must run backwards from the last line to the first, rather than the traditional way round, and there should be no sex scenes.

Once all of the groups have back-pedalled through their love story call time. Invite each group in turn to present their storyboard, from finish to start, remembering to join in with the final line in true fairytale tradition, 'once upon a time'.

Congratulate the young people on their stories and point out that relationships are the basis for lots of different types of documentaries, plays and movies. Often traditional stories are taken and adapted to set them in another time or place, which is exactly what is going to happen next.

3. Development activity

Allocate each group a sticky note that has on it a different film/TV genre to adapt their story to. The characters must stay the same, along with the basic storyline of love and romance, but the action is likely to change. This time they have ten minutes in which to complete the task.

Again, call time and ask each group to present their new version, this time from start to finish, leading a round of applause after each one.

Review the adaptations to discuss the following:

- How easy was it to keep love as the central theme in the 18+ movie genre? Point out that sex is central to a porn film, rather than the story of the relationship.

- How do soap opera love affairs differ to those in real life?

- Are the type of relationships shown in musicals/rom-coms realistic?

- Which type of relationship is most likely to offer a 'happy ever after'?

4. Reflection and review

Although we all understand that fairy stories are just make believe, some people find it harder to distinguish between the type of relationships shown in porn films and real life. Ask:

- How do we know that the events and relationships shown in porn are unlikely to reflect healthy, positive relationships in real life?

  For example, because lots of the things shown in adult movies, such as casual sex, domination, aggressive behaviour, sex involving more than one person, would be likely threaten the happiness of one or both partners in a real relationship. Sex within a loving relationship is about emotions too and this is not shown through porn; in real life both partners should know their own personal boundaries and feel comfortable sticking to them.

Finally, reinforce the importance of both partners giving consent to sex in real life. Without it, the perpetrator is committing a sexual assault or rape.

5. Summary

- A romantic relationship does not have to be a sexual relationship.

- A great relationship is not always about what you look like, there is physical attraction but also an emotional attraction too.

- Relationships built on respect, care, mutual trust and getting to know someone well, as friends as well as romantic partners, are far more likely to last than those built simply on physical attraction or self-gratification.

ACTIVITY 4.7: GOSSIP, RUMOURS AND LIES

(Years 7–13+)

Aims

- To question how decisions are made to pass on different types of information and discuss the potential consequences of doing so.
- To build empathy for the victims of untrue gossip and rumours and understand the potential impact they can have on someone.

Time: 30 minutes

Learning outcomes

- To know the basic difference between gossip, rumours and lies.
- To understand the potential impact each might have on a victim.
- To understand the personal responsibilities involved in the giving and receiving of information.

Key vocabulary

- **Choice**
- **Personal responsibility**
- **Keeping safe**
- **Consequences**

You will need

- Three large sheets of paper
- Marker pens

How to do it

1. Introduction

- Establish/revisit ground rules (see pages 42–43 for guidance).

Write the headings 'Gossip', 'Rumours' and 'Lies' on three large sheets of paper and stick them up around the room. Write and read aloud the following examples under the correct heading.

Gossip – Sarah, in Year 12, has been caught sending texts to her boyfriend during French.

Rumours – Someone told me that they know a girl who became a famous glamour model through texting naked selfies.

Lies – Why won't you send me a topless selfie? I know a girl who became a famous glamour model because she sent a picture to her boyfriend.

Divide the young people into three groups, allocating each a different pre-prepared sheet (gossip, rumours or lies) and a different coloured marker to make it easier to identify who comments belong to later. Ask each group to give a quick definition of what the word on their allocated sheet means.

- Gossip – a conversation or reports about other people, usually involving details which are not confirmed as true.
- Rumours – a currently circulating stories or reports of uncertain or doubtful truth.
- Lies – false statements made with deliberate intent to deceive; intentional untruths.[2]

---

2   All definitions based on those in the online Oxford Dictionary, www.oxforddictionaries.com

2. Opening activity

On the shout, 'Go!', set each group the five-minute task of writing down as many examples of whatever is on their sheet as they can under their heading. The examples previously written can be used as a prompt. Call time and then invite each group to move on to the next sheet of paper, setting the same task, but asking them to read what others have written first.

Rotate until everyone is back in front of the sheet they started with. Here they will be able to review everything that has been added since their original ideas to see if everyone has a common understanding of the different terms and to consider the different ways that information can be passed on.

Invite each group to share at least three examples from their sheet and then discuss the potential consequences of each particular rumour, gossip or lie, including the harm that may be done to an individual or to other people.

3. Development activity

Ask:

- What is the difference between gossip and passing on information?

  Answers could include the different motivations behind sharing information and repeating gossip; gossip is not always true, while information is likely to contain facts.

- Where do rumours come from?

  Answers could include rumours spread by gossip, people sharing information without knowing if it is true, rumours that become 'urban myths', i.e. everyone has heard them but no one actually knows who it allegedly happened to, celebrity gossip and malicious rumours that seek to harm somebody or their reputation.

- Why might someone lie about information they share?

  Answers could include to deliberately deceive someone, to justify an argument, to persuade someone to do something they don't want to do, to make someone appear more interesting or to hurt someone.

Point out that passing on any information that includes information or pictures which could considered sexual or that have an adult content could result in laws being broken. It is also illegal to knowingly tell lies about someone else to discredit them or ruin their credibility or reputation.

4. Reflection and review

Conclude with a short whole-group discussion to draw up some basic principles about passing on information. These could include:

- If in doubt, do not pass on information.
- Only pass on information that is definitely true.
- Do not present rumour or gossip as facts.
- Think about the potential consequence of passing on information before doing so.
- Consider how it might feel to be a victim of gossip, rumour or lies.
- Be assertive and refuse to take part in or pass on gossip.

5. Summary

- Passing on untrue gossip can lead to unfair assumptions being made and cause misery to the victim.
- Perpetuating rumours about a person's sexual activity, or lack of sexual activity, is a form of bullying.
- Telling lies about sexual behaviour can have far-reaching consequences and could break privacy laws.

ACTIVITY 4.8: RELATIONSHIP BULLYING

(Years 8–13+)

Aims

- For young people to explore what constitutes bullying behaviour within an intimate or dating relationship.
- To demonstrate different types of pressure or coercion that one partner might apply to another.

Time: 45–60 minutes

Learning outcomes

- To understand that relationship bullying is a form of domestic abuse.
- To understand that relationship bullying is not dependent on gender, age or sexuality.
- To be aware that domestic abuse is not always linked to physical violence.
- To know where to go for help and support.

Key vocabulary

- **Positive relationships**
- **Bullying**
- **Domestic abuse**
- **Gender and sexuality**

You will need

- Sticky notes and pens
- Flipchart paper and a red and black marker pen
- Two sets of the *Relationship bullying cards*
- Information about local and national support for domestic abuse

How to do it

1. Introduction

- Establish/revisit ground rules (see pages 42–43 for guidance).

Draw a large red heart onto a sheet of flipchart paper and write in bold letters across it 'LOVE HURTS'.

Hand each learner a sticky note and pen, introduce them to the popular saying written on the red heart and then ask everyone to take a minute and write down what they think it means.

One at a time invite young people to come up to the heart, read out their definition and then stick it on. Acknowledge ideas but do not develop them into a discussion at this point.

Reflect that the phrase is widely used in slogans, songs and so on and probably refers to the emotional anguish that can be experienced as part of the highs and lows of a relationship. It is not endorsing or normalising domestic abuse or relationship bullying.

2. Opening activity

Begin to challenge any stereotypical ideas held about relationship bullying or domestic abuse by asking:

- Is it only women who can be bullied or suffer violence within a personal relationship?

   One in four lesbian and bi women have experienced domestic abuse in a relationship. Two thirds of those say the perpetrator was a woman, a third a man. Almost half (49%) of all gay and bi men have experienced at least one incident of domestic abuse from a family member or partner since the age of sixteen.[3]

- Does relationship bullying happen within a same sex relationship?

   About 25 per cent of LGBT+ people suffer through violent or threatening relationships with partners or ex-partners, which is the same rate as domestic abuse against heterosexual women.[4]

- Does relationship bullying and domestic abuse happen to those couples under 18?

   The British Crime Survey 2009/10 found that 16–19-year-olds were the group most likely to suffer abuse from a partner, with 12.7 per cent of young women and 6.2 per cent of young men in this age group reporting that they experienced it. This led to the government extending the legal definition of domestic violence to include people under 18 from 2013.[5]

Explain that domestic abuse and violence can take many forms, which is what the following exercise is going to explore.

3. Development activity

Divide the class into small groups and give each a set of *Relationship bullying cards*.

The group task is to read and discuss each scenario or action described before agreeing if it constitutes relationship bullying, or not. Once agreed, they can place the cards into two piles, 'relationship bullying' and 'not'.

Remind the class that these discussions should not include any personal disclosures and explain that anyone who is worried about anything raised during the lesson should speak in private afterwards. Allow up to 20 minutes for discussion and then bring everybody together in a large group.

Read out each of the cards and ask each group to reveal which pile they have placed it on, encouraging discussion and debate on any conflicting decisions. Point out that arguing or simply being unpleasant to a partner does not necessarily mean that bulling or domestic abuse is occurring.

4. Reflection and review

Review where the line is crossed between a volatile relationship, where arguments do happen but there is mutual trust and respect and problems are resolved, and a relationship where one person controls, bullies or dominates the other either emotionally or physically or both.

Give out information and contact numbers for domestic abuse support and who to tell if they are concerned about a situation or person. This includes contacting the police, who have been running wide campaigns to promote the support that they offer victims and families. There are also national support groups for the perpetrators of domestic abuse. Organisations who can help:

National Domestic Violence Helpline
www.nationaldomesticviolencehelpline.org.uk
Freephone 0808 2000 247

The Freephone 24-Hour National Domestic Violence Helpline, run in partnership between Women's Aid and Refuge, is a national service for women experiencing domestic violence, their family, friends, colleagues and others calling on their behalf.

---

3   www.stonewall.org.uk/help-advice/criminal-law/domestic-violence
4   www.endthefear.co.uk/information/help-and-advice/same-sex-domestic-abuse
5   www.gov.uk/government/news/new-definition-of-domestic-violence-and-abuse-to-include-16-and-17-year-olds--2

Men's Advice Line

www.mensadviceline.org.uk

Freephone 0808 801 0327

Men's Advice Line is a confidential helpline for any man experiencing domestic violence and abuse from a partner (or ex-partner).

Galop

www.galop.org.uk

020 7704 2040

Advice and support for people who have experienced biphobia, homophobia, transphobia, sexual violence or domestic abuse.

Supportline

www.supportline.org.uk

For children and young people witnessing domestic violence in the home.

Respect

www.respectphoneline.org.uk

Freephone 0808 802 4040

A confidential and anonymous helpline for anyone concerned about their violence and/or abuse towards a partner or ex-partner.

Call 999 if it's an emergency or you're in immediate danger.

5. Summary

- It is never acceptable to bully, threaten, coerce or be violent to a partner.

- The police take domestic abuse very seriously and will act on information given.

- Sexual bullying that includes the making or sharing of indecent images should be reported, either to local police or if it is online through the CEOP website.[6]

- All reports are confidential and the welfare and safety of the young person is the first priority.

Extension

Set young people the task of finding more about organisations that offer support for domestic abuse. These could include:

- www.galop.org.uk – confidential help and support for lesbian, gay, bisexual and transgender people suffering from domestic violence by their current or former partner.

- www.endthefear.co.uk – support, information and advice for anyone experiencing domestic or sexual violence or who knows someone who may be being abused.

- www.nationaldomesticviolencehelpline.org.uk – the Freephone 24-Hour National Domestic Violence Helpline, run in partnership between Women's Aid and Refuge, is a national service for women experiencing domestic violence, their family, friends, colleagues and others calling on their behalf.

---

6   http://ceop.police.uk

ACTIVITY 4.8: RELATIONSHIP BULLYING CARDS

I have told my partner, the reason I shout and smash things is so I don't hit her.	My partner wants to know where I am all the time because he loves me.
It is my fault we argue. I wind her up.	I have told him he has to choose – me or his friends.
My boyfriend says that if I love him I will let him film us next time we have sex.	My partner never says 'I love you', I always have to say it first.
I send sexy messages to my partner telling him what I want him to do to me later.	My partner has shared intimate photos of me that were supposed to be private.
My ex keeps stalking me on Facebook and turning up at the same places.	I have warned my partner I have an anger management problem so she shouldn't argue with me.
My partner says I don't need my family now that we are together.	My partner gets aggressive if another man even talks to me.
My partner says that if I ever try to leave her, she will kill herself.	My partner split up with me by text and won't take my calls.
When we argue we hurt each other. We have both had cuts and bruises after our fights.	My boyfriend keeps comparing me to the girls he fancies online. How can I compete with a porn star?
I have sexual fantasies and feel frustrated that my partner doesn't want to try them out.	I have told my girlfriend I will stop watching porn if she will have sex with me.
My partner has told me that her ex is better looking than me.	My partner makes me feel insecure by not calling me every day.
I often provoke an argument with my partner because I like making up.	My partner is often rude to me but says it is just 'banter'.

ACTIVITY 4.9: POWERS OF PERSUASION

(Years 7–13+)

Aims

- To experience the powers of persuasion used to incite someone to do something they are not really comfortable with.

- To develop assertiveness skills to say what you want and try out simple techniques to set and maintain personal boundaries.

Time: 45 minutes

Learning outcomes

- To be aware there are different ways to persuade or coerce someone, including emotional blackmail.

- To recognise that saying no is not always easy, especially if you like the person or seek their approval.

- To learn how to be assertive and maintain personal boundaries.

Key vocabulary

- **Consent**
- **Personal boundaries**
- **Assertiveness**
- **Personal relationships**

You will need

- A packet of small sweets
- Sets of *Persuasion cards*
- Paper and pens

How to do it

Elements of this lesson are shown as role-play activities but if young people are uncomfortable with this then adapt to a small group discussion.

1. Introduction

- Establish/revisit ground rules (see pages 42–43 for guidance).

To work effectively this icebreaker needs a second person to play the role of 'persuader'. This can be a young person.

Hand each young person a sweet, telling them that it is theirs but they must not eat it until you give permission for them to do so. Then invent a reason to leave the room for a few seconds.

At this point the second person should step forward to cast doubt on this instruction. They should gradually question the reasons why they shouldn't eat the sweet, before openly eating it and encouraging the rest of the class to go ahead and do the same.

Return to the room and ask who ate their sweet and who conformed to your instruction.

Ask:

- What made you eat the sweet?

  For example, someone else did, it seemed OK to do so, didn't understand the reason for giving it in the first place, wanted to, etc.

- What prevented you from eating the sweet?

  For example, didn't want to get into trouble, didn't like the sweet, didn't want to get caught, was told not to.

Quickly review the techniques that the second person used to persuade the class to disobey instructions. For example, presenting a good case for ignoring the instructions, appealing to the impulsive side of people or group loyalties, challenging authority, sounding confident, finding it hard to ignore, offering reinforcement for what you wanted to do anyway.

Conclude that these are all methods employed to persuade people to do things in other situations too, regardless of whether it is right or wrong.

Start by acknowledging that while everybody is responsible for their own behaviour in some circumstances it can be very hard to refuse to do something, even if you are uncomfortable with what is being asked of you, or know it is the wrong decision for you. This can provoke feelings of anxiety and anger, especially if someone else is using their powers of persuasion.

2. Opening activity

Invite the young people to either stand or sit in a large circle. This is important, as they do need to be able to see each other.

Open the game by explaining that communication is not just about speaking and listening. While it is really important to speak clearly and listen actively – i.e. not jump to conclusions or 'second guess' what someone is going to say – body language and tone are just as vital. Suggest that changing these, for example making eye contact, using hand gestures, smiling or frowning, can change the whole context of the conversation and meaning. Offer an example to show what you mean – the word 'whatever' works well!

The game is to go around the circle as many times as possible to demonstrate different ways of saying, 'No!' After each person's turn the rest of the group should try to guess the mood from the tone of voice and body language used, for example shouting could be angry or a cry of amazement; you could beg someone to stop or encourage them not to stop.

See how many ways it can be said – young people will practise saying no and gain confidence in saying it assertively.

3. Development activity

Introduce this assertiveness framework and write it up to aid learning:

- Use direct language to describe your concern.

- Use 'I' statements to describe emotions and feelings, for example 'I feel angry', rather than 'You make me angry'.

- Actively listen to the other person's point of view.

- Make up your mind (if you cannot do that ask for more time or refuse to do anything until you can make a decision).

- Express your decision – without apologising, making excuses or justifying it.

- Once you have set a personal boundary, stick to it.

Explain that to practise this, learners are going to work in groups of three to role-play a series of situations where one person is trying to persuade the others to do something they don't want to do. Give each trio a set of *Persuasion cards*. It doesn't matter who has which card as each person will have the opportunity to experience all three roles. Each role-play will take three minutes and then there will be one minute for feedback, before swapping roles to work through the next scenario.

There are three roles:

1. *The Persuader* – who is going to use charm, reasoning and every skill they possess to persuade the other person to go along with whatever they suggest.

2. *The Subject* – who is going to use the assertiveness framework and try to resist any pressure applied to persuade them.

3. *The Observer* – who is going to make notes based on the assertiveness framework throughout the role-play to feedback at the end of three minutes.

Facilitate the activity, keeping people on task ensuring that each person participates fully.

Once everyone has experienced each role invite feedback, asking which techniques worked well and to give examples. Ask:

- How easy or hard it was to resist pressure applied by the Persuader?

- What else could you do if someone is putting pressure on you?

    For example, tell someone, walk away, refuse to discuss it, etc.

4. Reflection and review

Ask young people to suggest some examples where it might be hard to refuse to do what is asked of you. Answers could include:

- When the person asking is someone you like or love.

- You feel too embarrassed to say no.

- You are frightened or worried about what will happen if you say no.

- When you are unsure of what to do.

- When all of your friends are doing it.

- When you think you will look silly by refusing.

5. Summary

- Everyone has the right to say no.

- It can be hard to say no in some situations, especially if the person asking is a partner or someone you like.

- It is wrong to apply emotional or physical pressure to try and make someone do something they are unhappy with

- In certain situations this is illegal, for example putting pressure on someone to have sex or engage in anything that is illegal.

ACTIVITY 4.9: PERSUASION CARDS

Persuader 1:

You are trying to persuade the other person to text you a naked selfie.

Persuader 2:

You are trying to persuade the other person to make an intimate film with you.

Persuader 3:

You are trying to persuade the other person to watch a porn movie with you.

ACTIVITY 4.10: FLIRTING OR SEXUAL HARRASSMENT?
(Years 9–13+)

Aims

- To consider the difference between flirting, banter and crossing the line into sexual harassment.
- To raise awareness of personal boundaries and develop empathy.

Time: 60 minutes

Learning outcome

- To define the boundaries between acceptable behaviour and sexual harassment, as defined by law.

Key vocabulary

- **Personal boundaries**
- **Assertive behaviour**
- **Sexual harassment**

You will need

- Flipchart paper and markers
- A set of *Flirting or harassment? cards* for each group

How to do it

1. Introduction

- Establish/revisit ground rules (see pages 42–43 for guidance).

Ask the young people to share with a partner a time when they have misunderstood the meaning of a text or message sent to them, including:

- what happened
- how the misunderstanding occurred
- how it was resolved.

As a whole group, invite comments on how it feels to get it wrong, or misunderstand the intentions of another – even when it doesn't really matter. This could include things like feeling embarrassed, ashamed or confused.

Conclude that it can be easy to misunderstand the meaning behind a text, which can lead to arguments or resentment if it is not resolved. Suggest that this can be the same in real-life romantic situations where the intent of someone else is not clear, and messages are mixed or misunderstood, as well as when the attention is unwanted and requires courage and assertiveness to challenge.

2. Opening activity

Divide a sheet of paper down the middle with a thick line. Write 'Appropriate' on one side and 'Inappropriate' on the other. Now invite learners to call out suggestions for both appropriate and inappropriate ways that someone might show that they fancy someone else. Write down all of their answers and talk about any that raise queries or discussion. Ideas could include really simple things like smiling or sending a friendly text, which can be placed on the 'Appropriate' side of the paper, right through to less acceptable behaviour on the 'Inappropriate' side, such as sending intimate selfies, stalking or using sexualised language.

Conclude that some of the ideas on the 'Inappropriate' side include unwanted physical or verbal advances and those that have clear sexual undertones. Suggest that this can be considered sexual harassment, and that is unacceptable morally as well as victims being protected by law.

Make sure you point out that it is not just males who sexually harass females; females can harass males, males can harass other males and the same applies for women – it unacceptable behaviour whoever does it. The kind of behaviour that can be considered a form of sexual harassment includes:

- telling or texting sexual jokes

- sending porn or links to porn websites

- inappropriate touching

- inappropriate gestures or hand signals

- spreading gossip or rumours about another person's sexual behaviour

- taking pictures without permission

- passing on photos without permission

- calling people names with sexual connotations.

3. Development activity

Divide the young people into small groups and hand each group a set of *Flirting or harrassment cards* to work through. Each scenario depicts something that someone might do to get the attention of someone they find attractive and want to get to know better. The young people should discuss each scenario and decide whether they think it is 'flirting', 'sexual harassment' or neither of these. Once all the cards have been discussed, invite feedback from each group, stopping to discuss any cards where agreement has not been reached.

4. Reflection and review

Finish by considering the following:

- What are the best ways to show someone you find them attractive?

- Where is the line between flirting and sexual harassment?

- How can we make sure our actions are not misunderstood?

- What should happen if a person feels sexually harassed?

Reflect that there is nothing wrong with telling or showing someone you find them attractive, but it is important to look carefully for the messages that demonstrate whether the attention is welcome or not. However, it is important to give clear messages back to people so that they know where they stand.

5. Summary

- Sexual harassment should be reported, especially where the relationship is unequal, for example in the workplace, as it is unacceptable.

- Equally, if someone is making it obvious that they are interested in being more than just friends it is a good idea to be honest if those feelings are not reciprocated.

- Messages sent should be clear both ways and accepted by both people, regardless of if this leaves one person feeling sad, angry or upset.

- Dependent on the young person's age and the nature of the harassment, for example sending genital shots to someone under 16, laws may have been broken and the police could become involved.

ACTIVITY 4.10: FLIRTING OR HARRASSMENT? CARDS

Try to make them laugh.	Ask for their mobile number.
Find reasons to put your arm round them.	Say something nice about how they look.
Whisper the sexual things you would like to try with them in their ear.	Lend them your hoodie if they are cold.
Text them every hour telling them how much you like them.	Try to take photos of bits of their body you admire.
Show interest in the things they like doing.	Text a naked selfie with a cheeky message.
Wink at them.	Make up a nickname about their breasts/genitals.
Give them a high score out of ten in front of your friends.	Tell them your best dirty jokes.
Draw a cartoon of you having sex with them and post it online.	Boast how many sexual partners you have had.
Make disrespectful comments about your ex-partners to impress them.	Press your body close to theirs at every available opportunity.
Keep bumping into them 'accidentally'.	Tell their friend that you are interested.
Invite them to go with you to a party.	Pretend to be upset so they comfort you.
Hang about outside their house so you can watch them.	Smile and start a conversation.
Ask to be friends on social media.	Follow what they are doing, with whom and when on social media.
Smile when you see them.	Check out their relationship status on social media to make sure they are single.

ACTIVITY 4.11: PERSONAL BOUNDARIES

(Years 9–13+)

Aim

- To help participants recognise feelings that the body sends to signal personal boundaries.

Time: 45 minutes

Learning outcome

- To experience reaching personal boundaries and then transfer this learning to discuss ways to be assertive about setting and maintaining them within a personal relationship.

Key vocabulary

- **Personal boundaries**
- **Assertiveness**
- **Sexual consent**

You will need

- Flipchart and markers

How to do it

1. Introduction

- Establish/revisit ground rules (see pages 42–43 for guidance).

Begin by explaining that personal boundaries are made up of beliefs, opinions, attitudes and past experiences, as well as things learnt from family, faith and society. Different people have different boundaries, but the body sends signals when these are being threatened through feelings. This can range from feeling a bit uncomfortable to full on embarrassment or anxiety and it is important to learn what your signals are and then listen and act on them. This includes communicating where your personal boundaries lie within a personal relationship rather than accepting or putting up with something you are not happy with or do not want to do. In a positive relationship the personal boundaries of both partners should be respected and not pushed.

2. Opening activity

Now, ask the young people to call out a list of personal questions and record them onto sheets of A4 paper, placing them face down on the floor once written. These should range from general questions through to more intimate questions but should not involve questions of a sexual nature. Examples could include:

- Do you have a boy/girlfriend?
- Have you ever exaggerated to make yourself sound better?
- Who is your celebrity crush?
- Who do you fancy and what do you find most attractive about that person?
- What is the most embarrassing thing you have ever done?

Ask for a volunteer to step forward and pick up one of the questions. If they are happy to answer it then they should do so. If the young person feels that this is an 'off limits' question, or feels uncomfortable answering, then they should raise a hand to show that a personal boundary has been reached, and without reading it aloud place it back face down on the floor and choose another. Everyone has the right to pass, and young people should be reminded of this as the exercise progresses.

3. Development activity

As the activity progresses, develop it further so that when a question is answered, the rest of the group are encouraged to ask extra questions to find out more. Once again, set the proviso that if a personal boundary is reached they should signal with one hand and the questions must stop.

4. Reflection and review

Once everyone has had the opportunity to ask and answer questions, facilitate a feedback session to review what happened and consider how this might translate in other circumstances.

- How does it feel to reach a personal boundary?

- In real life what pressure might be put on someone to cross a personal boundary? How and why?

- In a personal or sexual relationship, who sets the boundaries?

- How can these be explained to a boy/girlfriend?

- How can you make sure personal boundaries are respected by both partners?

5. Summary

Everyone has personal boundaries which, if threatened or crossed, send signals to the body via thoughts, feelings and ultimately actions, such as running away or getting aggressive. It is important to listen to these internal signals and also to recognise and empathise with those of others. You may have different boundaries but each person's are valuable and should always be respected.

ACTIVITY 4.12: GROUND RULES IN RELATIONSHIPS

(Years 8–13+)

Aim

- To consider the use of ground rules and personal boundaries within a relationship.

Time: 30 minutes

Learning outcome

- To learn that ground rules are a useful tool in relationships.

Key vocabulary

- **Ground rules**
- **Personal boundaries**
- **Consent**

You will need

- Large sheets of coloured paper
- Flipchart paper and pens
- A set of *Profile cards*

How to do it

1. Introduction

- Establish/revisit ground rules (see pages 42–43 for guidance).

Start by asking the young people to consider why there are rules in any society. Are rules a good thing? What would happen if there were none? Would people know how to behave without them, or would the world descend into chaos?

2. Opening activity

Ask the young people to suggest some of the rules that they think affect them. These can be at home, school and work, or in their social life.

Move on to consider the difference between laws for which there is a judicial punishment if you break them, such as stealing, and unwritten laws that people live by within society, for example not jumping a queue. Then ask everyone to turn to the person next to them to discuss any family ground rules they have. These could include things like household chores, discipline or bedtimes. Are these ground rules used in other relationships, for example with friends or a partner? These could include things like calling when you say you will, not being late when you meet up and supporting each other's hopes and dreams.

3. Development activity

Divide the young people into fours and allocate each group one of the *Profile cards*. On it, they will see that the scenario features a couple caught in a relationship dilemma. The group task is to write a set of ground rules to help this couple communicate better and enable them to improve their relationship. Encourage people to think about the positive impact that having rules, or boundaries, could have on the couple but also about any negatives.

For example:

Positives: *each person will know where they stand and should be able to say how they feel without fear of an argument or upsetting their partner.*

Negatives: *things could get worse if they have different personal boundaries and expectations of each other.*

Invite each group to introduce their couple and the dilemma outlines before presenting their relationship boundaries and their discussions about the impact these might have.

4. Reflection and review

Move on to facilitate a discussion that considers:

- How helpful in a relationship would it be to know the boundaries?

- When is the right time in a relationship to discuss personal boundaries and agree some ground rules?

- What should happen if one person persistently breaks the ground rules?

- Can you put 'sanctions' or punishments' in place in a relationship?

5. Summary

Having some basic ground rules in place within a relationship could help each partner understand the boundaries and enable them to talk through disagreements in a more positive way without it becoming an argument or escalating into conflict.

ACTIVITY 4.12: PROFILE CARDS

Ava and Edward

Both Ava and Edward work full time and have lived together for two years. Despite working longer hours, Ava does all of the shopping and most of the household chores. After cooking dinner and doing the washing up, Ava is tired and all she wants to do is have a hot bath and go to bed early.

Edward comes from a very traditional family. At home his mum did all of the cooking and cleaning and seemed proud to do it. Edward's dad calls housework 'women's work' and although he likes cooking, Edward never does it as Ava gets angry when he makes a mess in the kitchen.

Now they seem to argue every night. Edward wants Ava to be the fun girl he first met, rather than going to bed early every night. He fears she simply doesn't fancy him anymore.

Ava feels resentful that Edward doesn't do more around the house – surely he can see she does all the work? She has tried telling him how she feels but it always ends up in an argument – especially when he reminds her of how loving they used to be.

Sam and Alex

Sam and Alex have been together six months and it is the first serious relationship for both of them. Sam came out to his parents ages ago and they are both supportive of him and pleased that he has found someone he cares for.

Alex says he has always known he was gay, but has hidden it from his dad because he is afraid of rejection. He told Sam that his dad holds very old-fashioned views and has been heard making homophobic comments about TV shows featuring gay couples. Because of this he has asked Sam not to make it too obvious that they are together in case someone finds out and tells his dad.

At first Sam was OK with this but now that things are getting serious he sees no reason why he should sneak about. He tells Alex that he is not happy living a lie and wants to tell everyone, regardless of what Alex's father thinks. He has told Alex that if he does not tell his dad about them soon, then he will do so himself. He has already changed his relationship status on social media and has started posting pictures of them as a couple.

Alex is mortified that Sam has gone ahead without his consent. He is not ashamed of Sam and wants them to be together, he just doesn't want his dad to know.

Niles and Divya

Niles and Divya have been married for ten years and have two children. They met at school and have been together ever since. Although they have always been a loving couple, since the birth of their second child Divya has gone off the idea of sex. She still loves her husband but just feels that sex is now not as important.

Niles loves his wife and wishes they could have sex more often. He has taken to watching online porn on his tablet downstairs when Divya has gone to bed, but last night she came down unexpectedly and caught him.

Divya is furious and has told Niles she is disgusted with him. How can he still love her if he is secretly watching porn? It feels as if he has been unfaithful and she is uncertain if she can ever forgive him.

Niles is very upset. He does not think that he has done anything wrong. He would never be unfaithful to his wife and it makes him angry that she could ever think he would be.

Siobhan and Thomas

Siobhan and Thomas have been dating for ages and are in a committed relationship. They love each other but have agreed not to have sex until after they are married in accordance with their religious beliefs. This decision was made together, although Thomas has secretly been feeling increasingly frustrated at not being able to demonstrate his emotions in a physical way.

Thomas has suggested that once they are engaged they take things further, but Siobhan is furious and deeply upset with him for even talking about it. As she sees it, they both have the same faith and follow the religious practices so he should understand why she is so adamant about being a virgin on her wedding day.

Thomas doesn't understand why she is so upset. He agrees they should wait to have penetrative sex until after the wedding, but says there are lots of other things they can do to become intimate, which will bring them closer. It's not as if he's trying to make her have sex.

ACTIVITY 4.13: HOW TO SAY WHAT YOU WANT TO SAY
(Years 8–13+)

Aim

- To build on the previous activity to explore different types of responses to a series of challenging situations.

Time: 45 minutes

Learning outcome

- To practise expressing what learners want to say in a way that is assertive, rather than aggressive or passive.

Key vocabulary

- **Consent**
- **Assertiveness**
- **Positive relationships**
- **Domestic abuse**

You will need

- Copies of the *Just say it worksheet* (photocopied to A3)
- Pens

How to do it

1. Introduction

- Establish/revisit ground rules (see pages 42–43 for guidance).

This is a sensitive topic that could provoke an emotive response or safeguarding disclosures. Ensure that the limits to confidentiality are reinforced and that information about local and national support is available, as well as details of support for the victims or perpetrators of domestic abuse and contact details for the police.

2. Opening activity

Ask and agree examples of passive, assertive and aggressive behaviour. For example:

Passive *behaviour can look like: remaining silent or withdrawn, refusing to say what is wrong or explaining feelings or opinions; going along with things even if you don't really want to do them; not taking responsibility for yourself and/or the things you do.*

Assertive *behaviour can look like: confidently saying what you think or feel, while respecting other people's thoughts and feelings that may be different to your own; listening to what is being said before offering your own opinion; making it clear where your personal boundaries lie.*

Aggressive *behaviour can look like: bullying; ignoring the feelings, wishes or rights of others; disrespecting personal boundaries of others and using physical or emotional strength to try and enforce your will on others. It can lead intrusive body language and/or physical aggression.*

Write these up to refer to later.

3. Development activity

Divide the young people into groups of three and hand each trio a large copy of the *Just say it worksheet* and pens. For each situation one person should respond in an aggressive way, another gives a passive response and the third assertive. These different roles can be rotated so that everyone takes a turn at responding to a difficult situation in each of the three styles. Inform learners that although you will be discussing the effectiveness of the different styles, you will not ask people to repeat what was actually said, which should encourage learners to experiment with tone, words and expression without the pressure of having to perform later.

4. Reflection and review

Invite feedback and then facilitate a discussion that considers:

- Which style is most likely to lead to a challenging situation?

- Which style is most likely to get your voice heard?

- Which style is most likely to lead to feelings of frustration or lack of self-worth?

- Which style is most likely to make the situation worse?

- Which is likely to make you feel best?

- What other options are there if someone is trying to put sexual pressure on you to do or be something you are not happy with?

Conclude that while being assertive does not guarantee that you will get what you want, it is more likely to resolve a situation, get your point across and help you set and maintain personal boundaries. People are also more likely to respect assertiveness and listen to what you say, even if they do not agree. This is true for home, school or work as well as within friendships and personal relationships.

5. Summary

Remind young people that putting sexual pressure on someone else, or using emotional blackmail to get your own way, is wrong, and in some of these examples if that pressure continued it would be illegal.

Suggest that if a young person is worried about themselves or someone else being a victim of relationship bullying they should confide in a trusted adult, such as a teacher, parent or youth worker, or go to a local or national youth support service which can offer confidential information and advice (see contact details on pages 185–186). If someone is worried about their own safety or the risk of immediate harm, or that of someone else, advise them to contact the police.

ACTIVITY 4.13: JUST SAY IT WORKSHEET

1. Your boy/girlfriend has been watching a porn movie and is putting pressure on you to try some of things he/she has seen. What do you say/do?

2. Your boy/girlfriend suggests filming you both having sex saying, 'If you loved me you would...' You don't want to. What do you say/do?

3. You want to have sex, but your partner refuses. He is worried that you will be disappointed by the size of his genitals compared with those seen in porn films. What do you say/do?

4. Your friend is desperate to have the largest breast implants possible because she wants to get into glamour modelling. You think she will regret it. What do you say/do?

5. Your partner keeps asking you to have a threesome with your best friend. When you refuse he tells you that everybody does it and you are just being boring. What do you say/do?

6. Your colleague keeps watching online porn whenever the shop you both work in goes quiet. She keeps asking you to watch too, but you're scared you might get caught. What do you say/do?

7. Your partner has bought a sex toy online and wants to try it out with you. You feel embarrassed and confused. You have only seen pictures before and are not sure you want to go further. What do you say/do?

ACTIVITY 4.14: IDENTIFYING RELATIONSHIP BOUNDARIES

(Years 9–13+)

Aim

- To introduce the idea of personal boundaries within an intimate relationships and the right to set and maintain these.

Time: 60–75 minutes

Learning outcomes

- To understand the importance of knowing and communicating your personal boundaries within a relationship.
- To know that personal boundaries can differ between individuals, but should always be respected.
- To consider that it may be emotionally healthier for a couple to part if they have incompatible personal boundaries and values.

Key vocabulary

- **Communication**
- **Consent**
- **Personal boundaries**
- **Positive relationships**

You will need

- Large sheets of paper
- Coloured marker pens
- Sticky notes
- Pens

How to do it

1. Introduction

- Establish/revisit ground rules (see pages 42–43 for guidance).

Explain that this lesson is going to explore the things we share within a relationship and the things that are kept private, before moving on to discuss personal relationship boundaries and how to maintain them.

Stress that this is appropriate for single people as well as those already in a relationship. Alternatively it could be used to explore what someone wants in a future romantic relationship, even if they are not ready to date yet.

2. Opening activity

Hand each young person a large sheet of paper and provide a good selection of coloured markers.

Task everyone with drawing the outline of a simple house on the paper, large enough to cover most of it, then add four windows and a front door. This house is going to represent their hopes, dreams and aspirations for a positive relationship. This will include their personal boundaries.

Along the bottom of the house, ask each young person to write things about the 'foundations' that their life is built on. This means the things that they believe influence their vision of what a positive relationship looks like and the type of partner they are looking for, for example family, peers, culture or faith.

Once this is done, ask them to write the things they look for in a romantic partner onto the house, for example trust, respect, sexual attraction and shared values. The windows, roof and doors should still be left empty.

Next, in each window ask the young people to write one word that they believe describes a positive skill or quality they have, (which they are happy for others to know about) that they offer a potential partner, for example a sense of humour, honesty, generosity or kindness. In the door they can write a wish or a dream they have for a future relationship, for example true love, marriage, children or commitment. For those already in relationships this can be a shared aspiration or goal, if appropriate.

The roof should now be the only empty space in the house. Explain that even in the closest relationship everyone is entitled to keep a little bit of themselves back and being part of a couple does not mean that you have to share every single thought. Taking a pen, they should use a symbol or symbols to mark personal things they prefer to keep private and are not happy to share with others. Reassure everyone that these will not have to be explained later and can be anything that is personal to the person drawing the house.

Once everyone has completed their house ask the young person to choose a partner and share 'houses'. Make a point of saying that while most of the information on the houses is for discussion, some is not, and this should be respected. Without saying what the roof symbols mean, encourage learners to discuss why some things are private and not for discussion, and introduce the concept of personal boundaries and the individual right to decide where these lie.

3. Development activity

Still in pairs, ask:

- How might personal boundaries be challenged within an intimate relationship?

Allow five minutes for discussion and then invite ideas from each couple. These could include:

- one partner wanting to do something the other is uncomfortable with
- having different values
- wanting different things
- having different expectations of the relationship.

Invite each pair to join another couple, so they are now in small groups of four. Explain that now the young people have explored their own personal boundaries and considered how they might be challenged, you are going to allocate each group a relationship scenario to analyse. Write up the following guidelines for them to work within:

- The couple are having arguments because their personal boundaries are being challenged.
- They care for each other.
- They want to be able to stay together.
- Can this challenge be resolved?

Encourage each group to consider their allocated scenario from both people's point of view, how and why they may feel the way they do, what personal boundaries are being challenged and if a compromise is appropriate or even possible without one partner having to back down and ultimately betray or abandon their stance. Finally, decide if resolution is achievable for this couple, or whether their differing personal values and boundaries mean that for one person to be happy the other has to go against their personal boundaries. If this is so, should they still be together?

Allow up to 20 minutes for discussion time and then invite each group to read out their scenario, summarise their discussions and announce if they think this couple can stay together and be happy.

4. Reflection and review

Suggest that when it comes to relationships couples have to make compromises all the time, for example whose friends to see that night, where to go on a date, where to spend family celebrations like Christmas or even where to live. This will happen throughout the relationship, whether they are together four weeks or 40 years. Learning to compromise can be hard, but is not impossible if both parties want to make the relationship work.

However, everyone has personal boundaries, based on values, beliefs, experience, faith and culture and so on, and sometimes these cannot and should not be compromised. In a positive relationship, no one should feel forced into doing something they are unhappy or unwilling to do, and both partners' boundaries should be respected.

Hand out the sticky notes and pens. Ask each young person to write down one thing they think is non-negotiable in a positive relationship. This could include:

- keeping it exclusive and not seeing other people

- mutual respect

- listening to each other's point of view

- valuing difference

- loyalty.

Once done, stick the notes up to review.

5. Summary

- Everyone has their own personal boundaries based on values, beliefs, experiences and attitude.

- In a healthy relationship these are communicated and respected.

- Some personal boundaries are negotiable but some are not.

- Nobody should ever try to force or coerce, for example by using emotional blackmail, a partner into doing something sexual they are uncomfortable, unhappy or unwilling to do.

- If a couple have widely different personal boundaries and their values conflict in a way that is only resolvable by one person 'giving in' or going against their beliefs, then it is probably healthier to split up.

ACTIVITY 4.14: RELATIONSHIP SCENARIOS

1	One person wants to have penetrative sex, the other does not feel ready yet.
2	One person wants to watch live stream porn together, the other finds the idea disgusting.
3	One person wants to send and receive naked selfies, the other doesn't like the idea.
4	One person likes sending 'sexts', the other finds it really embarrassing.
5	One person wants a proper commitment before sex, the other thinks the sex should come first.
6	One person has a sexual fantasy they'd like to explore, the other thinks it's too funny to be sexy.
7	One person wants to film intimate moments, the other feels disrespected.
8	One person wants to be married before penetrative sex, the other doesn't want to wait.
9	One person wants to buy their partner an adult themed costume, the other feels cheapened by the idea.
10	One person wants to watch an R18 DVD, the other believes that these films exploit women.

ACTIVITY 4.15: SOMEONE TO TRUST

(Years 7–13+)

Aim

- To identify a personal network of people who can offer support, correct information and appropriate advice about sex and relationships, including pornography related concerns.

Time: 25 minutes

Learning outcome

- To understand the importance of having a personal network of trusted people who can provide accurate and appropriate information, advice and guidance on relationship issues.

Key vocabulary

- **Sex and relationships**
- **Trust**
- **Information, advice and guidance**

You will need

- Leaflets and information about local support for young people
- Pieces of business-card size paper or card and pens
- Flipchart paper and markers

How to do it

1. Introduction

- Establish/revisit ground rules (see pages 42–43 for guidance).

2. Opening activity

Start the session by inviting young people to call out qualities and skills that they would look for in someone they would ask for help with a sex and relationships dilemma or problem. Encourage wider thinking than just going to the GUM clinic about an STI or a one-stop-shop to sign up for the C-Card scheme for free condoms. You may want to offer the following examples to help focus thinking:

- Someone is putting pressure on you to do something you are not comfortable doing.
- You receive an unwanted sext or a sexually explicit image.
- You have done something and are worried about the potentially negative consequences for yourself or a friend.
- You have been told a secret and you think it should be shared to prevent harm to someone else.

Record all ideas for qualities and skills onto flipchart paper, for example non-judgemental, safe, honest, confidential, knowledgeable, caring, supportive.

3. Development activity

Suggest that it is important to think in advance of people who we can turn to for support when we need it, rather than waiting for a crisis to occur. Facilitate a short discussion that considers:

- Who are the people you trust most?
- How do you know you can trust them?

Hand out the small pieces of card and ask each young person to reflect on the list of qualities and skills compiled and then note down at least two contact details of people who meet the profile. Alternatively they could design a contact card on their mobile phone or online.

4. Reflection and review

Conclude that we may take different problems to different people, including family, friends, faith or community leaders and professionals such as teachers or youth workers, and that this card is a prompt to remember that we are not alone, and that there is always someone there to help.

5. Summary

- Everyone needs help at some time.
- It is good to identify at least one person you trust for sex and relationships information, advice and guidance.
- There are professionals who can offer advice and information within a confidential relationship. This includes not informing parents, unless the law dictates otherwise.

CHAPTER 5

Sexting, Revenge Porn and Online Sexual Bullying

Digital communication is an exciting, ever-changing platform available 24/7. This chapter offers lessons to raise awareness about risks and identifies ways to stay safe.

ACTIVITY 5.1: PLEASE SHARE

(Years 7–13+)

Aim

- To discuss the ethics of sending, receiving and sharing text and social media messages.

Time: 20 minutes

Learning outcome

- To be aware of the speed with which information can be shared and the personal responsibilities inherent in choosing to forward it.

Key vocabulary

- **Personal responsibility**
- **Privacy**
- **Text**
- **Social media**

You will need

- Access to mobile phones

How to do it

1. Introduction

- Establish/revisit ground rules (see pages 42–43 for guidance).

To begin this activity the facilitator needs to make sure that everyone has access to a mobile phone and has the number of at least one other person in the group. If this isn't possible, divide the group into pairs with access to a phone between them.

2. Opening activity

To demonstrate the speed with which a piece of gossip can rage through a group, ask for a volunteer and take them outside the room, or away from the class. Instruct them to send the following text to at least one person in the main room:

> When you get this don't speak, don't show anyone, just sit down. Please forward.

Allow a few moments for it to send and then go back into the class. Dependent on the signal strength, by the time you return at least one person should have received the text instructions and be seated. As the texts zap around the room and people begin to sit down keep an eye on the time to be able to tell them how quickly this particular piece of information circulated.

As the last person sits down, call time and notify the group how long it took for the first person to receive the message to the last. If anyone does not comply, don't worry as this can be used as a discussion point later. Ask the first and last person to read out the text they received. This should be the same. Point out that now everybody knows your request, regardless of if you told them or not.

3. Development activity

For those who did exactly as the text requested ask them:

- Why did you comply?

  For example, other people were, because the text told you to, because it seemed the right thing to do, etc.

- How did you know that the text was genuine?

  For example, you expected it, it was from someone you trust, etc.

For those who did not comply, ask why they decided not to. Answers here could range from simply not wanting to participate to not being sure if it was a trick of some kind – all of which are relevant to the next part of the discussion.

4. Reflection and review

Ask people to raise their hands if they usually comply with requests to forward text and/or social media messages in real life. Then refer back to the previous questions about how and why and defining authenticity, suggesting that there is a responsibility on a person forwarding any text, social media or email message to ensure that it is from a genuine source and an appropriate request, before deciding to go ahead:

- even if you think it is a joke
- even if the message does not include information or pictures of anyone you know
- even if it contains superstitious threats, for example of good or bad fortune
- even if it sounds official.

If it is a picture or information about someone you know then always check with the subject of the message before forwarding or cutting and pasting something to pass it on. Again, the responsibility is with you, as the sender, to find out before circulating inappropriate material; saying you didn't know is not really a defensible decision in law.

Point out that if you do decide to forward a message then you have a responsibility for whatever happens (or doesn't happen) as a consequence of it, including the distribution of any content that is breaking the law.

5. Summary

- Stop and think before forwarding messages.
- Just because a message tells you to share, you don't have to.
- By forwarding material that is inappropriate, such as porn or intimate pictures, you could be breaking the law.
- This could include being charged with distributing pornography, and if the subject is under 18, child pornography.

ACTIVITY 5.2: SEXTING AND THE LAW

(Years 7–13+)

Aim

- To introduce the concept of 'sexting'.
- To explore the potential legal consequences of making, sending or receiving intimate texts.

Time: 45 minutes

Learning outcomes

- To be clear about what sexting is.
- To better understand the laws that govern the making, sending, receiving and passing on of sexually explicit texts or pornographic images via text.

Key vocabulary

- **Sexting**
- **Explicit texts**
- **Pornography**
- **The law**

You will need

- Flipchart paper and markers
- A5 paper and pens
- A bag or bucket (to collect questions in)
- *Facilitator's 'sexting' information sheet*

How to do it

1. Introduction

- Establish/revisit ground rules (see pages 42–43 for guidance).

2. Opening activity

Start by writing the question below in big type in the middle of a sheet of flipchart paper, inviting young people to call out responses:

What is sexting?

Record ideas around the question on the flipchart paper so that everyone can see, at this stage recording all ideas. Offer this definition, from ChildLine,[1] to see how it fits with those from young people:

Sexting is when someone sends or receives a sexually explicit text, indecent image or video on their mobile phone, usually in a text message.

3. Development activity

Hand out sheets of paper and invite young people to write down any question they have about sexting. This can be about a sexually explicit topic, but remind them to use respectful language

---

1   www.childline.org.uk/explore/onlinesafety/pages/sexting.aspx

where possible and stress that if it is a question about a real-life situation then no names should be used. Dependent on the group, you may want to check this before putting them in the bag or bucket.

Once written, all of the questions can be folded up and collected in a bag or bucket to be shuffled and discussed as a whole group. This provides anonymity for the questioners and will, it is hoped, encourage young people to feel safe enough to be open about the things they want to know. If questions are a bit thin on the ground then consider using some or all of the suggestions below, written onto paper, folded and mixed in.

- Is it illegal to send a sext?
- Is it only young people who send sexts?
- Is it still sexting if you forward an image of a person you don't know?
- What should you do if you receive an unwanted sext?
- How can you report a sext?
- What is considered an indecent image?

Bring the group to sit in a circle and place the bag (or bucket) with the questions in the middle. Pass the bucket around the circle, inviting each person in turn to take out a question and read it to the group. If it is something they are not comfortable reading out, suggest they simply re-fold and return it to the bucket for someone else to draw.

Guided by the facilitator, the whole group can then discuss the questions. There is a facilitator's information sheet provided with this activity. Any questions that cannot be answered should be put to one side to be looked up online later.[2]

4. Reflection and review

Ask:

- What is the difference between sending a love letter and 'sexting'?

Record answers underneath two headings, 'Love letter' and 'Sext' on a whiteboard or flipchart paper so they can be seen and the distinctions clarified. Example answers:

Love letter – about love not sex, personal message outlining feelings and emotions, romantic love, respectful, heartfelt, written to tell someone how much you love them, can be destroyed if the love affair ends.

Sext – picture or words intended to sexually arouse, can be sexually explicit, can be an expression of sexual fantasies, can relate to intimate moments already experienced, not romantic, can be disrespectful, can be illegal dependent on the content and age of the sender/receiver.

Point out that some people keep their love letters, including Valentine cards forever as a romantic reminder of someone they love or loved. Suggest it is unlikely that someone would keep a sext in the same way.

5. Summary

- Do not to send anything that you would not be happy for a parent, carer, or teacher and so on, to see, no matter how much you trust someone.

- Once a message or picture is sent the sender has no control over it.

- It is never OK to put pressure on anyone to send a sext.

- There are laws in place to protect under-18s and keep them safe from harm. This means that the maker, sender and anyone who forwards texts containing indecent content to or from someone under 18 is breaking the law and could be in trouble.

---

2   Useful websites include: www.childline.org.uk, www.thinkuknow.co.uk and www.ceop.police.uk

ACTIVITY 5.2: FACILITATOR'S SEXTING INFORMATION SHEET

This is intended as a basic guide to support questions that may be asked through this activity, based on example questions given.

- Is it illegal to send a sext?

  It is illegal to take, possess or share 'indecent images' of anyone under 18 even with the consent of the person or if the picture is of yourself.

- Is it only young people that send sexts?

  No, but according to research it is particularly prevalent among young people under 19.

- Is it still sexting if you forward an image of a person you don't know?

  Yes, and the same laws could apply to distributing pornography.

- What should you do if you receive an unwanted sext?

  It is not OK for anyone to make someone feel uncomfortable or upset by texts sent. If it is one text, you could delete the picture and contact the person sending it to tell them that it is unwanted and not to send another. You could remind them that sending texts like this could be considered distributing pornography. It is also possible to block the sender. If the sexts become persistent this could be considered as sexual harassment so tell a trusted adult, such as a teacher, guardian or youth worker, or consider reporting it straight to the police.

- How can you report a sext?

  If the sexts are from an adult (i.e. someone over the age of 18) they can be reported directly to the CEOP site.*

- What is considered an indecent image?

  Pictures and images considered indecent include those of naked bodies, a topless female, pictures of genitals or sex acts, including masturbation.

---

*　www.ceop.police.uk/ceop-report

ACTIVITY 5.3: USING SOCIAL MEDIA
(Years 7–13+)

Aim

- To assess knowledge and experience of using social media.

Time: 30 minutes

Learning outcome

- To reach a common understanding of popular forms of social media and begin to discuss potential safety issues.

Key vocabulary

- **Social media**
- **Online safety**
- **Personal responsibility**

You will need

- Paper and a pen for each team

How to do it
1. Introduction

- Establish/revisit ground rules (see pages 42–43 for guidance).

Begin by asking young people to show who has at least one social media profile by a show of hands. Tell them to keep hands raised if they have more than one, two and so on, to see how popular social media is within the group. Conclude that social media is an exciting and fun thing to use.

2. Opening activity
Divide the group into small teams of three or four players and give out paper and pens. Explain that this exercise is a bit like a quiz to test out existing knowledge of social media and how it is used. On the count of three, each team will have three minutes to write down as many forms of social media as they can think of. The team with the most names will win.
This could include:

- Facebook
- Instagram
- Snapchat
- Twitter
- Instant messaging (IM)
- Vine.

Invite each team to count up their scores and congratulate the team with the most. Take ideas off each group, encouraging explanations about any listed that are unknown to others to create a common understanding of how each type of social media can be used and its purpose.

3. Development activity

Ask:

- What is the main purpose of different social media platforms?

  For example, Twitter sets users the challenge of sending and receiving messages, updates and news using only 140 characters each Tweet.

- Who is most likely to use it?

  For example, LinkedIn tends to be used by the business community.

- Is there an age restriction to open an account?

  For example, you have to be over 13 to open a Facebook account.

Next, ask each team to go back to their list and spend a few moments placing a cross by any social media that they think could be used to harass, humiliate, embarrass or target someone. It is likely that all of the suggestions made will be ticked, but remind everyone that this is not because of the social media itself, but how people choose to use it.

Invite each team to then select one type of social media in particular that they think has the most potential to be misused to harm (emotionally, socially or physically) or endanger young people. Set this as a ten-minute task and explain that you will be asking for feedback from each group.

4. Reflection and review

Call time and facilitate group sharing, inviting each group in turn to explain their choice of social media and the reasons why. Explore and discuss concerns before moving on to the next presentation, reminding young people of the need for:

- secure passwords that are not shared
- closing social media accounts when not in use
- using social media security and privacy settings
- reading the small print when downloading apps or accepting updates to see if these have changed as a consequence
- only accepting friendship requests from known people
- only posting information they would be happy to share in the real world.

5. Summary

- There are different social media platforms to choose from, dependent on what you want the main function of your account to be.
- Social media is a great way to share information and keep in touch with the world around you.
- However, despite all of the security and privacy settings designed by social media companies to keep people safe, it is open to misuse. This is down to human behaviour, not the technology.
- It is important to use social media wisely and to be mindful of keeping safe.
- Some misuse of social media, like. bullying and the sending and receiving of intimate and/or pornographic material, is illegal.
- If you are ever worried or unhappy about something on social media, use the support structure to report it, tell a trusted adult and/or contact the police.[3]

Extension

An extension activity for this would be for young people to research further and then design posters to advise their peers how to enjoy social media but keep safe online too.

---

3   To report online concerns go to http://ceop.police.uk/safety-centre

ACTIVITY 5.4: TRUTH OR LIE?

(Years 7-13+)

Aims

- To explore the sensitive issue of telling lies and reinforce the importance of truth and honesty when setting up a social media profile.

- To provoke discussion about the potential consequences of telling the truth or choosing to lie.

Time: 20 minutes

Learning outcome

- To understand the importance of telling the truth, despite any negative consequences, for example being 'told off', to ensure the safety of self and others.

Key vocabulary

- **Social media**
- **Online safety**
- **Honesty**
- **Choice**

You will need

- A copy of the *Truth or lies? worksheet*
- Pens

How to do it

1. Introduction

- Establish/revisit ground rules (see pages 42–43 for guidance).

This activity is shown facilitated as a personal worksheet to be completed prior to wider discussion, but can be easily adapted to a 'feet first' exercise for groups, asking young people to demonstrate their opinions by moving to different points in the room.

2. Opening activity

Start the session with a brief discussion about the difference between telling the truth and lying. Be prepared to explore issues raised, for example adults not telling the truth in the past or times when young people have lied to try and get out of trouble. Ask if anyone has heard the old saying that it is always better to tell the truth, and discuss examples of what has happened when this advice has been followed, both positive and negative.

3. Development activity

Hand out a copy of the worksheet and a pen and ask learners to read through the given scenarios and tick the box that represents their opinion best.

4. Reflection and review

Once everyone has completed the sheet, slowly go through each scenario asking people to show their response by raising a hand where they believe they would tell the truth.

Explore the possible consequences of withholding information and ask them to consider what the positive and negative outcomes might be. For example, a positive outcome of telling a lie may be avoiding any confrontation but a negative outcome could be that someone may be harmed or get into worse difficulties. Similarly, encourage empathy for everyone's feelings in the examples given, including the person who chooses to lie.

Conclude the activity by asking for some examples where the truth is vital to protecting the health and wellbeing of a person or people.

5. Summary

- It is important to tell the truth.

- Choosing to lie could put the health and emotional wellbeing of yourself or others at risk.

Extension

Design a graphic novel-style storyboard to demonstrate the consequences of someone choosing to lie when setting up a social media profile.

ACTIVITY 5.11: TRUTH OR LIE? WORKSHEET

Look at the statements before ticking the box you think is most like you.

	TRUE	MAYBE	UNTRUE
I would tell a lie if I thought it would get me out of trouble.			
I am not always honest with my parent(s)/carer(s) about sites I visit online.			
I tend to exaggerate about how good my love life is on social media.			
If I got caught with porn on my tablet I would probably blame someone else for downloading it.			
I think I am good at telling when someone is being genuine and honest.			
I sometimes lie about my age on my social media profiles.			
If a friend told me a secret I would keep it, no matter what.			
If I got a sext from my boy/girlfriend I would show my friends, even if I had agreed not to.			
If a friend asked me if I had ever searched online for porn I would say yes, even if I hadn't.			
If someone had a photo of an intimate part of my body and shared it without consent, I would tell a trusted adult or professional.			

ACTIVITY 5.5: SOCIAL MEDIA QUIZ

(Years 7–13+)

Aim

- To offer a range of social media dilemmas for young people to consider how they would be likely to react in similar circumstances.

Time: 30–45 minutes (dependent on discussions)

Learning outcomes

- To develop wider awareness of how social media can be misused.
- To learn about the potential consequences of actions and decisions made, both positive and negative.

Key vocabulary

- **Consequences**
- **Social media**
- **Personal responsibility**

You will need

- Copies of the *Social media quiz*
- Pens
- Paper
- A copy of the *Facilitator's guidance notes*[4]

How to do it

1. Introduction

- Establish/revisit ground rules (see pages 42–43 for guidance).

Define social media as websites and applications that enable users to create and share content. Once someone has a profile on their chosen platform, such as Twitter or Facebook, they can participate in social networking. Functions are constantly being updated and created and it is estimated that one billion people use Facebook everyday.[5]

2. Opening activity

Hand each young person a quiz and a pen and ask them to read the scenarios and consider which solution is most like the action they would take. Encourage honesty, explaining that this is a quiz that asks for a personal response rather than ticking the answer they think is right.

Once this has been done, invite them to choose a partner and discuss the results with them, looking for similarities and disparities in their responses.

---

4   Please note: this guidance is correct at the time of publishing but may change over time. It is suggested that facilitators check that it is still current and applicable before using.

5   http://newsroom.fb.com/company-info

3. Development activity

Bring the whole group together and work through the quiz, asking for feedback and any additional points that they have discussed in their pairs. Use the facilitator's guidance sheet to ensure that issues for each scenario have been discussed, and to discuss potential consequences of different actions.

Make sure young people are aware of the security settings and online reporting systems in place on social media sites.

4. Reflection and review

Back in pairs again, ask each couple to choose one of the quiz questions to focus on. The task is to identify different courses of action that are likely to:

- lead to the most positive outcome

- lead to the most negative outcome.

This can be recorded on paper to share with the whole group after ten minutes' discussion time.

5. Summary

- Using social media is fun but it is important to stay safe and make healthy choices. It is your personal responsibility to make sure that you only access things you are legally allowed to.

- To do this make sure you use the security settings and safety guidelines offered by the social media site you choose.

- All social media sites have a reporting system so that inappropriate content, hate crime and sexualised messages can be reported; use them.

- Filter messages and block anyone sending anything that makes you feel uncomfortable or that you know to be wrong.

- For more guidance about how to report online concerns go to the CEOP website.[6]

---

6   http://ceop.police.uk/safety-centre

ACTIVITY 5.5: SOCIAL MEDIA QUIZ

Please look at the scenarios below and circle the answer that best expresses what you think you would do.

1. You are setting up a new social media profile. Do you:
   a) Use your real name and a nice photo.
   b) Use your real name and a sexy selfie.
   c) Use a fake ID and a fake photo.
   d) Make up an online name but use a real photo.

2. You receive abusive messages from someone you consider a friend. Do you:
   a) Start sending abusive messages back – they asked for it.
   b) Ignore the messages.
   c) Tell someone you trust.
   d) Report them to the website.

3. You receive a photo attachment with the message line 'you should see this' from a friend. Do you:
   a) Open it – it looks interesting.
   b) Delete it immediately – you didn't ask them to send it.
   c) Message back to ask what it is.
   d) Open it and then forward the content to everyone you know.

4. You are chatting with someone new that you really like. They suggest using a different app so you can see each other while you talk. Do you:
   a) Decide it would be fun! Why not?
   b) Immediately block them – you have been warned about the dangers of this.
   c) Suggest you both take and send a selfie instead.
   d) Give them your mobile number so you can see each other that way.

5. You are on a dating app and flirting with someone whose picture looks hot. Do you:
   a) Suggest you meet up – there is no way you are giving up the opportunity of being with someone this good looking!
   b) Ask if they want to meet up with you in a public place – safety first.
   c) Not want to meet them – you don't know them.
   d) This would never happen, as you would never trust anyone on a dating app.

6. You get sexually abusive messages from an ex-partner. Do you:
   a) Delete the messages immediately and forget it.
   b) Panic – you don't want your parents to know you are sexually active.
   c) Try and speak to your ex and explain how upset you are.
   d) Speak to a youth worker or teacher and ask for advice.

7. You are missing your partner so decide to send a sexy selfie to show how much you like them. Do you:

   a) Regret it immediately, how could you have been so stupid?

   b) Feel pleased, you are sure your partner is going to like it.

   c) Send a text asking them to delete it.

   d) Not worry, you love and trust this person and plan to be together forever.

8. A friend confides that she and her partner have made a sex tape. Do you:

   a) Feel jealous that she has such a great relationship.

   b) Ask to see it.

   c) Feel worried about the potential consequences if anyone else sees the film.

   d) Not worry – lots of celebrities have done similar things and it hasn't harmed their career.

9. You see an intimate photo of a friend posted on social media. Do you:

   a) Think 'how stupid' for allowing the photo to be taken and do nothing.

   b) Laugh and click 'Like'.

   c) Phone your friend immediately to offer your support – they may not know.

   d) Feel embarrassed that you have seen something that is obviously private and avoid your friend.

10. You break up and your ex threatens to post naked pictures of you online if you don't get back together. Do you:

    a) Get back together – you believe their threat.

    b) Report the threat to the police – this is harassment.

    c) Respond with counter threats – this means war.

    d) Tell your ex that if they carry out the threat they will be breaking the law by posting pornographic images online.

11. You get tagged wearing swimwear and receive lots of negative comments about how you look. Do you:

    a) Feel ashamed of your body and retreat to your bedroom.

    b) Contact the person who posted the picture on social media and ask them to take it down.

    c) Feel really angry and start posting insults in retaliation.

    d) Close your social media account.

12. For a laugh you and a friend searched for porn online on your family computer. Now, cookies and explicit images keep popping up causing questions to be asked. Do you:

    a) Own up and confess all – you are sure they will understand.

    b) Keep quiet – they are making a fuss about nothing.

    c) Try and blame someone else so they get into trouble.

    d) Demand your own tablet so you can have the privacy to look at anything you choose.

ACTIVITY 5.5: FACILITATOR'S GUIDANCE NOTES

Please note this sheet is intended as guidance only and should *not* be taken as legal advice.

1. **You are setting up a new social media profile.**

   Use your real name and a nice photo. Obviously everyone wants to look their best, but it is not a good idea to use sexual images on social media. Additionally to stay safe do not give private details that you would not share with a stranger in the real world. Always use the security and privacy settings to ensure that you know who can see your profile and don't accept friendship requests from unknown people.

2. **You receive abusive messages from someone you consider a friend.**

   Do not respond by sending abusive messages back. Keep a record of the messages, for example by taking a screenshot or printing them, and consider showing someone you trust. If it continues, block the sender and report the incidents to the social media site. They will take it seriously. If messages become threatening then inform the police.

3. **You receive a photo attachment with the message 'you should see this'.**

   Never open attachments from unknown people as these may contain inappropriate images, spyware or a virus. If you open a pornographic image and then forward it to others you may be breaking laws that cover the distribution of porn and you could end up in trouble yourself.

4. **Using an app so you can see each other while you talk.**

   To keep safe it is best not to give out personal details or agree to use web or phone cams until you are absolutely certain who you are speaking to. If someone seems too good to be true, doesn't know any of your friends or family and you don't know how to find out more, then you should ask yourself why they have contacted you. If you have no answers, then it is best to steer clear.

5. **Using dating apps.**

   Most dating apps are for aged 18+, so if you are not old enough to have a profile, you shouldn't be using them. Dating sites are all about people eventually meeting in the real world, so if you are old enough and do choose to set up a profile, then make sure you adhere to all of the safety guidelines given on the site. Be careful about how much personal information your share and never post intimate photos. If someone sends you inappropriate pictures or makes you feel uncomfortable in any way, report them to the site. Do not meet up until you feel you have enough information to make an informed choice and always meet in a public place the first time. It is also a good idea to tell someone where you are going and who you are meeting.

6. **You get sent sexually abusive messages from an ex-partner.**

   If you think it will help then it may be worth trying to speak to the person who is sending the messages to talk about it. However, if this is unlikely to have a successful outcome then keep records of the messages and speak to a trusted adult to tell them what is happening. Dependent on your age they may not have to inform your parents, but should be able to offer you advice and support about what to do next.

7. **You are missing your partner so decide to send a sexy selfie to show how much you like them.**

If you are under 18 never be tempted to make or send intimate photos, no matter how much you feel for someone. If you have already done it then do try asking for it to be deleted, but it is impossible to know for certain that they have not kept a copy or taken a screenshot. Dependent on the type of picture taken, laws may have been broken too, meaning both you and your partner (if under 18 too) may be charged with indecency or even child pornography. If you are over 18, not sending explicit pictures is still the safest option. Remember, once a picture is out there it is impossible to take back.

8. **A friend confides that she and her partner have made a sex tape.**

As in the example above it is best never to make a sex tape, no matter how much you love and trust your partner. Although it may not seem to have harmed the careers of people like Kim Kardashian, most people would be horrified to think that something so intimate has been seen and shared by thousands of people, which can easily happen if a film goes viral. If either partner is underage, laws have been broken and even if they are both over the age of consent, laws about distributing pornography may be infringed if this tape is shown to others.

9. **You see an intimate photo of a friend posted on social media.**

A supportive friend is probably just what this person needs at the moment, especially if an image has been posted without their consent or knowledge. Ask for the help and advice of a trusted adult and contact the social media site to request that the picture is taken down.

10. **You break up with someone and they threaten to post naked pictures of you online if you don't get back together.**

This is a form of emotional bullying and blackmail, which should not be given in to. Any relationship based on fear of exposure is not going to work and this should be made clear. If the harassment continues then consider contacting the police as the law protects elements of this situation.

11. **You get tagged in a holiday picture wearing swimwear and receive lots of negative comments about how you look.**

Unkind comments both online and in the real world can be devastating and lead to victims feeling hurt, angry or both. It is easy to forget that online pictures are of real people and comments can snowball quickly without any real malicious intent behind the actions. Use approval options on social media before accepting tagged photos and think hard about how photos may be perceived by others. If you don't like a photo it is perfectly acceptable to ask the person who posted it to take it down.

12. **Cookies* and explicit images on a family computer.**

In a situation like this it is probably best to be honest and own up, rather than letting someone else take the blame. It is worth reminding people that any site accessed online will leave a 'digital footprint', so even if you clear the history it is possible to trace what you have been looking at, where and when.

---

*   Cookies are usually small text files, given ID tags that are stored on your computer's browser directory or program data subfolders. www.allaboutcookies.org/cookies

ACTIVITY 5.6: SHARE/NOT SHARE

(Years 7–13+)

Aims

- To discuss the potential consequences of posting personal information on an open forum.
- To consider who to share information with and how to enjoy social media but stay safe.
- To consider some of the risks of sharing or posting personal information

Time: 45 minutes

Learning outcomes

- To recognise the importance of taking time to decide how and where to share information before posting in an open forum.
- To realise that by openly sharing information on social media/online you relinquish control over who sees it.
- To be aware that there is a minority of people who use the anonymity of social media or online apps to target victims for their own purposes.

Key vocabulary

- **Personal information**
- **Privacy**
- **Social media**
- **Online apps**

You will need

- *Share/Not share cards* (cut up)
- Pens
- Paper

How to do it

1. Introduction

- Establish/revisit ground rules (see pages 42–43 for guidance).

Start by defining social media that can be used to communicate person to person, for example texts, emails, WhatsApp, etc., and those that relay information in a group forum, such as Instagram, Snapchat and Facebook.

2. Opening activity

Divide the class into small groups and hand each group a set of cards. Their task is to discuss the scenario on the card and decide if they would share this information using a one-to-one communication method or in a group forum. Alternatively, they may decide that it is not safe to share it anywhere or that it is something so concerning that they would report it.

Once all of the cards have been placed, invite group feedback and discuss any issues raised, especially for any cards deemed unsafe to share or that need reporting. Reinforce the message that if anyone is ever worried they should tell a trusted adult and get advice. Concerns about online content, forwarding messages with a sexual content or revenge porn should be reported to the police.[7]

Conclude that social media and texts are a great way to communicate quickly, but time should be spent deciding who you want to see it before choosing which platform to use. None is 100 per cent confidential and information can always be forwarded or uploaded, meaning that all control is lost over distribution.

3. Development activity

To demonstrate this visually, hand each person one of the cards from the set. They should read and then initial the paper before folding it up so that what is on it is no longer visible from the outside. This information now 'belongs' to them.

Ask everyone to stand up, shake the hand of the person standing next to them and then literally 'forward' the note they are holding by passing it on, and collecting a new one. The receiver of the note should open it away from the person they collected it from, read it quickly and then tick it to show that they have seen the information inside. Keep directing the group to repeat this until everyone has shaken hands with everyone else at least once (twice with a group of eight or less).

Finally, ask everyone to return the note they are holding to its owner who should then open it. As the young people read the number of anonymous ticks they have, announce that one of the people to have shaken hands (i.e. received and forwarded information) is a sexual predator. This person spends time searching and saving intimate and provocative images, often from social media, to share with a community of like-minded people.

Also among the group is a scammer who is willing to spend time romantically grooming young women, particularly lonely single mums, to get enough personal details to fraudulently borrow money and set up bogus accounts. This person uses a fake profile on social media and dating apps to build a relationship.

Finally, tell them that among them is a jealous ex-lover determined on revenge who is searching social media to find out where the ex and new partner go. The plan is to stalk the new relationship and then confront them in public for a show down.

Conclude that they will never discover who these people are, but should know that they have read their information. Encourage young people to share their initial responses and invite discussion about how it feels to know this. Ask:

- If you had known that predators, fraudsters and those with a grudge (as in the information given) were going to see your information, what could you have done to prevent it?

Make the point that unfortunately, just as you can't always tell if someone has harmful/illegal intent in the real world, it can be even harder (if not impossible) when using digital media. Point out that people are not vetted for things like a criminal record when they sign up for a social media account, or asked what they plan to do. Discuss security settings and the laws that protect against some of these issues and remind young people about telling a trusted adult or the police if they are worried or concerned.

4. Reflection and review

With this information, ask young people in the context of the scenario they were given on the note:

- How does it feel to know that lots of people have seen your information or pictures?

  This is not always done maliciously or to cause trouble, for example uploading photos onto Facebook and tagging the people in them. Ask for other examples to reinforce understanding.

- If you choose to put pictures and information into the public domain, do you have the right to say who can and can't see it?

  Point out that if you use your security settings properly on social media you can do exactly that.

---

7   Go to http://ceop.police.uk/safety-centre for more information and guidance.

5. Summary

- No matter how much you trust someone always think very carefully before sharing something you might later regret.

- Once posted on social media, private details can be quickly made public with no way of knowing who has seen it.

- Be sure to use all of the privacy and security settings available on your social media account(s).

- If something has got out of hand or you are worried tell a trusted adult or report it. Go to the CEOP website for more details.[8]

---

8   http://ceop.police.uk/safety-centre

ACTIVITY 5.6: SHARE/NOT SHARE CARDS

This is sexual gossip about a couple, you don't like. You are not sure if the information is true, but it is too funny not to share!	This is a romantic picture of you and your new partner having a picnic.
This is a selfie of you trying on a new bra – you are pretty pleased with how it looks. Better than a boob job!	This is a conversation between you and a friend where you confess to having a major crush on someone you both know.
This is a short video clip that you secretly filmed of your ex in the bath. Hot!	This is a conversation where you are repeating something that was told to you by a mutual friend in strictest confidence.
This is a message you are sending to tell your partner your relationship is over.	This is a tagged picture of you and some friends sunbathing topless by the swimming pool on holiday.
Your friend is gay but hasn't yet come out, apart from to a few close friends. This is you passing the confidential information on as gossip to someone else.	This is you sending a sexy message to your hot date.
Your partner has a changed social media status, 'Single', but hasn't spoken to you yet.	This is you boasting to your friends about your sexual conquests.
This is you confiding to a friend that you think you might be pregnant, but want to keep it secret.	This is you confiding in a friend that you are unhappy in your relationship.
This is a love poem sent to you by your partner.	This is you telling your friend how lonely you are since your parents split.
This is an intimate picture of you taken to show your partner.	This is a selfie of your naked biceps and chest – you are proud of all that gym work paying off.

ACTIVITY 5.7: PHOTO STORIES

(Years 8–13+)

Aim

- To create magazine-style photo stories about social media and sexting dilemmas.

Time: 45 minutes

Learning outcomes

- To consider different responses to risky situations.
- To understand the potential personal, social and legal consequences of misusing different social media.

Key vocabulary

- **Social media**
- **Sexting**
- **Decision-making**
- **Consequences**
- **Keeping safe**

You will need

- An A2 sheet of card or stiff paper for each group
- Paper and marker pens
- Digital cameras or phones and printers
- Glue and scissors
- Example magazine photo stories (printed or copied)
- *Photo story cards*

How to do it

Photo consent will need to be obtained for this activity. It is also important that boundaries are maintained during the making and taking of photos to ensure that no intimate or sexually provocative pictures are included.

To prepare go online to find magazines that contain traditional teen photo stories made up of a series of photos with speech bubbles. These will be used as examples so it doesn't matter if they are vintage.

1. Introduction

- Establish/revisit ground rules (see pages 42–43 for guidance).

Introduce the concept of photo stories, explaining that traditionally they tend to be in magazines designed for young women and are about love and romance. Point out that although this is the usual topic they are not dissimilar to graphic novels so the same method can be used to tell a story about anything.

Explain that in this lesson they are going to be the stars of their own photo stories.

2. Opening activity

Divide the young people into groups and hand each group a *Photo story card*, paper and markers. They should then spend time devising a storyline in ten frames, including characters, and plan this on to the paper using a storyboard.

Once they have decided what is going to happen they can start posing and making up sets before taking photos to illustrate their story.

Print out the photos and then the young people can add speech and thought bubbles. These can then be stuck onto the card in a series of frames to make a picture story.

3. Development activity

Invite each group to present their photo story, asking them to explain the choices made and why, promoting discussion afterwards.

4. Reflection and review

Call out the following statistics about sex, the internet and social media, asking the class to raise one hand if they think they are true, and to keep their hand down if they think it is false:[9]

1. Sixty-five per cent of British homes (16 million households) have internet access and 25 per cent of all five-year-olds have their own computer – True (and many children have online access without adult supervision, meaning that they make their own decisions about what the see and share).

2. A Channel 4 national sex survey revealed that 20 per cent of teens regularly watch porn – False (40 per cent admitted to regularly watching porn).

3. Seventy-five per cent of men who have come out as gay or bisexual have told a best friend or online friend first – True (and they expected the person they told to keep it confidential).

5. Summary

- Social media and access to the internet means that people can communicate and share information faster and more easily than ever before.

- However, this can mean that people can do things on the spur of the moment without thinking through the potential consequences.

- The likelihood of making risky choices increases if you have been drinking alcohol.

- Some things are very risky, such as taking and sharing naked or inappropriate pictures, sharing private information and watching online content that is illegal.

- Some poor choices will impact on personal relationships and emotional wellbeing.

- Therefore it is really important to understand the risks involved in hasty decisions and to think through the potential consequences in advance.

- That way, when a quick decision is required you are more likely to make a healthy, happy one.

Extension

Display the boards so that other young people can learn from them, and consider extending into a wider peer education campaign.

---

9   The answers for this quick quiz are taken from information on www.channel4.com/sexperienceuk

ACTIVITY 5.7: PHOTO STORY CARDS

Story 1	Ayesha is invited to a party she really wants to go to. She is busy getting ready to meet her boyfriend and has drunk some alcohol to relax her and get her in the mood for a good night. As she gets out of the shower she receives a text. It's from her boyfriend asking what she is doing. Ayesha giggles and picks up her phone – perhaps she should send him a selfie to show him?

Story 2	Angus has fallen out with his boyfriend George because George seems to spend more time posting updates and pictures online than he does investing in their relationship. Angus accuses George of being selfish and always putting himself first, while ignoring anything Angus might want to do. George says he doesn't want to split up but he doesn't intend to stop using social media. How can Angus show him that there is more to life than posting what you had for breakfast on Facebook?

Story 3	Donna has been sexting her boyfriend during lessons at school. She knows she should stop, especially as some of the messages are sexually explicit, but this is half the fun – telling him her fantasies while her teacher drones on about boring history. Now Donna has been caught and has had her phone confiscated. Her parents are not pleased about the phone and want to know why – how can she tell them without admitting what she has done?

Story 4	Saul has been streaming free porn to his tablet for the last few weeks. He likes the fact he can watch whatever he likes, whenever he likes, without anyone knowing. He has downloaded some of his favourite films and converted them to MP4 so he can share them with friends, for a small fee. The problem is that his mum has asked to borrow the tablet as her laptop has broken. How can he help his mum out but not have the embarrassment of having to explain his porn habit?

ACTIVITY 5.8: TAKING RISKS

(Years 8–13+)

Aim

- To explore the potential harm to self and others of risk taking behaviour in different online and social media situations.

Time: 30 minutes

Learning outcomes

- To consider that although risk taking can be exciting and fun there can be serious consequences that make it not worth it.

- To understand that some risk taking behaviour breaks the law.

- To recognise the importance of learning to assess potential short- and longer-term consequences before making a decision to go ahead.

Key vocabulary

- **Risky behaviour**

- **Social media**

- **Potential consequences**

- **Online safety**

You will need:

- A set of *Taking risk cards*

- Two A4 sheets entitled 'Very risky' and 'Not very risky'

How to do it

1. Introduction

- Establish/revisit ground rules (see pages 42–43 for guidance).

Explain that you are going to consider the levels of risk and potential consequences of a series of online and social media scenarios, some of which have malicious intent, i.e. they intend to harm, upset or humiliate someone else. Other risky situations include those affected by alcohol and those that started out as someone's idea of a joke.

2. Opening activity

Seat everyone in a circle and hand each person a risk card. Place one of the A4 sheets on the floor to one side of the circle and the other on the opposite side to create two poles. All of the cards will be placed between these poles by the end of the exercise.

Invite people to read aloud what is on their allocated risk card and then place it between the two poles to show how risky (or not) they consider the activity. Encourage participants to explain their decision, at this stage without allowing comments or challenge from the rest of the class.

3. Development activity

Go around the circle until all the cards have been placed and then ask if anyone wants to move any of the cards. Make sure that the concept of short- and long-term consequences is explained.

For example, being caught watching porn on the family laptop is likely to have an immediate consequence, but the risks in allowing a partner to take intimate photos increase dramatically if you later break up and the pictures are shared online.

Using this new definition ask the class to re-sort the cards into high, medium and low risk activities. For each ask:

- What are the risks?

- What are the potential consequences?

4. Reflection and review

Facilitate a discussion that considers:

- What factors might encourage someone to take these risks?

    For example, peer pressure, encouragement or pressure from a partner, the promise of excitement, thinking it is funny, having judgements influenced by alcohol or drugs, etc.

- What factors might prevent them?

    For example, thinking the consequences through, only making decisions when sober, education, empathy, having a positive relationship with your partner, etc.

5. Summary

- Before deciding to post or upload something that could be considered inappropriate consider the potential consequences.

- Some risks result in the law being broken and could lead to a criminal record.

- Some risks can have serious, long-term consequences.

- Things can quickly spiral out of control so if you are worried about any activity like those shown in the scenarios get advice from a trusted adult sooner, rather than later.

ACTIVITY 5.8: TAKING RISKS CARDS

Texting your partner your sexual fantasies.	Downloading an R18 porn film.	Typing 'porn' into your search engine to see what happens.
Lying about your age to set up a social media account.	Accepting a Facebook request from someone you don't know.	Using an air-brushed photo as your profile picture.
Using an older friend's ID to download an 18-rated video game.	Uploading a love poem to your partner on social media.	Breaking up a relationship by text.
Using an adult's credit card to buy sex toys online as a joke.	Creating a website and uploading Photoshopped porn pictures of your ex.	Uploading homemade porn on YouTube.
Agreeing to meet someone you met online.	Uploading a semi-nude selfie on Instagram.	Asking someone you fancy to send you a nude selfie on Snapchat.
Posting sexy selfies on your social media wall.	Following your favourite celeb on Twitter.	Threatening to share intimate pictures if your partner ends the relationship.
Getting drunk and texting an ex how much you love them.	Stalking your ex on social media to see where they are and who they are with.	Sharing porn via Bluetooth at school.
Using social media to ask someone out.	Secretly filming your partner during sex and keeping it on your phone to watch alone.	Taking naked selfies and keeping them on your phone.

ACTIVITY 5.9: SOCIAL MEDIA PROFILE REVIEW

(Years 7–13+)

Aim

- To raise awareness about the importance of reviewing social media profiles before uploading them.

Time: 30 minutes

Learning outcome

- To be aware of how online self-image can differ from the messages received by others within the context of social media vs. real life.

Key vocabulary

- **Social media profile**
- **Online safety**
- **Consequences**
- **Personal responsibility**

You will need

- Online access to social media
- Sticky notes
- Pens and markers
- Flipchart paper
- A4 paper

How to do it

1. Introduction

- Establish/revisit ground rules (see pages 42–43 for guidance).

Begin by asking young people if they have a social media account. Encourage them to call out names of different accounts they hold, such as Facebook and Twitter, and record these without discussing on a large sheet of paper.

Conclude that social media is popular with nearly everyone and that people often have more than one account. Facebook is now mainstream, with half of the UK population having an account; 15 million people have a Twitter account. Also popular are Pinterest and Instagram, and these platforms are enhanced with messaging apps such as Snapchat and WhatsApp – particularly popular with those aged 13–20.[10]

2. Opening activity

Ask young people to work in small groups to consider the following:

- What is the point of having a social media account?
- Have you ever exaggerated on social media to make yourself sound just a bit more interesting?

---

10   www.rosemcgrory.co.uk/2015/01/06/uk-social-media-statistics-for-2015

- Have you ever posted pictures that you think make you look attractive to potential love interests?

- Have you ever had to confess to lying online?

Invite feedback from each group and suggest that by setting up a social media profile you are potentially inviting lots of people to look at your words or pictures and judge them. This is why it is so important that the message received is the one you want to give.

3. Development activity

Hand everyone a sheet of A4 paper, pens and a wad of sticky notes. Ask each person to think about the words they would like people to use to describe them after seeing their profile. These should be written, one word per sticky note, and then stuck on named A4 paper.

Next, with the young people working in pairs, tell everyone to go online and open their social media profiles for their partner to see. Hand out another stack of sticky notes and a clean sheet of paper, this time asking participants to write the name of their partner at the top. In turns, each partner now has to review the other person's profile and write down ten words to describe what they see. This should include first impressions as well as information obtained through pictures, profiles and posts.

At the end of the exercise each person should have two sheets of paper, each filled with sticky notes. Invite them to compare both sheets to see if the way they see themselves matches with the way their partner saw them based on their social media profile. Ask:

- How similar are the words used to describe you on both sheets?

- Does your profile portray you in the way you want to be seen?

- What assumptions might be drawn from the pictures and information on your social media profile?

- What, if anything, needs to change to narrow that gap?

4. Reflection and review

Suggest that everyone goes back to their online profile and spends some time reflecting on the exercise before considering what needs to be done to improve it.

Remind young people that a social media profile might be the first thing that someone sees, including potential employers, friends and dates, so the way it is presented is their personal responsibility.

5. Summary

- Your social media profile should reflect the best version of you.

- Pictures and information can remain online for many years so don't put anything on there that might embarrass or hold you back at a later date.

- Never upload intimate pictures as they can be shared and used in unauthorised ways.

ACTIVITY 5.10: ONLINE DATING

(Years 10–13+)

Aims

- To consider the pros and cons of online dating.
- To discuss the risks of meeting a potential partner online and how to stay safe both online and in the real world.

Time: 30–45 minutes

Learning outcomes

- To consider why people might choose to sign up to an online dating site or download a dating app.
- To know how to stay safe when internet dating and meeting up outside the confines of cyberworld.

Key vocabulary

- **Positive relationships**
- **Online dating**
- **Consequences**
- **Staying safe**

You will need

- Large sheets of paper and pens
- A copy of the *Facilitator's guide to online dating*

How to do it

1. Introduction

- Establish/revisit ground rules (see pages 42–43 for guidance).

Start by asking young people to call out the names of internet dating sites and any information or preconceptions they have about them. This could include popular apps like Tinder as well as heavily advertised sites like Match.com and eHarmony.

Conclude that online dating is a popular way to meet potential partners.

2. Opening activity

Without asking who has or hasn't looked at these sites (or used them) invite discussion by asking:

Is online dating the 21st-century way to find true love?

Point out:

- Most online dating sites and apps are for over-18s only, so nobody under that age should be signing up.
- Online dating doesn't work for everyone and there are hundreds of reasons why things don't work out, the same as in the real world.

- The idea isn't to get as many people as possible interested, but to find one person that you connect with and would like to get to know better. For some people this takes just one date, for others hundreds.

Move on to ask: What are the risks of online dating?

Invite young people to call out ideas and record for use with the development activity next. Risks identified could include:

- Your date not looking anything like their profile photo.

- People lying about their age, for example their profile says they are 18 but in reality they are much older.

- Being stood up.

- Having nothing in common to talk about.

- Your date having sexual expectations that you have no intention of meeting.

- Your date pretending to be single when they are not.

- Meeting someone who is not who they say they are.

- Meeting someone who is potentially dangerous or a threat to your safety and wellbeing.

3. Development activity

Divide the young people into small groups and tell them that they are now going to write a list of ten 'rules' to advise those looking for love online how to date safely. These should be designed as a poster to be publicly displayed to raise awareness.

The *Facilitator's guide to online dating* has ten suggested rules on it.

Once done, invite each group to present their poster and then facilitate a quick class poll to decide the one that raises awareness most effectively.

4. Reflection and review

Research by online dating site eHarmony.co.uk anticipates that by the year 2031 'it'll be more likely that you'll meet a partner online than offline – in fact, just over half of relationships will have started on the web'.[11]

Invite each young person to suggest one positive reason for choosing to date online, and one reason for caution.

5. Summary

- Online dating gives you the opportunity to meet someone completely new.

- Most dating sites and apps are for people aged 18+.

- Not everyone who claims to be looking for love online is truthful.

- It is essential to keep important information private and never to send or receive intimate photos.

- If someone does send inappropriate or pornographic material, report them both to the site and the police.

Extension

Consider developing the posters into a wider online dating safety awareness campaign.

---

11   www.eharmony.co.uk/dating-advice/online-dating-unplugged/over-50-of-couples-will-meet-online-by-2031#

ACTIVITY 5.10: FACILITATOR'S GUIDE TO ONLINE DATING

Rule 1: Do your research.
Check out the different online sites and dating apps to see which one is best for you. Make sure it is appropriate for your age group. Have a look at online reviews to hear about other people's experiences and don't part with any money unless you know that you really want to invest in this.

Rule 2: Be prepared.
Choose a nice photo that actually looks like you, and write an honest profile (ask a trusted friend to check it).

Rule 3: Don't take everything at face value.
Accept that not everyone is going to be truthful. While this is true in the real world too, the difference is that it can be harder to tell online about things like age, physical appearance and relationship status.

Rule 4: Don't give out private information.
Do not give out private information, such as your bank account, online passwords or National Insurance number. Be wary of questions about your date of birth, mother's maiden name and where you were born. By giving information like this you could become the victim of online fraud.

Rule 5: Do not send or accept intimate photos.
Someone who is interested in a genuine relationship will not ask you to send pornographic pictures. If you are sent intimate photos stop all communication and report it to the dating site and/or the police.

Rule 6: Find out more.
Before meeting, get your date's full name. Many people use a profile or user name online and this may not be the same as their real world name. To find out more you could google your date's name, have a look at their Facebook page and any other social networking profiles, such as Twitter or Instagram.

Rule 7: Don't give out your address.
Do NOT let someone you have just met – online or otherwise – come to your home. Remember, no matter how many times you have talked to this person online, you don't know them.

Rule 8: Meet somewhere you know and feel comfortable.
Choose somewhere you know and feel comfortable for your first date.

Rule 9: Tell a friend where you are going.
Always tell a friend or family member where you are going. You could even agree a text or call if things are not going well to give you an excuse to leave. Listen to your instincts - if something doesn't feel right or you are not enjoying the date simply say goodbye and leave.

Rule 10: Have fun, but remember these 'rules' to stay safe.

ACTIVITY 5.11: BLAME AND EXCUSES
(Years 9–13+)

Aim

- For young people to experience and challenge a range of excuses that someone might make after forwarding something inappropriate and personal.

Time: 30–45 minutes

Learning outcomes

- To better understand the concepts of blame and broken trust within a relationship.
- To know how to respond assertively to a series of excuses.

Key vocabulary

- **Social media**
- **Personal responsibility**
- **Keeping safe**
- **Trust**

You will need

- Chairs for each participant, set out in two circles one inside the other, facing each other
- A set of *Blame and excuse cards*

How to do it

Set up two circles of chairs, facing each other, one inside the other, for the number of people taking part. If you have a group larger than 12 young people set up two circles.

1. Introduction

- Establish/revisit ground rules (see pages 42–43 for guidance).

2. Opening activity

Invite the young people to choose a partner to start the exercise and then sit opposite each other in the two circles. For the first part of this exercise those on the inside will each be given one of the first six *Blame and excuse cards*. Those seated on the outside will for this round be the person owed an explanation from the person sitting opposite who has broken their trust.

Read out the first scenario and allow a minute for the people on the outside to think about how they might feel if they were in this position, and those on the outside to think about their answers, prompted by the *Blame and excuse card* they have been given.

Then ask the person sitting on the inside of the circle to speak to the person opposite them, giving their opening blame or excuse from the card. They will have two minutes, speaking and listening, as both parties role-play what they think should happen next.

Call time and then ask each person in the outside circle to move one seat to the left, so they face a new partner and a new excuse. Repeat, until each excuse or blame has been heard and responded to and everyone has returned to their original seat.

3. Development activity

Review what has been said and heard using the following prompt questions as a guide:

- Was the situation resolved?

- How did it feel to hear the reasons given for breaking trust?

- What might be the reasons behind someone making these excuses or seeking to place blame in this way?

- What could be done to make this situation better?

For the next round, the people in the outside circle will be making the excuses or laying blame, so hand them one of the remaining six cards each. Those on the inside will be responding to scenario two.

Read the scenario out and then repeat the process. Keep rotating partners until all of the excuses have been discussed and participants returned to their original chairs.

Call time and review again, this time using these prompt questions:

- Who is most at fault in this situation?

- How easy is it to take responsibility for something you have done, on both sides?

- How might it feel to be in this situation?

- What would you advise a good friend if this happened to them?

4. Reflection and review

Reflect that, no matter how much you trust someone, if you pass on information, images or messages of a sexual nature, or allow someone to take intimate pictures, then you lose control over what happens to them.

5. Summary

- Do not allow anyone to take inappropriate pictures, as they may not always be kept confidential.

- Nothing is ever truly confidential and while it is never OK to try and pass the blame or make excuses for letting someone down by betraying their trust, it is also important to take responsibility for your own decisions, both good and bad.

- If someone has intimate pictures on their phone, delete them.

- If someone is worried about the security of private pictures or intimate photos that have got into the public domain, contact the Child Exploitation and Online Protection Centre (CEOP)[12] for help and advice.

---

12 http://ceop.police.uk

ACTIVITY 5.11: BLAME SCENARIOS

Scenario one

You went to a party with your best friend and both got very drunk. Along with other friends, you decided to go skinny-dipping in the river at midnight, which was great fun at the time but dangerous in retrospect. Apart from deciding never to go in a river while drunk again and suffering a massive hangover, you have thought no more about it. Until today, when you log on to social media to see graphic pictures of you and the others naked, including some intimate shots of your genitals, tagged and uploaded from your best friend's profile.

Massively embarrassed, you decide to challenge your friend. This is just awful – all your friends and family can see those pictures, as well as the friends and family of everyone else tagged in the shot. You just want to hide in shame and stay home forever.

Scenario two

You have just broken up with your boyfriend and are pleased that you were strong enough to break away from him. You thought he loved you and it has taken you over a year to see that your friends and family were right – he is a controlling bully. While you were together he was rude or argumentative whenever you went out with friends, so in the end it was easier to spend time together alone, which made him happy.

The final straw was when he deliberately made you late for your sister's birthday dinner. He knows birthdays are a big deal in your family and that your mum had made an extra special effort to cook something he likes. When you told him it was over he went mad, texting, calling and emailing you repeatedly, but you are determined not to change your mind.

Now you feel sick. You have just opened a text with a link to a page called 'myhotdoll' and on it he has uploaded private photos he promised never to share. You feel so angry, with him for doing it and yourself for allowing him to take the pictures. You decide to challenge him – those photos have to be taken down before anyone sees them.

ACTIVITY 5.11: BLAME AND EXCUSE CARDS

I didn't do it. You're telling lies.

It wasn't my fault – someone else must have used my phone.

It doesn't matter that much, you're making a fuss over nothing.

I can't see I've done anything wrong! Everybody does it.

It was just a laugh! Get over it.

Our friends encouraged me to do it.

It's your fault, you shouldn't have upset me.

I didn't mean to do it, it must have been sent by accident.

It is your fault, you allowed me to take the picture.

Don't you think I feel bad about it? I'm being punished too.

I only sent it to one person.

I only wanted to show people because I'm so proud of you.

Additional Information and Support

Laws and legislation

Any legal information contained in this book is intended as guidance only and should not be considered legal advice in any context. While every effort has been made to ensure that it is accurate and up to date, facilitators are encouraged to check to make sure that this has not changed since the date of publication. These websites may be useful:

- www.parliament.uk

- www.homeoffice.gov.uk

- www.ceop.police.uk/safety-centre

Pro- and anti-pornography campaigns in the UK

www.backlash-uk.org.uk – Backlash is an umbrella organisation providing academic, legal and campaigning resources defending freedom of sexual expression. Backlash supports the rights of adults to participate in all consensual sexual activities and to watch, read and create any fictional interpretation of such in any media.

www.safermedia.org.uk/blockporn.htm – Safer Media for a Safer Society is a campaign, headed by Claire Perry MP, which calls for UK-based internet service providers to provide anti-porn filters at network level. This would stop most pornography from reaching our computers and internet-enabled devices, particularly mobile phones, and protect children much more effectively.

http://sexandcensorship.org – the Sex & Censorship campaign sets out to challenge the myths and rumours. It aims to reach out to journalists and politicians and ensure that scare stories are not used to introduce yet more laws and regulations that further restrict our access to information that is freely available elsewhere.

Online information and support

The organisations in this section contain information, support and advice for teachers, young people and their parents and carers. However, the author can take no responsibility for the contents, and the views expressed are not necessarily shared or endorsed simply because they are included.

www.bbc.co.uk/schools – the BBC site has useful links to resources and information on a range of subjects related to sex and relationships.

www.brook.org.uk – Brook is a leading young people's charity with 50 years' experience of working with young people and professionals in schools and further education colleges, as well as delivery of nurse-based health services. Brook also publishes leaflets and teaching resources for SRE.

www.bullying.co.uk – young people's website offering information and support.

www.channel4.com/sexperienceuk – Channel 4 website which offers a series of documentaries and research on SRE, including pornography and its potential impact on children and young people.

www.childline.org.uk – the NSPCC has produced resources to make it easier for children and young people to get help with sexting.

www.childnet.com – advises on internet safety and has a range of leaflets for children and parents.

www.fpa.org.uk – FPA is a sexual health charity. The website offers information and resources to teach about sex and relationships, including sexual bullying.

www.galop.org.uk – advice and support for people who have experienced biphobia, homophobia, transphobia, sexual violence or domestic abuse.

www.legislation.gov.uk/ukpga/2008/4/contents – Criminal Justice and Immigration Act 2008. Part 5 details legislation governing the making and distribution of pornography, sexual offences and hatred on the grounds of sexual orientation.

www.legislation.gov.uk/ukpga/2003/42/contents – the Sexual Offences Act 2003 (and amended). As well as making illegal a range of sexual activity with children and young people under 16, the Act includes a number of clauses which have impact on young people and pornography.

www.mensadviceline.org.uk – Men's Advice Line is a confidential helpline for any man experiencing domestic violence and abuse from a partner (or ex-partner).

www.nationaldomesticviolencehelpline.org.uk – the Freephone 24-Hour National Domestic Violence Helpline, run in partnership between Women's Aid and Refuge, is a national service for women experiencing domestic violence, their family, friends, colleagues and others calling on their behalf.

www.pshe-association.org.uk – the PSHE Association is the leading national support body for PSHE teachers and produces PSHE resources, model policies and schemes of work.

www.respectphoneline.org.uk – a confidential and anonymous helpline for anyone concerned about their violence and/or abuse towards a partner or ex-partner.

www.sexeducationforum.org.uk – the Sex Education Forum is a group of organisations and individuals who believe that all children and young people have the right to good quality SRE. The website serves as a gateway to helping teachers and other SRE practitioners find resources to support the provision of good quality SRE.

www.stonewall.org.uk – Stonewall has produced a series of packs and information for schools to tackle homophobic bullying and hate crime.

www.supportline.org.uk – for children and young people witnessing domestic violence in the home.

www.thinkuknow.co.uk – CEOP (Child Exploitation and Online Protection) has developed this site, which contains a number of resources exploring the risks children and young people face online, including short films and teaching resources.

www.youngminds.org.uk – Young Minds is the UK's leading charity committed to improving the emotional wellbeing and mental health of children and young people. It campaigns, researches and influences policy and practice.

www.youngmindsvs.org.uk/sexual_pressures – Young Minds vs. Sexed Up is a campaign to challenge the hype about sex and relationships for young people. This includes sexual expectations, pornography and sexting.

Additional reading

These reports and briefings have provided interesting and invaluable information to upport this resource. However, inclusion does not necessarily mean endorsement so please read in this context.

Chief Medical Officer (2012) *Chief Medical Officer's Annual Report Department of Health*. www.gov.uk/government/publications/chief-medical-officers-annual-report-2012-our-children-deserve-better-prevention-pays

National Association of Headteachers (2013) *Research carried out in April 2013 by Research Now and commissioned by the National Association of Headteachers (NAHT) and press released by NAHT in May 2013*. www.naht.org.uk/welcome/news-and-media/key-topics/parents-and-pupils/parents-want-schools-to-manage-dangers-of-pornography-says-survey

Neil Carmichael, Chair of the House of Commons Education Committee (16 July 2015) Government response to sex education report is 'feeble'. www.parliament.uk/business/committees/committees-a-z/commons-select/education-committee/news-parliament-2015/comment-sex-education-15-16

Mumsnet (2011) *Survey of 1,000 parents*. www.mumsnet.com/campaigns/mumsnet-sex-education-survey#Results

Ofsted (2013) *Not Yet Good Enough*. www.ofsted.gov.uk/resources/not-yet-good-enough-personal-social-health-and-economic-education-schools

Sex Education Forum (2013b) *The Sex Educational Supplement, Issue 1: The Pornography Issue*. www.sexeducationforum.org.uk/resources/sex-educational-supplement.aspx

Written evidence submitted from the Sex Education Forum, National Children's Bureau (June 2014) *The Education Committee inquiry into Personal, Social, Health and Economic education (PSHE) and Sex and Relationships Education (SRE) in schools*. http://data.parliament.uk/writtenevidence/committeeevidence.svc/evidencedocument/education-committee/pshe-and-sre-in-schools/written/10259.html

Example letter for parents/carers – schools

Name and address of school (please insert)

Date:

Dear Parents/Carers

As a school we are committed to providing our pupils with opportunities to learn the skills they need for a happy, healthy life. This includes essential sex and relationships education, which is age appropriate and offered in a way that respects personal, family and cultural values as well as teaching the statutory parts of the National Curriculum.

Every so often a new concern arises for the safety and emotional wellbeing of young people. Of current concern are the high numbers of under-18s accessing pornography on a regular basis and the making and sharing of inappropriate pictures. Although not all young people will be directly involved in this, research suggests that it is likely to impact on collective perceptions of what is normal sexual behaviour and what constitutes a healthy relationship.

To challenge this we have developed high-quality PSHE lessons, which will be taught by (insert name) in line with government recommendations and guidelines from the PSHE Association. The aim of this is to deal sensitively with issues around pornography and the impact that it potentially has on real-life relationships, body image and attitudes to sex. This will include the law in relation to pornography and the making, sharing and distribution of explicit images, including social media and online safety.

We can assure you that under no circumstances will examples of pornography or anything of an explicit nature be shown.

The school is happy to provide opportunities for parents and carers to find out more about PSHE, and in particular how we teach this topic. We recognise that parents have expert knowledge when it comes to their children and we strive for a consistent approach from home and school to teach your child the skills to make healthy, safe choices.

I hope you now have all the information you require to give your consent to your child's participation by signing and returning the attached slip. Should you have any queries or concerns please do not hesitate to contact me.

Yours faithfully

(Name)

(Title)

Consent form

To: (insert name of school)

I/We give consent for our child to participate in the PSHE lessons outlined in this letter.

I/We understand that these lessons will include (please tick):

1. Accurate, up-to-date information about the potential impact that underage exposure to pornography can have on body image, personal attitudes and values and expectations about sex and relationships.

    YES ☐

2. Education about the laws that govern the making, viewing and distribution of pornographic material (including the use of social media).

    YES ☐

3. Online safety, appropriate use of social media and the taking and sharing of photographs (including those taken with consent).

    YES ☐

4. The promotion of healthy, loving, positive relationships based on mutual respect, trust and friendship.

    YES ☐

I hope you now have all the information you require to give your consent to your child's participation by signing and returning the attached slip. Should you have any queries or concerns please do not hesitate to contact me.

Yours faithfully

(Name)

(Title)

Pupil's name: _____ Year: _____

Parent/Guardian name (in capitals): _____

Signature: _____ Date: _____

Please return to: _____ by: _____

Thank you

APPENDIX 2

Example parents/carers consent form – youth services

Name of youth service/group (please insert)

Dear Parent/Carer

Every so often a new concern arises for the safety and emotional wellbeing of young people. Of current concern are the high numbers of under-18s accessing pornography on a regular basis and the making and sharing of inappropriate pictures. Although not all young people will be directly involved in this, research suggests that it is likely to impact on collective perceptions of what is normal sexual behaviour and what constitutes a healthy relationship.

To challenge this we will be engaging young people in social education activities in line with government recommendations and guidelines from the PSHE Association. The aim of this is to deal sensitively with issues around pornography and the impact that it potentially has on real-life relationships, body image and attitudes to sex. This will include the law in relation to pornography and the making, sharing and distribution of explicit images, including social media and online safety.

This will include:

- Accurate, up-to-date information about the potential impact that underage exposure to pornography can have on body image, personal attitudes and values and expectations about sex and relationships.

- Education about the laws that govern the making, viewing and distribution of pornographic material (including the use of social media).

- Online safety, appropriate use of social media and the taking and sharing of photographs (including those taken with consent).

- The promotion of healthy, loving, positive relationships based on mutual respect, trust and friendship.

I hope this gives you the information you require to give your consent to your child's participation by signing and returning the attached slip. Should you have any queries or concerns please do not hesitate to contact me.

Yours faithfully

(Name)

(Title)

Youth services consent form: person with parental responsibility (under-18s)

- I have read and fully understand the information.
- I understand that although pornography will be discussed at no time will anything of a pornographic or explicit nature be shown.
- I am satisfied that all reasonable care will be taken for the emotional wellbeing and safety of those participating.
- I have discussed with my child acceptable standards of behaviour and he/she has agreed to abide by them.
- I give consent for my child to participate in this area of social education.

Name of young person: _____

Date of birth: _____

Home address: _____

Postcode: _____

Contact telephone number(s):

1. _____

2. _____

Emergency number: _____ (This must be a parent or carer)

Signed: _____

Name (Print): _____ Date: _____

Please note: the adult signing must be a person with parental responsibility for the child and must have full legal rights.

Anyone *without* a signed consent form will *not be allowed* to participate in the planned activities and educational workshops. If you have any questions, please contact *(insert name, job title and contact details)* for further information.

APPENDIX 3

Example invitation to a parental PSHE information workshop

Name and address of school (please insert)

Dear Parent/Carer

We think that PSHE is one of the most important subjects taught in schools because it quite literally teaches children social skills for life. However, after listening to feedback from parents and carers we have come to realise that not everyone knows what it is or how we teach it.

We want to change that by inviting anyone with parental responsibility to a parental PSHE information workshop on _____ at _____.
We recognise that parents are the experts when it comes to their children and we need your help and support in reinforcing what we teach so they learn the skills to make healthy, safe choices.

This workshop will be giving you information about how we plan to tackle the sensitive subject of pornography and the potentially negative impact over-exposure to it can have on real-life relationships, body image and attitudes to sex. This will include facts about the law in relation to pornography and the making, sharing and distribution of explicit images, for example naked selfies, as well as how to keep safe on social media and online.

Please be assured that under no circumstances will examples of pornography or anything of an explicit nature be shown.

As well as a presentation and the opportunity to see the teaching materials we are going to be using you can ask questions and find out where to go for more information and support.

Please let us know if you are coming by completing the reply slip below.

We look forward to welcoming you.

Yours faithfully

(Name)

(Title)

Pupil's name: _____   Year: _____

Parent/Guardian name (in capitals): _____

Signature: _____   Date: _____

Please return to: _____   by: _____

Thank you

APPENDIX 4

Quick guide for staying safe online and social media for parents

Social media can be great fun for all the family, but to keep safe consider the quick checklist below:

1. *Before* opening a new social media account check to see if there is an *age limit*. If the site stipulates that you must be over 18 to join it is because the content is not thought appropriate for anyone younger.

2. *Preview* your profile, especially the main photo, to see how it looks to others. First impressions count so if you are not sure, ask someone you trust.

3. Have a *strong password* and *logout* when you are not using social media. This stops anyone else using your identity or changing the settings on your account.

4. Don't tell anyone your *password* and don't make it too obvious. Don't use the same password for all online accounts and change it regularly.

5. Check your *privacy settings* – do you know who can see your phone number, email address or where you live?

6. Edit the privacy settings of the *apps* you use and your *photo albums*. Your photos should only be accessible to you and the people you choose, not random strangers.

7. *Do not take, make, forward or share* any pictures or photos of nudity or anything sexual, *with or without consent.* If anyone in them is under 18 you are breaking the law and could be charged with distributing child pornography, even if the photo is of you and stored on your phone.

8. *Review posts and photos* that you are tagged in and if you aren't happy with them ask for them to be taken down. It is never OK to post pictures *without permission.*

9. Do not get into online arguments, retaliations or spreading malicious gossip, especially of a *sexual nature,* on social media or online. Social media companies *do not tolerate bullying or harassment* and you may be breaking the *law.*

10. *Report abusive or offensive content.* Reports are anonymous and you will not be identified.

11. Check your *online friends* are people you know in the real world. You can easily 'unfriend' or *delete* on social media without anyone knowing.

12. Always read the *terms and conditions* when you set up a social media or other online account (e.g. gaming) to make sure you know exactly what you have *given consent to share* and *who can see what you post.*

APPENDIX 5

Evaluation form

Name: _____ Date: _____

PLEASE RATE USING THE NUMBER THAT BEST MATCHES YOUR OPINION				
Strongly agree	←		→	Strongly disagree
1	2	3	4	5

_____   The **aims** explained at the start of the lesson were met.

_____   I feel more **knowledgeable** and **confident** in the subject area.

_____   A range of **learning methods** were used.

_____   The teacher actively encouraged **questions** and **discussion**.

_____   The answers given to questions were **easily understood**.

_____   The teacher **listened** to what people had to say.

_____   I learnt **practical skills**.

_____   Handouts and resources were relevant and of a high standard.

_____   Participants were **actively engaged** throughout the course.

_____   I feel more **confident** in my role as a result of the training.

_____   I would **recommend** this training to others.

Index